The Poet's
Daughter

The Poet's Daughter

Malek o'Shoara Bahar of Iran
and the Immortal Song of Freedom

Parvaneh Bahar

with

Joan Aghevli

Larson Publications
BURDETT, NY

ISBN-10: 1-936012-57-X
ISBN-13: 978-1-936012-57-2
Library of Congress Control Number: 2011935752

Publisher's Cataloging-In-Publication Data
(Prepared by The Donohue Group, Inc.)

Bahār, Parvānah, 1928 or 9-
    The poet's daughter : Malek o'Shoara Bahar of Iran and the immortal song of freedom / Parvaneh Bahar with Joan Aghevli.

    p. : ill. ; cm.

    Includes bibliographical references and index.
    ISBN-13: 978-1-936012-57-2
    ISBN-10: 1-936012-57-X

    1. Bahār, Muhammad Taqī, 1886-1951. 2. Poets, Iranian--Biography. 3. Iran--Social conditions--20th century. 4. Iran--Politics and government--20th century. 5. Bahār, Parvānah, 1928 or 9- 6. Iranian American women--United States--Biography. I. Aghevli, Joan. II. Title.

    PK6561.B3 Z68 2011
    891.5513/092   2011935752

Published by Larson Publications
4936 NYS Route 414
Burdett, New York 14818 USA

larsonpublications.com

20 19 18 17 16 15 14 13 12 11
10 9 8 7 6 5 4 3 2 1

DEDICATED TO THE MEMORY OF MY FATHER,

WHO TAUGHT ME THE ROAD TO FREEDOM.

CONTENTS

FOREWORD

MORE than anything else, what connects readers of *The Poet's Daughter* to Parvaneh Bahar's indomitable spirit is the clear love of humanity that shines through her words and illuminates her experiences.

The Poet's Daughter is essentially two stories intertwined. One is the story of her father, Malek o'Shoara Bahar, champion of democratic values and human freedom and a famous poet, and the world of turmoil into which Ms. Bahar was born; she reaches back into her Iranian roots to bring this world to her reader. The other is her own life story, a memoir of a courageous woman whose humanism and determination to leave the world a better place, learned in the company of her father and through his poetry and pursued all her life, led her to embrace the cause of the oppressed in her adoptive country, the United States of America.

The stories of the author and of her father's struggle for reform mirror one another, both singing the song of freedom for all human beings.

DR. MAJID TEHRANIAN
HAWAII, 2011

(Majid Tehranian was the first director of the Toda Institute for Global Peace and Policy Research, has taught at Harvard, Oxford, Tufts, USC, and Tehran universities, and is currently a professor in the University of Hawaii's School of Communications at Manoa.)

PREFACE

M Y STORY begins with my father. And I am sure it will end with my father—his will be the last face I conjure up, his words the last to caress my mind, his spirit the last to take leave of my soul. His was the seed from which I sprang, and he provided the fertile garden in which I grew. While I have lived a long and independent life, I feel that my father has walked by my side, even after his death, directing me toward the path of freedom, dignity, and compassion. His spirit imbues my life with joy, a passion for freedom and truth, and a sense of privilege at having lived on this beautiful earth.

Who was this man? Malek o'Shoara Bahar was a great—many say the greatest neoclassical poet in Iran since the fourteenth century—who very early in life was accorded the title "Prince of Poets." He was above all a humanist, a leading intellectual who used all his many gifts in pursuit of social reform and freedom for the people of Iran. While his determination to change the social order and see democracy flower in his country brought him several periods in jail and exile, it also earned him a place in the hearts and minds of those who have read and been touched by his beautiful and stirring words and his vision of freedom and human dignity.

ACKNOWLEDGMENTS

W E WOULD LIKE to thank several people whose support and skills paved the way for publication.

Anne Savage (Sydney, Australia) was the first to read the manuscript; her excellent editorial suggestions provided invaluable feedback in the early stages.

Jill Swenson was a strong ally as we prepared the manuscript for submission.

We are indebted to Majid Tehranian for his early encouragement and for his gracious foreword to *The Poet's Daughter*.

Hélène Saraj (Paris, France) shared her deep knowledge of Bahar's work as we prepared the poetry included in the book. We would also like to acknowledge the lifetime that she has devoted to bringing the work of Malek o'Shoara Bahar and other great Persian artists and intellectuals to Western scholars and readers through the foundation that she created, Fondacion Culturelle Bahar in Paris, France.

Hugh Rakhshan Bahar organized an accurate plan of "Paradise," the Bahar home in Tehran.

Chehrzad Bahar's excellent memory made recreating the plan of the Bahar home possible. We wish to acknowledge her dedication to preserving and publishing her father's literary heritage in Iran.

We are grateful to Abbas Milani, Marvin Zonis, Shahrnush Parsipur, Barbara Meade, Masoud Askari Sarvestani, and Carolyn M. Byerly for reading the book and providing comments.

IN MY FATHER'S HOUSE

THERE IS a new statue in Mashhad, an ancient city in the northeast of Iran. It is a tribute to the enduring legacy of a poet as well-known and beloved in Iran—a country that reveres poetry above all art forms—as Walt Whitman is in America. It stands in a park near the memorial to the eleventh-century genius, Ibn Sina, or "Avicenna," whose Canon of Medicine dominated Western practice for five hundred years.

While it is an honor for "The Prince of Poets," as he is known, to share the park with "The Father of Medicine," it was rumored that the poet's statue was intended for the center of *Maidane Aloom*, a circular park by Ferdowsi University. But even sixty years after his death, the authorities in Iran still fear the words of this poet.

The statue was erected in a less prominent position, putting a safer distance between the restive students and the man whose fierce words have become anthems to liberation, and whose uncompromising stand for freedom and human rights finds voice in today's democracy movement.

The man was Malek o'Shoara Bahar.

I am his daughter.

Bahar was a revolutionary thinker, a tireless democrat, and a committed humanist whose words and deeds continue to inspire. My own life has been full and rich, in large part because of the early lessons I received in my father's house: lessons in love of country and freedom, the equality of women and men, the rights of minorities, disdain for all forms of oppression, and reverence for life and the natural world.

My father's given name was Mohammad Taghi Sabouri. At a young age he chose the pen-name Bahar, which means "spring." He was born into a cultured, educated family in 1886 in the holy city of Mashhad, in the northeastern province of Khorasan. His aunt taught him to read and write, and to read the Koran. He learned the classical stories from Persian history by studying Ferdowsi's great tenth-century epic poem *Shah Nameh* (Book of Kings) with his father, who was himself a poet. At six, he started his formal schooling. At seven, he began to write poetry; but, fearing he could not live by poetry alone, the family apprenticed him, unhappily, to a merchant uncle at fifteen.

In a poem called "Random Thoughts," my father, looking back on this time of indecision, ponders his place in the universe and wonders how much control he has over his fate. The poem was written at a time when the revolutionary ideas of Charles Darwin, among others, were echoing around the world. The age-old question, "Who am I?" took on a whole new urgency as evidence of evolution shed new light on humanity's origins. I don't know if my father had read Darwin when he wrote the poem, but he was a voracious searcher after truth, and the ideas in the poem are very much of the time.

> Huddled in the huge blue arms of the universe,
> How very small is our Earth.
> And we humans—tiny, insignificant.
> And nobody, from the newborn to the ancient,
> Nobody is content with their lot.
> Why, then, should I alone expect happiness?
>
> I have sought so long the secret of existence.
> What does it mean, "I am"?
> On the dark horizon, just one small point of light
> And that carries no certainty.
> Beside that shiny seed of doubt, there is nothing.
> I was beguiled by the search for truths;

I sought them out, one by one
And turned my back on ignorance and lies.
To me, good and bad is really the same coin;
Healthy and sick, just different sides.
Sunset and sunrise, just the same.
My mind is quite lost in this universe.
I am like a shipwrecked boat, unmoored,
Starless, rudderless, quite lost.
I go up and down on the tide of destiny,
Powerless to influence its rise and fall.

The universe gave her creation two laws:
First Nature, the ineluctable it seems,
Second, Nurture, the wild card in the pack.
If my soul comes only from my ancestors,
God, who am I, this miserable person?
If both my soul and knowledge belong to me alone
Why should I let heredity dictate my path?

One ancestor was a great intellectual,
One wore the soldier's uniform.
My father was a poet, but because
His uncle was a solid merchant,
I was urged to follow suit.
But this safe course was all in vain and doomed;
It scarified my soul to be in trade.
Neither mystic, nor accountant, I,
No delicate aesthetic, nor cut from merchant's cloth.
I would never make an officer.
I *could* do all these things, even trade in rugs
But in none would I be true to myself.
It seems to me that I am but a small red target on a stone
Waiting for destiny to fire an arrow and tell me who I am.

Bahar tagged along with his father to democratic meetings, absorbing the revolutionary ideas of freedom and modern thinking that were flowering in Iran—just as they were in nearby Russia and other countries in the early twentieth century. As he says in the poem: *"I was beguiled by the search for truths."*

When my grandfather died suddenly in 1904, my father, only eighteen, became responsible for his mother, two brothers, and a sister. Pondering his new role as head of the family, Bahar was inspired to write a long epic poem, *In Praise of the Shah*, which he sent to the king, Mosafar o-din Shah of the Qajar dynasty. Ostensibly praising him, the poem identified the characteristics and actions of a great leader, subtly reminding the Shah that there was much he could do to improve his leadership. Greatly impressed, the Shah named the young poet Malek o'Shoara Bahar, (Prince of Poets), akin to Poet Laureate but a title held for life, and granted him a small stipend.

My grandfather had also held this title, but no other poet since my father has been nominated. The scholars in his own city of Mashhad questioned his qualifications for such high honor, but after putting him to many tests—including composing poems extemporaneously in front of a group of examiners—they could not deny his brilliance. Bahar began to gain a wide audience for his poetry, prose and essays. He is now famous to several generations of Iranians as Malek o'Shoara Bahar.

While his writing and the speeches he gave in the mosques and the bazaar in Mashhad were firmly grounded in Iranian culture, my father saw the issues he raised—the demands for a constitutional democracy to replace the absolute rule of the Shah, questions about the subordinate position of Iranian women—as part of the winds of change stirring in the wider world. To deepen his knowledge of Persian history and culture, he sought out one of the great classical scholars in Mashhad, Adib Neyshabouri, with whom to study. At the same time he read widely, not just in Persian but also in Arabic and in French, which was then the international language. The synthesis of old and new ideas in his work made him a greater poet than his father, his great-grandfather, or any of his contemporaries. His words rang with the ideals of freedom and equality, ideals that soon led him into politics.

As a co-founder of Iran's Democratic Party, my father started the newspaper

Noh Bahar, (New Spring), to disseminate the party's views. He sent a second poem to the Shah, "Justice for All," encouraging him to embrace constitutional monarchy. Father's first speech on behalf of the party, given in the Gohar Mosque in Mashhad, drew the unwelcome attention of the Russian consul. Like so many countries east of Europe, Iran was then a victim of the ambitions of the British and Russian empires. Russia had exercised control over the north of the country since its victory in the Iran-Russian War of the 1820s. Talk of freedom and self-determination, already a tense topic in czarist Russia, did not sit well with the occupying force. The British controlled the south of the country, in part to stop Russia from moving on India.

My father composed another epic poem, *May the Wind Blow My Message to Sir Edward Grey,* which he sent to the newly appointed British foreign secretary of that name, demanding that Britain leave Iran. Reactions were swift: The prime minister of Iran ordered that *Noh Bahar* be shut down, and the Russians placed a bomb in the Gohar Mosque that destroyed the building and injured many people.

Unhurt and undaunted, my father started an underground newspaper that he called *Tazeh Bahar* (Fresh Spring), in which he continued to promote both democracy and the liberation and participation of women, who at that time never left the house without a veil. The Russian consul shut down this newspaper and Bahar and the entire Democratic Party Committee were exiled to Tehran. On the journey my father was robbed of all he had, and he arrived in Tehran penniless. It was several months before he was able to rejoin his family in Mashhad.

In 1906, after years of unrest caused by the weak and profligate Mosafar o-din Shah's ruinous financial and political mishandling of Iran—a time in which foreign debt and foreign influence grew alarmingly—the Shah was forced to sign a new constitution that seriously limited royal power; a few days later he died. The constitution provided for an elected, representative parliament—the Majles—and a government with a cabinet to be confirmed by parliament. My father, still only twenty years old, was elected as Mashhad's representative to the Majles and returned to Tehran to take up his duties. His newspaper *Noh Bahar* reopened. It was shut down again within months and once more he was sent into exile by the prime minister.

The Constitutional Revolution promised other significant democratic reforms, including freedom of the press and speech; but, sadly, few were realized. Six times *Noh Bahar* opened, only to be closed time and again because the content was considered inflammatory. Constitutional monarchy did not suit Mosafar o-din Shah's successor, Mohammad Ali Shah, and he put all kinds of obstacles in its way. He tried to revoke the constitution his father had signed, blew up the Majles, and arrested many representatives and their family members. Bahar countered by writing the poem, *Aeneh Ebrat* (The Mirror of Experience), about these terrible abuses of power. This extremely long epic poem, addressing the two Qajar shahs and holding up a mirror from the past to show them examples of good leaders, begins:

Guardians of the people,
Awake from your moral stupor and look around.
Our people are like sheep without a shepherd.
On the one side is a lion, on the other a wolf[1]
Tearing their prey one from the other
With bloodied hands.
The guardians are drunk,
The sheep are simple,
But the enemy is cunning.
Everything is being lost.
Our only hope is to wake up and look around.

These translated excerpts give just a hint of the original, as Persian poetry is very hard to translate. Its rolling, sonorous quality, especially when recited, is impossible to capture, and the many-layered references, ironies, and nuances of language cannot be expressed in English. Much of my father's poetry is especially dense with meaning and artistry.

The Democratic Party organized all over Iran in reaction to the formal division of Iran into spheres of influence by Britain and Russia in the Anglo-Russian Convention of 1907, by which national assets were divided up under the pretext of safeguarding Persian sovereignty. In 1909 they moved to take over the capital. Mohammad Ali Shah first sought refuge in the Russian embassy, then went into exile in Russia. His son, eleven-year-old Ahmad, became the last shah of the Qajar dynasty, which had ruled Iran for more than two hundred years. The boy shah was sent to Europe with a tutor (who years later became my father-in-law) to study.

There was much celebration as the institution of constitutional democracy was restored in principle, but my father feared that the powerful presence of Britain and Russia would impede its actualization as they played out what Rudyard Kipling called "The Great Game." The Qajars had already auctioned off most of the country's resources and industries. In 1901, the Shah sold exclusive rights to petroleum and natural gas to a British financier for sixty years, a decision that was to shape the future of Iran.

The stakes in The Game were raised considerably in 1908, when the Anglo-Iranian Oil Company found oil in commercial quantities, in southern Iran. As G.D. Turner noted in a 1913 lecture at the (British) Persia Society, "It is the misfortune of Persia that the course of her history is determined far more by events and personalities outside than by happenings within."

An American economist, Morgan Shuster, was invited to Iran to assume the post of Treasurer. The changes he advocated to reorganize the country's finances and remove the favored tax status of the Russian and British syndicates would have put the reformist parliament on a strong footing to govern. But the British and Russians struck back, demanding that Shuster return to America. Russian troops marched on Tehran. By the end of 1911, the country was in a state of anarchy; parliament was shut down and many of its members were in jail. The hard-won constitution was suspended and tribal rule reasserted itself. The ambitious Constitutional Revolution had ended.

Through his poetry, which blended classical Persian references and the modern song of freedom, my father hoped to remind people of their glorious past and give them the strength to seize their own destiny from the many hands that reached in to exploit and rule. He returned to Mashhad and reopened his newspaper. Over the next decade he embarked on many projects in addition to his poetry, including studying Sanskrit with a German professor and writing histories of the Qajar Dynasty and the Russian Revolution.

In 1921, he was elected to represent Mashhad in the fourth Majles. On his return to Tehran, he wrote one of his most famous epic poems, *Damavandieh*, a revolutionary work employing the powerful image of Iran's largest mountain, Damavand, beloved of poets. The slopes of this snow-clad peak, northeast of Tehran, form the backdrop to some of the country's most stirring classical stories, including the *Shah Nameh*.

This is an excerpt from *Damavandieh*:

O white Damavand with your feet in fetters!
O Dome of the world, Damavand!
A warrior's silver helmet adorns your head,
But a slave's iron band encircles your waist.
That no man read your face,
You have veiled it in cloud.
As revolution raged, the Earth recoiled in horror,
Cold, silent and grief-stricken.
She thrust her angry fist towards the sky.
And you are that thrust, O Damavand!
You are the heavy fist of Time,
Heaved up by centuries of simmering resentment.
O fist of the earth, pound the sky!
Land some smashing blows on Rai![2]
No, no, you are not the fist of Time, O mountain!
I have painted the wrong image of you.
You are the world's anguished heart,
Swollen with power and poisoned by corruption.
You have tried to hide the infection and salve the swelling
With a plaster of snow that drifted soothing down.
O fiery heart of Time, burst forth!
Deny not the raging fire within.
Lie not mute, but rather howl your message!
Do not withdraw, but rather shriek in protest.
Listen to this advice from a heartsick poet:
If the fire within is suppressed, the spirit within will be consumed.
I swear by my life this is true.

Burn down this facade to its very foundation.

For the monument to oppression must be completely destroyed.

Then on behalf of the wise and the good,

Wrest justice from the base and the ignorant.

World War I brought occupation, with British, Russian, and Ottoman forces competing for control of the country and its increasingly precious oil. Into this turbulent situation stepped Reza Khan-e Mir-Panj, an uneducated but fiercely ambitious member of the Persian Cossack Brigade. Supported by the British, he rose rapidly through army ranks to the position of army commander, then minister of war.

With the young Ahmad Shah still in Europe and with the help of his British sponsors, Reza staged a *coup d'état* in 1921. He became prime minister in 1923, then consolidated his power by pushing through a parliamentary resolution dissolving the Qajar dynasty and placing himself on the Peacock Throne in 1925 as Reza Pahlavi, Shah of Iran. He took the name of the ancient Persian language, Pahlavi, presumably to co-opt some of its power.

Reza did not like the talk of freedom coming from people like my father. During one of Bahar's speeches in the restored parliament, a journalist who bore a resemblance to him was beheaded by two of Reza's men as he left the Majles. The word went out that Bahar had been assassinated even as he was finishing his speech; friends helped him to leave by a back door before the mistake became known. Many other opposition parliamentarians were not so fortunate.

In 1924, my father was re-elected to represent Mashhad in the fifth Majles, the same year that Mossadeq, the much-admired nationalist and future prime minister, took a seat in parliament for the first time. After the *coup d'état*, Tehran was the only city that still exercised some degree of freedom; Reza had put his puppets in control in the provinces. Despite keeping a low profile after the assassination attempt—he was teaching and avoiding politics—my father was elected as the representative for Tehran in the sixth Majles in 1926. He had not finished the two-year term when Reza imprisoned him for twelve months, determined to prevent him from attending parliament. During his year in jail, Bahar wrote

some of his most powerful poetry, including this excerpt from a poem he sent
to Reza Shah when I was a baby:

The power of the king is no stronger than the helplessness of the people.

The palace of the king is no more secure than the little shack of the poor.

A beautiful man is one who never disappoints those who depend on him.

A potent ruler is one who never breaks a poor person's heart.

If a little of my blood, even a drop, makes you happy,

If it is that important to you, go ahead, spill it.

But don't also pretend I have done wrong.

The only crime I have committed is to love my country.

While you put me in jail, you sit in your palace in Tajrish.

But if my perception of you is correct,

My jail is no worse than your cage in Tajrish.

It is unwise to be attached to worldly things—

In this world we cannot predict the future.

The good side of life is always shadowed by the bad.

My captivity is neither better nor worse than Massoud's or Bu'ahmad's.[3]

A humanist thinks of others; only animals care just about themselves.

On his release, my father stayed home and worked on a number of books;
but within a few years he was back in prison. I was then three years old. Father
was released only to be exiled to Isfahan in southeast Iran. My mother and the
children, then numbering five, followed him into exile, enduring a period of terrible
isolation and poverty. Maman tried to sell our house in Tehran to raise funds to
support the family, but she found no buyer. In Isfahan, few dared even to visit us.
Were it not for the kindness of friends who came late at night to sneak food and
money through the back door, we would probably not have survived.

After a year of this desperate existence, we returned to Tehran. My father
remained at home for many years, writing, until Reza Shah was forced to abdicate
in 1941. He was unpopular at home for his despotism and, more importantly,
had come to be viewed with suspicion for his tilt towards Germany that had
put Iran's rich oil reserves within reach of the Nazis. Reza saw his meteoric rise

succeeded by an equally meteoric fall when the U.S.S.R. and Britain invaded Iran and combined to push him from the throne, replacing him with his twenty-one-year-old son, Mohammad.

I remember so well the night someone telephoned to tell us the news. My mother raised her hands to the late summer sky and thanked God for the vindication of Bahar's cry for freedom, so mercilessly rewarded with jail and exile and the suffering of his family. Reza Shah died in exile in 1944.

The years in prison had taken a heavy toll on my father's health. But when he died of tuberculosis in the spring of 1951, he left behind a rich legacy of poetry and scholarly works. His voice still rings out from the pages of his writings, while the voices of his persecutors have fallen like ash from the pages of history.

In most civilized nations, when a great artist dies the state acquires his or her residence and works of art and preserves them for succeeding generations. To the great loss of Iran, this was not the practice under Mohammad Reza Shah.

The death of my father left my mother almost destitute. To support herself and my younger sister Cherry, Maman was forced to sell not only our beloved family home but also my father's magnificent library—the collection of a lifetime and renowned among scholars. We were heartbroken to see these treasures going to auction, but the reality of need made any other course impossible. The house, the garden, and the library were the essence of who my father was. Everything—the rooms, the flowers, the trees, the books—was imbued with his spirit. And they were the source of his inspiration.

The many books and articles written about Bahar have focused on his work rather than on the man, on his fame as one of the greatest neoclassical poets in Iran since the fourteenth century, and his pursuit of social reform and freedom for the Iranian people through his writing, politics, and academic work.

I would like to take you by the hand and lead you back in time, through the rooms my father inhabited, the flowers he gazed upon, the books that sustained him, the trees under which he sat, and the family that he loved. By taking this journey with me, I hope you will gain a sense of my father and his family within our private world, a world we affectionately called *Paradise*.

PARADISE

THE HOME into which my two brothers, three sisters, and I were born was at that time on the northern outskirts of Tehran, outside the city gates and surrounded by the dry foothills of the Alborz Mountains. Our only neighbors were the American embassy and the house of a general. Now this area is part of downtown Tehran, a city of about eight million people, with over twelve million in the greater Tehran area that extends all the way up to the snow line.

On a recent visit to Iran, I sought out my birthplace, my beloved Paradise. I was excited to recognize our street, named for my father—Malek o'Shoara Bahar Avenue—but all other connections to the past had disappeared. Instead of a dirt lane shaded by small groups of trees planted along the *jube*, a deep gutter along which water from the mountain springs gurgled, there was asphalt. Gone were the earthen walls surrounding our house and garden, gone were the house and garden themselves. In their place a huge ugly building clawed at the sky. Gone, too, the shady trees along the street and the murmur of the water in the *jube*, once the only sound to break the mysterious near-silence of the desert. I found myself enveloped in the cacophony of noise, the pollution, the oppressive heat, the almost unthinkable chaos that is modern Tehran.

I could hardly bear the feelings of loss that I experienced there on Malek o'Shoara Bahar Avenue. As I stood, looking at the monstrosity that had replaced my Paradise, I closed my eyes and was transported back to a time when Paradise was still intact. In my mind, I saw so clearly the green wooden door to the garden with its gold inscription, *Malek o'Shoara Bahar*. As I did so long ago, I push the door and walk in, my feet crunching over the cobblestones. Just to my left, a glorious honeysuckle vine climbs up and over the wall and I pluck one of the soft, warm flowers. Inhaling its heady fragrance, I walk into the garden whose perfumes had greeted me even before I opened the door.

To the right, an area of fruit trees—pomegranates, peaches, apricots, figs, quince—flavors the air with hypnotic, syrupy sweetness, competing with the profusion of flowers to delight and enfold me in the familiar sensual atmosphere that has defined "home" to me since my birth. Even as I stand in this coarse and oppressive modern street, a deeply ingrained memory that I can evoke as a physical presence sustains me. Wherever I find myself, I can always draw upon the smell of a ripe apricot, the scent of a rose, the tinkle of water in a pool to take me back to the hallowed place.

Walking into the middle of the garden in my mind again, I see three interconnected olive-shaped pools. Upon their surface, water lilies unfold in the filtered sunlight—purple and pink in the central pool, white and yellow in the other two. Rose bushes encircle the pools, each carefully selected by my father for its beauty and perfume. A keen gardener, Father was like an attentive lover to these prima donnas. We were forbidden to cut the blooms, but were rather instructed to appreciate their glory and allow them a full, uninterrupted life. As my father noted in a poem entitled "Jamal Tabiyat" (The Splendor of Nature):

Walk slowly and joyfully through the lush greenery and the roses.
If your soul does not shy at the beauty of a rose bush,
If you are not harassed by doubt, you will see
A hundred flowers but not one thorn.
If a thorn pricks the finger of one who plucks the rose,
The fault is not of the thorn, but of the gatherer.

Beyond the roses, a line of deep green cypresses separates the flowers from the orchard. White and yellow honeysuckle mass on the tall wall to the right.

To the left, the broad leaves of our mulberry trees create a cool retreat during the summer months and promise a bounty of sweet and delicate fruit.

At the furthest end of the garden stands the *laneh kabutar*, the pigeon house. Father loved those pigeons—their innocent company a metaphor for a purer world than the villainy he witnessed beyond our garden walls. One of his great joys was the daily release of the birds in the afternoon. He wrote a marvelous poem called "Soroudeh Kabutar" (The Music of Pigeons), about their pure beauty and grace as they took to the air, a glorious, free white cloud against the deep blue sky, transformed into angels as they soared towards heaven, then drifted back towards him like snowflakes.

I see our gardener, Asghar, who lived behind the fruit trees in a small room next to the greenhouse that became, at the beginning of each winter, the repository for all our potted flowering plants. I spent many winter hours in that warm greenhouse, where the colors and scents of summer lingered all through the cold months.

Turning towards the house, I mount the four familiar steps that lead inside. Father's study lies to the right of the central hallway. Despite the absence of light within, I am drawn to this room, the center of his intellectual life and where he spent almost all his waking hours. The study, with its wonderful library, was the most respected room in our household. It was of medium size, with a large folding window looking straight onto the garden. During the summer, he opened the window early in the morning to capture the last of the cool night air, and closed it as the day heated up.

Bookcases of rich brown mahogany, some glass-fronted to protect their precious contents—hundreds of original manuscripts, most of them very old, many illuminated and illustrated with glorious artwork—claimed every available space on the walls and reached right to the high ceiling. It was arguably the best manuscript collection in Iran, and the nation lost a treasure of inestimable worth when it failed to secure this literary marvel on my father's death. My mother approached the government many times to buy our home and the library and preserve it as a museum for the nation. Fortunately, in 1952, the head librarian of the Iranian Parliamentary Library bought the manuscript collection. Today it is housed in the old Parliament building—now a museum—in a room named for my father. Sadly the books, many of which were rare and valuable, dispersed into the hands of many individual collectors.

While the manuscripts and most valuable books were kept in my father's study, in reality the whole house was a library. Father received or bought a copy of every volume published in Iran and also had good collections of works in French and Arabic. They were all available to us as children and we grew up respecting and loving books for the knowledge they convey, their beauty, even their smell. No wonder I became a librarian!

The floor of the study was covered wall to wall with Persian rugs. I do not recall their design and colors very clearly. They must have been very lovely, as my father was a connoisseur of carpets, appreciating them both for their beauty and for the particular knots and designs that reveal their origins. Whenever he bought a new one, he would proudly lay it out in the interior courtyard and sit on it for hours, touching its velvety surface and getting to know this new part of the household.

Art is integral to Persian daily life. Glorious carpets are walked on and sat on, decorative porcelain is used for food and drink, delicate inlaid boxes contain everyday items, etched silver trays carry tea. In the West, art tends to be thought of as a separate element, to be hung on walls, put behind glass, even stored in bank vaults. In Iranian culture there is no separation between beautiful objects and daily living, between form and function. Much of the artistic creative process aims to incorporate the beauty of nature into the home. The difficult, even harsh climate and the hot, often arid, landscape inspire the creation of a softer natural world inside, with "garden" carpets, floral motifs, images of water and indoor fountains, poetry, and miniature paintings of deer, rabbits, and green, flowered places. Even paintings portraying bloody combat have delicate, lyrical settings where flowers bloom, animals and birds frolic, and nature reasserts herself.

Against the wall in one corner of the study was a covered mattress with colored pillows and a khaki army blanket (khaki is the Persian word for earth) where my father sat while he worked and thought. He would go to his study right after breakfast, rejoin the family for lunch, and then return to his study. There in the afternoons he would often receive visitors—friends, students, writers, poets, politicians, and other intellectuals.

On this particular afternoon of memory I am surprised to find him sitting alone in his study, lost in thought.

"Hello, Father. Why are you sitting in the dark?" I ask him. He looks up at me with obvious pleasure, his eyes shining

"Oh! It is you, Parvaneh, my butterfly. Come and sit next to me." I sense, more than see, tears in his eyes. I open the folding windows onto the garden so that light and the perfume of the flowers wash into the room.

As I seat myself beside my father, he begins to compose a poem about me called "Parvaneh," which is both my name and Persian for butterfly, expressing feelings of great loss. I had been married only the day before. I had no idea that he would miss me so much, so soon. I was just sixteen years old.

> The candle whose glow illuminated my house is gone.
> Now that my butterfly has flown, what use have I for flowers?
> I am the oyster, robbed of its treasured pearl,
> Left with parched lips and a worthless shell.
> Although the summer sun still lingers
> The garden of my soul has slipped into autumn
> Since the harvesting of its most perfect bloom.

I remember it all as though it were yesterday. I experience it again as though it is today. The noise and heat of the street reclaim my senses. The wall, the gate, the garden recede. Paradise is lost, but I can go back whenever I choose. Throughout my life, through meditation, I strive to return to that state of grace. In conjuring up images of that happy place, I find peace.

Our family home was typically Persian in style, hidden behind high walls that from the outside gave the effect of a small fortress. It was quite a large house, laid out as a series of connected rooms around a central courtyard. At the center of the courtyard was a square, shallow pool, and in each corner a fan-shaped flowerbed filled with cheerful flowers. A few tall cypresses stood guard along the edges. The simple tapestry of the design, the reflection of the trees in the pool, created a sense of tranquility only disturbed by the happy laughter of children at play.

At one end of the courtyard lay the servants' quarters and our enormous family kitchen, charming and very old-fashioned, dominated by several wood-burning stoves. A huge wooden table occupied the center, while a spacious storage alcove several steps up on one side held the fruits of my mother's creativity—small miracles of color and shape, ranks of gleaming jars filled with fruit preserves of many kinds, pomegranate juice and sauce, and *torshi*, a spicy vegetable and herb pickle. Nothing of the bounty from our garden went to waste. We enjoyed the fragrance and color of its fruits, vegetables, and herbs year round.

When my brothers and sisters and I came in from school, ravenous after a dusty walk of five or six miles, we headed straight for the kitchen. It was the center of our lives for about an hour each day. We wolfed down leftovers from lunch or the previous night's dinner and caught up with each other's doings before settling in for a few hours of study.

Once a week, we all lined up in the kitchen to have our hair washed by our nanny, whom we called Nani. She was terrified of lice. Big kettles of hot water would be waiting for us on the stove, and one by one we submitted our heads to Nani's close inspection and energetic scrubbing before being sent off to our studies.

Like all but the very wealthy, we had no bath or shower in the home. Once a week, usually on a Thursday, our servant Hassan would pick us up from school to meet Maman and Nani at the *hamam*, the public baths, for our weekly wash. The bathhouse that was used by our neighborhood was called Hamam Valiabad and was about a mile from our home. It was available on alternate days for women and men. Up to the age of six, boys could accompany their mother on women's days. Far more than a simple bath, these ablutions were a social occasion that took four or more hours. Many of our neighbors would go on the same day, so a visit to the baths was like an extended party with lots of gossip and laughter. It also provided the perfect occasion for women to check out the physical attributes of a prospective marriage partner for their sons.

The *hamam* comprised two large rooms, a square anteroom with a decorative pool in the middle, and the bathroom itself. Families reserved an area of the anteroom as well as a favorite section of the bath. By the time we arrived at the *hamam*, Nani and Maman had already set up our section of the anteroom with rugs, sheets and pillows carried from home, and our clean clothes were laid out. We eagerly ate the food they had brought and then raced naked into the bathhouse, a huge, round, steamy room off which fanned many small alcoves for family bathing. In the center was a pool for those who didn't wish to pay extra for privacy.

Each alcove had a shower and a faucet. The floor was heated from below by coal and was too hot to sit on, so we all sat on inverted round copper trays that functioned as low stools. Maman had a standing reservation with our favorite *dalak*, or washing lady, who came into the alcove to wash us one by one.

First you were washed off, and then you sat there in the steam to warm the skin and open the pores. Next, the *dalak* applied a white granular exfoliant called *sefidab*, brought from home along with coarse, bag-like, woolen gloves called *kiseh*. Our choice of *kiseh* depended on how vigorously we wanted the dead skin rubbed off our bodies. Glowing from the ministrations of the *dalak*, we rinsed off under the shower, and presented ourselves to Nani, who would wash our hair with the same suspicious concentration she applied in the kitchen. Back to the shower we would troop, and then off to the anteroom where warm towels were waiting. The whole enterprise of scrubbing, rinsing, and washing took us to well after dark, and we would arrive home at about eight o'clock. It was great fun and we looked forward to bath days immensely. We fought and played and ate and ran around naked—what more could a child want?

In our house the room next to the kitchen was a large storage room. When my oldest sister, Mamak, a bright student, was in high school, the storage room was converted into her study so that she could remove herself from the clamor of the younger members of the family. Mamak went on to become a respected translator and a businesswoman, so her time alone was well used.

Beyond this was a second locked storage room used to keep dry foods such as rice and dried vegetables, and cooking oil—items purchased in bulk several times a year. Every morning Maman would unlock the door and take out what was needed for the day.

Next in line lay a formal dining room. This room was so cold in winter that it was unusable other than for food storage. Two big cupboards were used to keep cooked foods, just as a refrigerator would be used today. In summer, when we had company for lunch, we ate here, as the room somehow managed to retain an unseasonable degree of coolness. It was actually a somewhat scary place to us as small children. Two windows looked onto the shaded area of the garden where the mulberry trees stood, but their dark bamboo shades were always drawn and the room seemed to us to have a gloomy, ominous atmosphere. Nevertheless, my brother Mehrdad and I (usually at my instigation) would quite often creep in and help ourselves to the food stored in the cupboards.

Beneath the dining room, and possibly the source of the room's peculiar chill, was our water storage, a huge concrete tank called an *abembar*. From the courtyard, many steps—perhaps twenty—led down into the dark to the open *abembar* (*ab* means water). Two or three times a year, the tank was refilled from the spring water flowing down the *jube* out in the street. Maman would add charcoal and powdered lime to purify the water. Water for washing, cooking, or drinking was drawn from the faucet in the side of the tank into clay jugs. These were left outside at night to stay cool and brought into the house in the morning. Water for the gardens and pools came straight from the *jube*.

The story of my entry into this world is closely tied to that *abembar*. When Maman was pregnant with me, she fell down the steps one day when she went to get water and I was born, a month prematurely, that evening. Like all children at that time, I was born at home with the help of a hastily summoned midwife. My mother, a healthy woman, bore eight children, of whom six survived beyond infancy—Hushang, Mamak, Mali, myself, Mehrdad, and Cherry.

From the formal dining room, a doorway led to the room of my older brother, Hushang. He was the only one with his own room, although he sometimes shared it with our youngest uncle, Mussa. Tall and good-looking, Hushang had beautiful diction. We all called him *Dadash* (brother). As the oldest son in a male-oriented society, Hushang was worshiped by my parents and had great authority over the rest of us. He was a wonderful older brother, always very kind and loving.

Hushang's room was furnished with a table for studying and a couple of chairs. The floor was covered with a Persian rug. A tall window opened onto the area of the garden where the mulberry trees grew. A second doorway connected his room to the hallway leading to Father's study, the big family living room, and my parents' room. These three rooms were the most esteemed part of the house.

To walk into the light-filled living room was to enter an enchanted realm. On one side, tall folding windows opened onto a spacious balcony that overlooked the formal front garden and its three pools. On the opposite side, big windows framed a view of the courtyard. A large, coal-burning open fireplace, with a carved mantelpiece above it, occupied one part of the inner wall nearest to my parents' room. Over the mantel, a beautiful rug, woven with a pattern of animals and birds, hung above an old Russian clock. To each side stood tall green crystal vases—always empty, for we cut no flowers from our garden.

On the floor was a matched pair of large Persian rugs. With a background of earthy beige, these exuberant and colorful floral carpets brought the garden inside, their tones echoed in the pink and beige floral velvet armchairs arranged around two low, square, dark wooden tables. A beautifully carved wooden side table placed in front of the windows onto the balcony was always massed with fragrant potted flowers from the greenhouse. Views of the garden and the cypress trees in the courtyard were reflected in the opposite windows, the effect a gorgeous celebration of nature and art intertwined in a single room. It was a truly beautiful space, filled with harmonious colors that danced before the eyes and created a feeling of immense joy in all who spent time there.

Two glorious paintings presented to my father by Mohammad Ghaffari, a famous twentieth-century Persian artist better known as Kamal-ol Molk, hung to the sides of the windows onto the courtyard. One depicted a blind woman being led by her two boys, her face suffused with love for these children, the other a famous Persian mystic, a woman called Gorat-Alayn.

During, *Nowruz*, the Persian New Year, a celebration of the rebirth of the earth after winter that has been observed in Iran for thousands of years, the carved table near the balcony held the traditional display of *sofra-ye haft sin*. *Sofra* means a special cloth that is spread on the floor or table in a room used for entertaining guests; *haft*, which means seven, is a sacred number, and *sin* is the letter "s". *Sofra-ye haft sin* is a display of seven symbolic items that, in our family, typically included apples (*sib*) to represent health; coins (*sekeh*) for wealth; vinegar (*serkeh*) for patience; *sumaq*, the reddish gold powder from sumac berries, for joy; garlic (*seer*), esteemed for its medicinal properties and power to ward off the evil eye; *samanu*, a thick reddish pudding painstakingly prepared by the women of the household (who make wishes for children or a husband as they stir) from sprouted wheat, flour, oil, and nuts, and considered an aphrodisiac; *senjed*, the dried fruit of the lotus tree, for love; and *sabzeh*, a dense circle of young green wheat or barley shoots to represent rebirth.

Most families have more than seven *sin* items on their *sofra*, and the specific number may have been a recent addition to the custom. My family usually added sweet-blooming hyacinth (*sonbol*); brightly painted eggs; a small brazier smoldering with the seeds of wild rue, or *sepand*, to ward off evil; and goldfish swimming in a small bowl of rainwater. There would also be honey, fruits, sugar, and bowls of sweets, sugar-coated almonds, and puffed rice.

On either side of a large mirror placed at the back of the table, candleholders held a candle for each child in the family. Father's treasured volume of the *Shah Nameh* (Book of Kings), the magnificent story of Iranian history by the revered tenth-century poet Ferdowsi, completed our *sofra-ye haft sin.*

The *Shah Nameh* brings the rich history of Iran's glorious past to life in poetry, unparalleled in its beauty, beloved and memorized by all Iranians. In my father's tribute to the great Ferdowsi, he wrote:

He conjures up the great ones from our past—
　　Cyrus, Darius, Xerxes—
And breathes fresh life into their heroic deeds.
　　His years of devoted toil, his love of country,
Made Iran's long proud history bloom anew.

The story of Ghaznavi[4]—who cares? He's gone
　　While the one who remains with us is Ferdowsi.
These stories belong to our whole nation.
　　But the one name that will last forever,
Linked through his words with our glorious heritage,
　　That one is the poet Ferdowsi,
Reminding us of what we were in centuries past.

Father's handwritten copy of the *Shah Nameh* was a real treasure. It had wonderful hand-painted illustrations and illuminations, as well as his detailed annotations. After my father died, the book went to my mother, and then to me when I came to the United States in the 1950s. Feeling that this masterpiece belonged not to me but to the Iranian people, I presented it to Iran's National Archives in 2000. A facsimile version has since been published, so that many people can enjoy their own copy of this magnificent volume and read to their children the stirring tales of kings and queens, love and battles from the distant past.

As the exact spring equinox approached, we would gather around the table. Father, known for his powerful lyric voice, would recite from the *Shah Nameh* and from the beautiful works of Hafez, a much-loved poet of the fourteenth century also known in the west as Hafiz. We would take it in turns to make a wish, then open Hafez at random to see what this great philosopher could offer us as an answer to our wish. Father or Maman would read the chosen verses and we would all interpret them to see what guide they provided.

We loved Nowruz. Apart from the customary gifts and gold coins children received from the adults in the family, we were all outfitted in brand new clothing from head to foot in recognition of the new beginning.

The spirit of celebration went on for twelve days after the official start of spring. On the thirteenth day, *Sizdeh-bedar* (*sizdeh* means thirteen, and *bedar* means outdoors), we would find a field with running water and trees and have a picnic. We took along our sprouted grain, or *sabzeh*, now about a foot high. Throwing the *sabzeh* into running water marks the rebirth of the year and the new cycle of growth beginning.

All over Iran families act out this ancient ritual, and the streams and rivers flow green with offerings to nature. Even transplanted Iranians carry on the tradition. I have seen little rafts of *sabzeh* bobbing merrily on the Potomac River in Washington and the Seine in Paris on the thirteenth day of spring. And there are signs that these symbolic circles of green shoots have become springtime favorites of florists and decorators outside the Persian culture.

During Nowruz, our family would visit all the older relatives to congratulate them on the new year. Every house was filled with flowers and decorated with its own *sofra-ye haft sin*, and we would be offered tea, fruits, cookies, and other treats. It was the responsibility of younger people to show respect to older relatives and friends by paying a visit. This was the time when friendships were affirmed and enmities forgiven, so that everywhere, as the earth renewed itself, human beings renewed their commitments. As with the communion with nature that art and literature celebrate, Nowruz reminds us that we are here on earth for a short while and have an obligation to give back some of the richness that we receive by being alive.

My father wrote a lovely description of Nowruz in a long political poem called *Bahar e Isfahan*, written while we were in exile in Isfahan. The title is a double entendre: it could at once be spring (bahar) in Isfahan, or more darkly, Bahar (the exiled poet) in Isfahan. The poet laments the sad state of the nation and sets out his hopes and dreams for the future. He shakes himself out of his reverie to remind himself that life goes on and it is spring.

It is spring. The garden is filled with joy and blossom.
The new-grown grass is fresh and fragrant.
All of the flowers are blooming but my heart is still in winter.
All hearts should rejoice in the new year;
It is a shame to be despondent on this happy day of rebirth.
At least that's what a Black-eyed Susan keeps telling me.
Don't look for "*shin*" instead of "*sin*"[5]
Because *shin* means everything bad: complaint, screams, destruction,
    corruption, gossip, deceit, cruelty.
Choose instead seven "*sin*" which are sweet and positive:
Fresh greens, hyacinth, fragrant apples, music,
samanu, bright eggs and happiness.
Arrange the *haft sin* on a beautiful table
And throw the *haft shin* out of the window.
It is the dawn of spring. Forget about your pain. Rejoice!
Visit your friends and ask God for a blessing.
Celebrate the miracle of life and leave the rest to the Universe.

Below our living room was the *zir zamin*, a vital part of our lives during the summer months. *Zir* means under, *zamin* means earth, and this semi-underground room was our refuge from the fierce summer heat, for we had no air-conditioning in those days. From the courtyard, six steep steps went down into this space; from the garden, another set of five steps gave access. Two windows opening on the garden side allowed light into the room. In the garden, a deep well provided sweet underground water for drinking. The cool depths of the well offered a wonderful bonus: a short underground passage leading to the side of the well brought deliciously chilled air drifting into the *zir zamin*, making it a heavenly retreat from the heat outside. My father used the cool passageway as a cellar for his collection of wines from various parts of Iran. My mother kept a big basket of fruits there.

The *zir zamin* was a large white room, with a plaster ceiling hand-carved in an intricate pattern of ornate rectangles. Wall-to-wall Persian rugs covered the dirt floor. Over the carpets were spread blue and gray cotton *jajim*, hand-woven cloths, cool and comfortable to lie on. In the middle of the day, we would all go down the stairs into this room, take off our shoes, pick up a pillow and a sheet from a pile in the corner, and take a nap.

The side of the *zir zamin* nearest to the passageway and thus the coolest part of the room was where my father would set his pillow down to sleep or read. Even though our mother was the one in charge in our family, the best place was always given to my father. Maman loved him deeply, and was very proud to be married to him. She would put her pillow nearby.

Two large columns supporting the ceiling provided a wonderful opportunity for us children to escape the watchful eyes of our parents. Only two or three of us could fit into the small spaces behind the columns, so we would race each other after lunch to lay claim to these prime locations. The last thing we wanted was to find ourselves lying in the open central part of the room. Being behind the pillars also meant we could sneak into the passageway to help ourselves to the fruit basket. Probably our parents knew perfectly well what we were up to, but we felt very clever.

On some afternoons, relatives or close friends, among them our family doctor, came to join us. Special pillows and sheets were provided for these guests, who did not always come to sleep but rather to talk. The overheard conversations, ranging from literature to science to politics, were a background to our growing up and kept us up to date with what was going on in the world beyond our house.

If any of us wanted to escape the afternoon routine of the *zir zamin* we had to make sure we had our *giveh*, woven cotton slippers, hidden under our pillow. Even two steps barefoot on the fiery cobblestones of the courtyard would blister the soles of our feet and make us yelp with pain. So as not to awaken our parents, I would always be sure that my *giveh* were under the pillow. Poor Mehrdad, younger and more naïve than I, often got caught as he tried to get his shoes and follow me outside.

Our parents' bedroom served a multitude of purposes; it was next to the living room, with a door connecting the two. The only time this door stood open was when one of the children got married. Then all the women in the family would gather in the bedroom to prepare the bride for marriage, while the men gathered in the living room.

Two large windows opened from the bedroom onto the garden. A simple, wide metal bed stood in one corner of the room, but it was hardly used. My parents preferred to sleep on the floor, like most Iranians then, and many today. During the day, the bed was piled with the mattresses and pillows that at night were placed on the floor. In the summer, mosquito nets were hung above the mattresses and the windows were kept open to let in the cooler evening air. Each morning, all was piled back on the bed, and the room became a family room.

Two red Isfahani rugs were the only other furniture in the room apart from the wardrobe of dark wood that held Father's clothing. Maman kept her clothes folded in the storage room.

At noon and again in the evening, the bedroom became a dining room. A large white tablecloth was spread on the floor and all the children joined my parents for these family meals. The room was the center of our family life.

From this bedroom a second door opened onto a hallway that led on one side to steps down into the courtyard, and on the other to the children's bedroom that I shared with Mehrdad and my sisters.

In the hall stood a wooden table covered with a heavy, fringed cotton cloth.

The fabric was printed in a paisley design in blue, red, beige, and white in the traditional wood-block style of Isfahan. On the table sat a large copper samovar on a copper tray. A white china teapot perched on top of the samovar held strong, fragrant, brewed tea to which boiling water from the samovar was added when it was served in small tea glasses, or *estekan*, that were grouped to the side. The samovar, fueled by coal, was lit by our servants early in the morning before we woke up, and again in the afternoon.

In the morning, the table was laid with our breakfast. Aromatic flatbread of various kinds—*sangak, lavash, barbari*—was cut by Nani and ready in a basket. Hassan went out before dawn to buy fresh bread from a baker in town. Boiled eggs were cooked on a special rimmed section of the samovar and served in china eggcups. Then there was feta cheese, eaten with the still-warm bread and herbs such as mint, basil, tarragon, and parsley picked fresh from our garden. Small dishes of my mother's jam rounded out this very typical Persian breakfast. My father, who usually worked late into the night, would get up after we children had left for school. But the rest of us and Nani would gather around a big white cloth on the floor of the children's room, drawn from sleep by the fragrance of the tea, the irresistible aroma of the fresh bread, and the spicy tang of the herbs.

The children's room had two windows overlooking the courtyard. In most Persian households, the whole family would share one room; but in our family, my parents and Hushang, and later Mamak, had their own rooms. Our room was large, particularly for an Iranian house, about twenty-five feet long on each side, with two windows overlooking the courtyard. The windows began about three feet off the floor and were hung with white curtains. A rug with a floral design covered the floor. Against the wall between the windows stood a wooden wardrobe that held our clothing and all our possessions.

Nani slept in the room with us. When our baby sister Cherry joined us, the room was full of life, and we had lots of fun there together. I long for those days of closeness and love.

Tehran is built in a valley at the foot of the Alborz mountain chain, the tallest peak of which is the volcano, Damavand. Winters are cold and were even colder back in the days when the city was little more than a town. We often had a foot of snow.

Our only transportation in those early days was a donkey (they were very cheap then). When there was snow on the ground, the three oldest children would ride the donkey to school, wrapped all around with blankets. Hassan—we children called him Baba Hassan (literally, father Hassan, but actually a term of endearment)—led the donkey down the mountain and through the city.

The funny little group was quite well known in the neighborhood and people would say, "Here come the Bahar children!" as they made their way through the lanes and streets. Sometimes the donkey slipped on the snow and the bundle of children, tied up together in blankets and thus condemned to a common fate, tumbled to the ground. Hassan would separate the bodies from the blankets, put them back on the donkey, wrap them up, and off they would go again.

One of the saddest moments of my life was when, years after I had left Iran, it came to me with piercing clarity that Hassan—our beloved Baba Hassan—was a spy in our midst, paid by the authorities to report on my father's activities. Even as a child it had sometimes puzzled me that Hassan, whose pitiful salary we sometimes could not afford to pay, seemed to live quite well whereas I went a couple of winters without a coat. He eventually acquired a plot of land near to us, and built a three-story house there for his family, quite unusual for those times. We younger children were in and out of his house, playing with his children. It was like a second home to us.

It was a sad, but not shocking, realization. For a man like Hassan, life was not easy. It would be very hard to refuse a steady income. Nothing was done secretly at our house, and it probably seemed of little consequence to report from time to time on the many people coming to visit my father. Moreover, it would have been easy for the authorities to intimidate Hassan should he refuse to cooperate; everyone in Iran was terrified of their power to arrest, torture, even "disappear" people who somehow crossed the regime.

I wonder that my parents were oblivious to this enigma. I can imagine that my father, who had no head for financial matters, would not even give it a thought. But my careful mother, who held the purse strings close to her chest and accounted for every *rial* that came in or out of the family coffers? Perhaps they were both aware of the situation and chose to ignore it. Maybe they used it to their advantage. Maybe they modified their behavior accordingly, although

I very much doubt it, as Father refused to make any concessions to his right to freedom and free speech. For me, though, it was painful to recall the love and intimacy we enjoyed with Baba Hassan, and try to reconcile it with a treacherous Hassan, accepting money to spy on us. Sadly, this is one of the inevitable products of oppressive dictatorships, where people's humanism is stripped away by fear and necessity and they turn on their fellow sufferers to save themselves.

During the winter, the house was very cold. The living room was warmed by a coal-burning fireplace and most of the other rooms had a coal stove. In our room, however, we had a *korsi*, a low square table under which a deep metal tray holds burning coal. Our mattresses were laid out, one on each side of the table. A huge wool comforter, or *lahaf*, was spread over the whole thing to keep the heat in. When we sat at the table to study, we would pull the comforter around us, and at night when we slept, the comforter would be over all but our heads.

Maman always warned us not to put our feet under the table while we studied, or we would become too cozy and be sure to fall asleep. So we knelt at the table, leaning on our elbows. Probably we were lucky not to suffer carbon monoxide poisoning!

I loved the *korsi*. I loved the close companionship, with Mehrdad to my left, Mali opposite, and Nani—and later on, Cherry—to my right. I loved the warmth and comfort it provided. I don't recall ever feeling cold in winter, as there were so many sources of heat—the *korsi*, the fireplace, the coal stoves, the samovar, the wood-burning kitchen stoves—that every part of the house had its own heating personality.

In the summer we had the opposite challenge—to keep cool. At night our mattresses were set up under a large mosquito net in the courtyard outside our room. On the other side, my two older sisters had their mosquito net. Hushang had a netted area of the balcony and my parents slept under a net in their room, or on a wooden bed set up in the garden.

So this was the house I grew up in. This was the paradise to which my spirit returned that day as I stood in the hot, noisy street. This is where I go when I close my eyes. It is the fertile ground from which I sprang, like one of my father's beloved roses. In a poem called "The Splendor of Nature," my father immortalized our Paradise:

Look at this beautiful spring blossom!

Its delicate beauty outshines the face of my beloved.

Look at the fruit ripening on those trees!

Nothing could be sweeter or more inviting.

Look at that adorable little girl!

In her heart there is nothing but love.

Look at that sweet-faced boy!

He is too young to have experienced anxiety.

Just look at those innocent children!

They deserve nothing but love and kindness.

Look, too, at their father and mother.

In their hearts is no hint of bitterness or revenge.

These people represent the world, a glorious world,

A place with no room for darkness or deceit.

If you want to find bad things in this world, go ahead.

But the fault will lie in your blindness to its magnificence.

If you can look upon such beauty and still be heartsick,

What can I say? That you are angry with the Creator Himself?

And if you find His creation empty of delight,

Your life will remain a hollow shell.

With every spring, as new life emerges from the winter soil, as the grass fulfills its green promise and flowers reassert their place in the garden, my soul flies back to the sweet paradise of my youth. I hear again my mother's soft voice, feel the warmth of my father's loving glance, laugh once more with my dear brother, recall our happy play in the garden. And my heart yearns for the simplicity, the innocence, the beauty that nurtured us in Paradise.

MY MOTHER

W HEN MY father was in his early thirties, he was in a position to afford a wife and family; but, having left the society he knew in Mashhad when he moved to Tehran to attend parliament, he was not acquainted with any suitable women. Given the strict social constraints of the time, it was almost impossible to find a partner without a go-between. His father, who might have acted as a matchmaker, had died and his other relatives were in Mashhad. He told a close friend, who happened to be married to my mother's sister, that he was seeking a wife who was strong and tall, educated, and from a very good family. The qualities he sought were unusual: Most men would look for youth, beauty, virginity, perhaps wealth; but my father was looking for a life partner, not an ornament.

My mother, born in 1895, was twenty-three at the time. In those days, any woman who did not marry in her teens was considered quite a tragic figure, as neatly summed up in the old proverb, "We can only weep for the girl who finds herself unmarried at twenty."

Despite her advanced years and pitiable spinsterhood, my mother possessed all of the qualities my father sought in a wife. Although there was no formal schooling for girls—education for women was considered "un-Islamic" by most religious leaders—my mother was educated at home by private female tutors. I am not sure how extensive her education was; she could read and write and was sufficiently comfortable with mathematics to manage our household finances. I never saw her reading books, even the Koran, but perhaps that was because she did not have time. She was able to check our homework up until the sixth grade, but by junior high we were on our own.

My aunt suggested that Bahar accompany them to a wedding party that her sister Soodabeh was to attend, and arranged that Maman walk past them. Father later complained that this was not equality, as she could see him but he could only catch a glimpse of her in her veil. Nevertheless, their wedding ceremony was duly arranged and they entered the period of *aghd* (like an engagement). In those days, couples could not see each other during this period, but my parents kept a correspondence of beautiful love letters. Judging by my father's responses to her love letters, Maman was able to express herself well; but unfortunately, the letters she wrote were lost.

After Father died, my mother gave me his letters with instructions to keep them safe, just as he had begged her to do during their courtship. He had written: *Please don't show my letters to anyone. Guard them with your life and keep them somewhere safe. These letters are souvenirs of our youth and our love.*

When she died, I presented them to the National Archives of Iran, where archivists preserved and displayed them, and they were published as a small volume.

In my father's first letter to my mother, where he is introducing himself, he wrote:

My dear companion for life

> *Although I have not really seen you yet, I am absolutely sure of my good fortune: in you I have found a great treasure. I know in my own heart and soul that I have chosen the best. Now let me introduce myself to you. I am a young man with a good heart, hard working and passionate. Friendship is sacred to me. If ever I had an enemy, I would deal honorably with him as befits another human being.*

> *I was born into a family that prizes, above all, moral thinking. My mother, besides being a well-educated woman, is just. In my family, stinginess, lying, exaggeration and gossip do not exist. We have been taught by our parents to be pleasant, industrious, and independent. My father died when I was eighteen and I became the head of the family. I have worked hard to take care of my mother, two younger brothers, and one sister. Today, all of them are very proud of me. Whatever I have achieved, it was through my own hard work; and I have made money too.*

Because until now I have not had a loving partner to guide me, whatever I have made, I have spent. I live alone in Tehran, because my mother's bad health has confined her to Mashhad. I had a good life in Mashhad—a nice house and all the belongings a family needs. I have five hundred family members on my father's side and my mother's side, all living in Mashhad. But because of my way of thinking and my political views, I had no choice but to live in Tehran. Now that I want a family of my own, I hope that I can make them as proud of me as is my other family in Mashhad.

I am offering my hand to you, and swear that I will be true to you until the day that I die. I promise that you will be the only woman in my life, now and forever. I am not like some other young Iranian men, with no experience and moving from one woman to another. I believe that women deserve the same rights as men. I know that you will be like minded, because you come from a very great family. I knew your father and I know your mother and the rest of your family. I know that we will find great happiness together. You have chosen me because I have all the qualities that I described to you. I shall promise you that you will never be unhappy with me. You can ready yourself to move into my life, my heart, and my soul. You are the owner of my wealth, the head of my house, and the conqueror of my heart. You are my master in every aspect of my life. I only pray and hope that your heart will cleave to mine, and that we will never become two. We remain one, one heart, through all our life.

I hope I can see you, that I can talk to you and tell you in person what is in my heart. Then I could see how you respond to my feelings. I am, to my friends and my family, a symbol of love, friendship, and loyalty. If you are of the same opinion, it will be a blessing for both of us. I don't believe a marriage is only what two mullahs recite in Arabic. The true marriage is what is between two hearts and souls. Well, we have no other choice but to wait to see each other when you finally come to my house. At least we can write to each other. You are all I think of, all day long.

I am renovating my house. It is a good house, newly built. I have three bedrooms, a living room, and dining room, as well as a room to entertain visitors. There is a big garden and I don't imagine you will have a bad time here. You will have to hire a good cook and a maid and bring them with you.

I hope you answer my letter as soon as you can. Please give my regards and respect to your mother, the Princess. I will kiss her hand because I am so happy that she said "yes" to my request to marry you.

M. Bahar

In a later letter, father wrote:

I beg you to write more about yourself. Since we cannot see each other, these letters are the only way we can communicate our feelings. We should never lie to one another, neither in our correspondence nor after our wedding. If I were allowed, I would come every day just to glimpse your beautiful face. I would kiss both your hands and kneel down in front of you to tell you how much I love you. When I received your last letter and I saw your handwriting, my soul flew toward heaven. I wish I could hide myself in a corner of your heart, somewhere safe, and feel what you are feeling towards me. I can never express my own emotions well on paper—I could do better if I were with you.

My mother must have used a petulant tone in one of her letters, for Father wrote:

Your last letter was beautifully written. Writing should be like talking: it should be simple and express feelings. I beg you to try to use fewer Arabic words and rely on your Persian vocabulary. In one of your letters you say you are a victim. I don't understand what you mean by "victim." Who has ever hurt you? Or is this an exaggeration? A person who sees herself as a victim has relinquished self-determination. How could the person I have chosen to be my wife be seen as a victim? Embracing victimhood shrinks the heart and extinguishes the fire of the soul. From now on, you will not be a victim.

It must have been difficult for the young couple to wait to meet each other in person, and it appears that Father kept requesting a meeting. Finally my grandmother gave permission for them to see each other at her house. Father sent the following letter after their meeting:

How happy I am that we finally saw each other. You are absolutely the woman I thought you were—beautiful, educated, and well-bred. The bracelet I gave you was not really the one I would have chosen. But I had too little notice and so wanted to bring a gift. Today I went to a jeweler and I chose a ring—an emerald surrounded by diamonds. I also noticed that you did not have a necklace, so I chose a beautiful necklace of diamonds for you. I have asked my younger brother to bring them today so that you can see if you like them. If they are to your liking, give them back to my brother; I will buy them right away and bring them myself tomorrow. I will put the ring on your finger myself and I will hang the necklace around your beautiful neck and I shall give you a kiss on both cheeks.

Your loving husband

The period of waiting was over. Their home was ready. A big party was held in my grandmother's house, at the end of which the bride began her new life in her husband's house. Although they had come to know each other through their letters, they had seen each other only twice. They were to live together for thirty-three years in harmony and mutual dedication.

After marrying my mother, Soodabeh Qajar, Father began to call her Bahar or Bahar-*joon*, "Dear Spring," because he loved her so much and saw her as a new beginning to his life. A tall woman with large, very black eyes and olive skin, my mother inherited the title of princess from both her parents, descendants of Fath Ali Shah, the second shah of the Qajar dynasty who reigned from 1797 until 1834 (and first cousins, a marriage arrangement prized in Iran at the time). Her father, Prince Safdar Mirza Qajar, died early, in his forties; but her mother, Gohar Taj Qajar—tall, slim, erect, aloof and very strict—lived on until she was 100. One day, my grandmother asked all her children and grandchildren to come to her to say good-bye, saying that she had lived long enough. She died that night. She had been in good health, walking unaided and living a normal life. She just decided it was her time to go.

My mother was a powerful woman and a good manager. Her domain included everything in our household, from the food and the servants to the children. She was like a rock in difficult times, always managing somehow to see us through. Father had no idea how a household worked; he did not even know when or how he got his pay. My mother would send Hassan to collect my father's salary from the University of Tehran at the beginning of each month and then put the money in her big black money box. Once, overwhelmed by the management of our big household, Maman took the money box to Father and said she couldn't do it anymore. Father said he would take over; but after a day of enduring people parading though his office wanting money for this and that, he picked up the box and threw it into one of the pools, saying, "I can't—I *won't*—do this anymore! It is too hard!"

If it were not for Maman, our family would never have thrived and I am sure my father could never have pursued his writing with the dedication he was able to bring to it. My mother stood beside Father during good and bad times, and there was often a lot more bad than good. When not in jail or engaged in intellectual and political pursuits, my father was in his study reading and writing. Maman's life work was to make life as calm as possible for him. She adored my father unconditionally, a type of love I have rarely seen again in my life. He always came first. She called him *Agha*, which translates as "sir" but is a common form of addressing a man, particularly in those more formal days.

Very early on in her marriage, she realized that she had married an unusual and creative man. Throughout her life she was proud of her tall, lean, aesthetic, sensitive, tense husband and she set out to make his life comfortable. No sacrifice was too much, from traveling to Tehran from Isfahan innumerable times when he was exiled until she extracted a pardon, to selling all that she had inherited to pay for his trip to Switzerland in search of a cure for tuberculosis.

A key element of the relationship was that Maman never condemned Father for his risky political activity and never complained about the repercussions on the family. She knew that if he conceded just a little to Reza Shah and later, to Mohammad Shah, we could have a much better life. We were at times almost penniless, but still she stood next to him. In truth she was Father's partner and I believe that she was also a partner in the creation of his literary work. Like the women behind many great men, she created the environment that made the work possible. Father worked at home, sometimes until very late at night, and Maman enjoined us to respect his need for peace and quiet.

When she tired of her children's antics, our mother put on a solemn face.

Then we would tell her she looked like her ancestor, Agha Mohammad Khan, who was always portrayed with a very long, sad face. The first of the Qajar kings, the cruel Mohammad Khan seized the throne in the 1790s but was soon assassinated. There was a good reason for his famously sad and bitter face: when only a child, he was castrated by enemies who tried unsuccessfully to prevent his succession. When we saw his expression appear on our mother's face, we knew it was time to behave.

It was easy to see where my mother got her role model. My grandmother, who ran her own large household singlehanded for almost sixty years after her husband died, was also undemonstrative, even distant to our family. Perhaps it was because of Maman's marriage to a man who not only had no status or wealth, but was in and out of jail and exile. Eventually my father's status outstripped all of the Qajar family, but during my childhood we were definitely the ugly duck-lings amongst my grandmother's brood. Her other children and grandchildren lived in her household, and she seemed to show more affection to them than to me and my siblings, particularly to her oldest grandson on whom she doted.

I remember our visits there as tense, obligatory affairs. We children were instructed to sit silently and not to accept any food offered to us, as this would be considered impolite. At home, we ate well but only had treats like cakes and pastries on special occasions like Nowruz, so it was hard not to be tempted by the lavish table. I am sure that my grandmother's keen intelligence noted our longing; we must have made a strange picture, six silent children sitting cross-legged in a row, staring solemnly at the table.

When I was in junior high school, I started dropping in on my grandmother by myself during the long lunch period that was typical of Iranian schools. I was curious about her, and wanted to establish a relationship of my own. No doubt I was also hungry for love. Her home was then quite close to my school and after eating my lunch—I never broke the rule about accepting food—I would walk over for a visit. The family was usually at lunch when I arrived and I would join them, not saying much, just being a part of the group. Perhaps this was the main attraction—our family was perforce rather solitary (officially ostracized, so that at times even friends were afraid to be seen with us) and it was comforting to enlarge my sense of belonging. After a number of these visits, my grandmother asked me why I came. When I told her that I loved her and wanted to get to know her better, she seemed to soften in her attitude toward me; and while she never became particularly friendly or gentle, I could see that I had sparked her interest and she seemed pleased when I appeared.

As children, we never really understand our parents' relationship. There must have been affection in the privacy of their room—after all, there were six children! What we saw was enormous respect and consideration, loyalty, and pride in each other's achievements. My father certainly admired my mother's prodigious managerial skills. In a long poem called *Khanehvadeh* (Family) about our family, he wrote of her:

> The lady who is mother to my children is the head of the household.
> Truly, she has a beautiful soul.
> Extending her command from the kitchen to my study
> She takes care of the money and anyone who comes and goes.
> She owns us all and we all adore her for what she does.
> She gave birth to our children and raised them
> Like a lioness who nurtures her cubs.
> Her dedication to her children's health exceeds that of a doctor.
> When the children return from school she helps with their homework.
> Though kind and good to the people who work for her
> She looks and acts like a general in the army.
> Rising early in the morning and working past midnight
> She is just like the sorceress who creates the world.

Father's views about women were radical for his time. He always believed women and men were equal, and he was unafraid to speak out for women's rights to freedom and equality. Everything we owned was under my mother's name, another unusual feature of the household. In those days, men and women did not interact outside of prescribed circumstances—usually within family gatherings—and women were veiled and cloistered. After marriage, my mother never observed *hejab* (modesty in attire) by wearing a veil or *chador*, the full-length, all-enveloping piece of cloth that hides all but a woman's face and hands: Father would not countenance it. He saw the *chador* as a symbol of captivity. So even before Reza Shah forced its abolition in 1936 as part of his drive to modernize Iran, my mother went without it.

Many women—probably most—were mortified by the precipitous ban on the *chador* and many simply stayed at home rather than experience the shame of appearing in public "naked." I did not grow up in a sea of *chadors*, as the young women in today's Iran did. Certainly there were women who covered their hair, but in the north of Tehran where I lived, these were mainly servants. I can remember being shocked when the *chador* became a political symbol in the late 1970s as Khomeini, the exiled cleric, unified the opposition to the Shah from Iraq and then Paris. The symbol of solidarity and resistance so defiantly worn by brave and strong women in the street demonstrations became mandatory soon after Khomeini forced the Shah into exile, and continues as a form of oppression today.

One telling story about my mother is the time that she was en route to the United States to be with me when my second child was born. It was her first trip abroad alone and she had to change planes in England. My brother Mehrdad was in London at that time and he went to Heathrow to meet her. As he waited for her outside the customs hall, he saw a small commotion going on inside and in the middle of it was Maman. She was waving her arms and speaking very emphatically in Persian to a bemused group of British officials. He later found that she had been displeased with some aspect of her treatment and resorted to her fail-safe phrase, "I am the wife of Malek o'Shoara Bahar!" While this was an "Open sesame" in Iran, it did little to solve her problem at Heathrow, not least because she spoke no English. But so confident was she of her husband's fame and stature and the respect that his name generated that it was this talisman for which she had reached. She spent her life nurturing his genius and was proud to the end that she, indeed, was the wife of Malek o'Shoara Bahar.

Maman lived for twenty-eight years after Father died, succumbing to a long illness at eighty-five. It was sad to watch her—she didn't go out, she gained weight, didn't exercise. Essentially she said to herself, "Life is over for me."

My mother was in her mid-fifties when she was widowed. Her marriage must have been very hard on her, but when it ended, it wasn't just that she was in mourning, it was as though the core of her being had been ripped away and she withered inside. Joy in existence simply evaporated. Throughout her married life our family had been ostracized, so she did not have friends. For the next three decades she isolated herself, seeing only the family, or what was left of it. Mehrdad was in jail and later went to England. I soon went abroad, and Hushang—the light of her life—was incommunicado and in the United States.

Maman always hoped to be buried next to her husband and bought a plot next to his in the cemetery where all the writers and artists were buried. But by the time she died, the cemetery was closed and with great regret we had to bury her elsewhere.

I admire my mother enormously. She was very strict and demonstrated very little physical affection for her children, characteristics that were more common in the years of our growing up than they are today. When I think of what she had to deal with—the really awful periods of poverty, ostracism, and separation from her husband—I am filled with respect for the way she held the family together. Most people would have fallen apart or walked away. She was a masterful manager, so that even when we had little or no money, we were always fed, clothed, and housed. Her bookkeeping and planning were meticulous and her frugality legendary—nothing was ever wasted. She made sure we went to school and did our homework, and she tended us when we were ill.

Sometimes we found her ways puzzling or burdensome. As I grew older and became more aware of the huge effort required to keep everything going, my admiration increased. I think, above all, what gave her the strength and courage to never give up and to live to the age of eighty-five was her love for my father and the commitment she made to him at marriage. To me she is a giant of a woman who taught me the power of endurance.

But she also taught me the dangers of totally immersing oneself in husband and family. In this, I did not want to emulate her. Family, marriage, and children are certainly important to me, but I wanted more. I never thought that a man could be my whole life. I have had many friends, friends that I have made myself, and I cherish these friendships and nurture them.

I wanted independence, a career. I value my health and work hard to keep fit, knowing that I have inherited my mother's genes for gaining weight and developing leg problems. Maman almost willfully refused to exercise, so that the last ten years of her life were spent in partial paralysis. She closed the door behind her when Father died. In contrast, I never stop. I think the only time I will stop is when I am dead.

CHILDHOOD MEMORIES

MEHRDAD and I were best friends. We were born just a year apart, I in 1928 and he in 1929. We grew up together and started school on the same day. We climbed trees and planned mischief together. When we got into trouble with our demanding mother, we would both run like the wind together to escape punishment. Everything we did, we did together. It never crossed my mind that we were any different. Of course, I knew he was a boy and I a girl, but somehow I felt we were the same. I grew up with a boy and felt like a boy.

When we wrestled together—which we did frequently—we offered entertainment for the whole family, who would bring rugs to the garden and provide us with an enthusiastic audience. The winner of our bouts received a round of applause. This form of theater continued until I was thirteen. Up to that point I usually won, but suddenly Mehrdad, who was just reaching adolescence, began to develop. When he trounced me for the first time, Mehrdad decided that he didn't want to play that game anymore. At the time, I had no idea why he stopped wrestling me after one victory. I wanted to have a rematch but no, that was the end of it.

One night, when Mehrdad was about sixty—I had brought him to the Mayo Clinic to seek a cure for his leukemia—he finally told me why he had abruptly terminated our wrestling matches. It was the day the doctor had broken the sad news that there was no cure for his condition. We left the Mayo Clinic and walked to an Italian restaurant for dinner. We ordered our food and a bottle of wine, but neither of us had an appetite. We sat looking at each other, our tearful eyes mirroring our sadness at the knowledge that he had only two more years to live. He asked me, "Did you know why we stopped wrestling?" I told him that I had no idea. He said that the moment he felt physically stronger than I was, he knew he could no longer wrestle with me. I had always been the winner up to that point and he wanted it to remain that way.

That night was probably the most painful of my life. I saw that I was losing a brother, my best friend, my soul mate, my confidante, just as Mehrdad had apprehended what he was losing when he stood so sadly in the doorway to our garden the night of my wedding. But this would be a permanent loss. I told him that half of me would die with him. Neither of us had ever been alone as we grew up, except for the times that I accompanied Maman to Tehran from our exile in Isfahan.

Mehrdad was a symbol of humanity, courage, and goodness to me. He was so like my father. I always hoped that I would find a man who combined the qualities of my father and Mehrdad, but I never found one who came close.

When Mehrdad and I started school we were both in the first grade, but I had been studying at home and was soon promoted to the second grade. Mehrdad was unhappy that we were separated. He was a very serious student and as we went through the grades, he was the one who brought home the academic medals. I was nutty and naughty, but smart enough to do well and be promoted.

Father always found time to listen to our efforts to write when we were young. If we had an assignment for school, he would drop everything to sit and hear what we had to say. If he felt the writing was good, he would reward us with some money.

One day we decided we wanted to buy chewing gum and lemonade, the luxuries of the day. We had spent our small allowance and so sat in our tree and plotted. A brilliant idea came to us: we figured that Father, who was teaching literature at Tehran University, had probably forgotten the poetry that was taught in the first grade. We chose a poem by the poet Parvin Etesami. She was actually very famous and accomplished, but to our first-grade minds her poem was obscure and, we hoped, unknown or at least forgotten by our exalted father. We wrote out the poem in our best hand and marched together to the study. We found Father sitting on the floor in front of one of the bookcases, researching as usual. He raised his head from the book he was studying and asked, "Children, what do you want?"

Like a little chorus of birds, we chirped, "We have just written a poem together. We would like you to listen to it." Father closed his book, and said, "Wonderful! Wonderful! Would you read it please, my darlings?"

We started, in unison, to read "our" poem, which was about a spider and a fly that has become entangled in its web. It is a very famous poem, but we of course were blissfully unaware that a poem about a fly assigned in the first grade might ever reach the lofty ears of the Poet Laureate.

A fly, caught in a web, started talking to the spider . . ."

We got no further. Father starting shouting, "You thieves! This is not your poem! You are thieves! You have stolen the words!" He reached out to grab us, but I was too quick, and anyway, Mehrdad was sitting in front of me. Although my heart beat fast and my face went red, I escaped. Poor little Mehrdad was caught and punished. For several nights, neither of us appeared at the dinner table. We were so ashamed. Never again in our lives would we ever steal someone's work.

Mehrdad went on to become a great scholar of Persian mythology, his work a respected source for academics all over the world. I am sure he never plagiarized. As for me, forever afterwards, even when I quote someone with full attribution in any of my work, a feeling of dread will come over me. The memory of the shame is still there to prickle my mind, so powerful was the experience. And not only did we not get the hoped-for reward of money for "our" brilliant poem, we received no allowance for months! So there was no chewing gum and lemonade for some time. How small were our aspirations in those days, how simple the treats. How big the lessons.

Beyond Father's study were our mulberry trees. The trees were tall and bore heavenly sweet white mulberries. One of our favorite pastimes was to climb these trees and help ourselves to the delicious soft fruit. Because of his respect for the trees, Father didn't like us to climb them. But we did it anyway.

One day, we were sitting like birds in the top of the tree, gorging ourselves on the berries. We heard Father saying to Asghar, "Please bring some chairs into the shade of the mulberry trees. I have some guests coming and it will be cool there." I climbed down right away and went inside. But Mehrdad stayed on his perch. He assumed that the friends would come only for a short time, since it was nearly lunchtime. It was his bad luck that Father not only decided to invite his guests to stay for lunch but to have the meal served there under the trees. Poor Mehrdad; he had to stay quietly up there for hours! He knew that if he made his presence known, Father would be angry.

When lunch was served for the family inside, there was no Mehrdad. Maman fretted because she couldn't find him anywhere. I was too afraid to tell her that he was in the tree, because then she would go and call him down. Of course no one was truly worried, because we knew that a child was always safe in the house or the garden. There was none of the modern anxiety about the safety of children, and it was assumed he had fallen asleep somewhere.

Finally, as the afternoon grew late and the guests departed, Mehrdad reappeared, his face swollen from the many bee stings he had endured in silence while sitting among the mulberries. He was tired and thirsty. Maman applied some ointment that she made herself from herbs to relieve the swelling. Mehrdad did not appear for dinner, so Father never knew the little drama that had played itself out above his head.

It was not that we were severely punished by our father; we were in fact left alone to do as we liked, completely free. It was more that we respected Father so much that we didn't wish to displease him. There were just a few things that Father didn't like us to do—picking the flowers and climbing the trees being among them.

I can't remember how old I was when Father made the announcement that a german shepherd dog was joining our family. We were so excited. A dog! Keeping a dog is not a typically Persian custom and dogs are generally considered unclean, so the prospect of having a dog was very novel for us. She was a beautiful dog, jet black and trained by a Russian family that was leaving to go back to Moscow. Her name was Reba. She quickly became the seventh child of the family. We all loved her. She ate with us, slept with us, played with us, and traveled with us as one of the children.

Wherever we went, we went with Reba, even to the outdoor movies shown in summer. As we were a large group, Father would get a box for the whole family. Reba would rest her chin on the ledge of the box and watch with us. She was a very smart dog. When we traveled, we always rented a small bus and a driver. Reba would take up her place on the floor of the bus. She was just one of us.

When Reba heard the cry "*Nahar!*" (lunch) or "*Sham*" (dinner), she responded just like the rest of us. She would put her head through the handle of her food pail and trot to the table, waiting to be served. There was no special dog food; Reba ate what we ate.

On our trips north to the Caspian Sea, Reba appointed herself special guardian to Hushang, whom she adored. He was the only one who knew how to swim and Reba would watch him like a hawk from the sand. Whenever she thought that Hushang had swum too far from shore, she would charge into the water and swim like crazy to rescue him, dragging him back by his clothing despite his protests.

A wooden house was built in the garden outside Hushang's room for Reba. She usually slept there, but sometimes she would sleep with us. She lived with us for several wonderful years, then one night she must have suffered a stroke because she became paralyzed. A few weeks later, knowing that she was about to die, she managed somehow to drag herself from her house, up the stairs, and into Hushang's room. She rested her head next to Hushang's on the bed and died.

The whole house went into mourning. It lasted for months. We all, including Nani and Asghar, wept with grief at the loss of our magnificent friend. There was a lovely cherry tree in the garden and Father suggested we bury Reba under that tree. We had a ceremony there in the garden and put Reba into the earth. The next spring, the cherry tree was amazing. It flowered profusely, masses of glorious, fragrant pink blossoms that far excelled earlier years. We felt sure that Reba had come back to us, in a different form, to grace our lives. Father wrote a poem to commemorate her passing, "Reba the guard dog":

A wolf dog once shared my life.
But to my great sorrow, she suddenly died.
Her ears stood up like two black jewels.
Her deep black eyes could penetrate your soul.

When she bared her teeth to protect you, she might be a shark.

Her tail conducted the music of friendship with an acquaintance

But when someone threatened, she was vicious.

Reba was leonine and lean with beautiful black velvet skin.

Her paws were elegant and refined, but the nails were long and sharp.

Her four legs were poised to protect you from attack.

In Russian Reba means fish and she was as quick and lithe as a trout.

I tried to find a mate for Reba so that she could have children

And found a perfect candidate as black and beautiful as she.

When Reba fell pregnant I thought all my hopes had come true

But the evil eye spied our happiness and the pups were never born.

When she sickened I shed many tears

And sought the advice of everyone I could find.

But nobody could suggest a remedy.

Finally I lost my Reba and buried her beneath a beautiful tree.

Most evenings at around sunset, Father would take a long walk. Mehrdad and I always accompanied him, as did Reba while she lived. First would go Father, then Reba, then Mehrdad and I would trail behind. Father walked very fast. We tried to keep up. He set out on the dirt road close to our house, went past the American embassy and into the desert, then headed south into the city on the first paved street we came to, Shah Reza Avenue. About halfway down, we turned right and made a beeline for the bookstore on the corner of Istanbul and Saadi Avenues. The bookstore was called "Danesh" (Knowledge), and it was the best one in Tehran. It carried all kinds of books, chosen with care by the owner, Mr. Danesh, a very learned man and a close friend of my father. As soon as we arrived, Father would reach into his pockets and fish out some money for Mehrdad and me to buy lemonade and chewing gum, with instructions to stay away as long as we wanted. Of course, he wanted time to talk with his friend about books, but we set off eagerly with Reba in search of our treats.

The bookstore provided a long table and a number of chairs for people to sit and read. Father would claim one of these chairs and hang his cane behind him. If it were summer, he would take off his jacket and hang it on the back of the chair with his cane. When Mr. Danesh joined him over tea, the two would eagerly discuss the new books that had arrived.

Mehrdad and I happily spent quite a bit of time roaming around the streets. In the 1930s this part of Tehran was more like a small town, with few people in the street, and it was quite safe for two children to be on their own. Now it has been overtaken by the enormous growth of the city and is part of downtown.

In his eagerness to occupy us, Father usually gave us a good deal more money than we needed for lemonade and gum. We were able to buy ice cream and even something for Reba to eat. After a couple of hours of playing and eating, we slowly made our way back to the bookstore to find Father and Mr. Danesh still bent intently over their discussion. But when he saw us, Father said his farewells and we would make our way home.

On the way back, we took a shorter route straight along Saadi Avenue to Dowlat Avenue and then to the city gate. Tehran had been a small town famed for its mountain springs and fruit before the Qajars made it their seat of government. It was fortified with a city wall through which several gates allowed access. Our house lay beyond one of the gates; even by then Tehran had escaped its walls. In the urban explosion of today's Tehran, almost all traces of the old boundaries have been obliterated in the scramble to house the metropolitan area's more than twelve million people. When we took our evening walks, the gate was still a landmark. Once outside, we walked again on the dirt road to our home.

The return trip was a time for talking. We were always encouraged to speak our minds and Father would answer our childish questions in a forthright manner. We felt free to ask questions such as, "Is there a God?" His answer, I recall, was, "I have no idea." We would walk into the house around nine o'clock in the evening, in time for dinner.

In the summer, our evening meal was laid out in the garden. A big rug was placed beneath the mulberry trees and a white cloth thrown over it. In the center, a hurricane lamp with multi-colored glass threw a magical light over the immediate area. The rest of the garden lay in darkness, with the occasional sound of *gur bagheh*, frogs, the only disturbance to the deep silence of the night. *Gur* is the sound that frogs make and *bagheh* means garden, so *gur bagheh* are those who say "*gur, gur, gur*" in the garden.

If Father was in a good mood, which he usually was, these post-bookshop summer meals were wonderful. There was rice and a dish with meat and one or more of the vegetables or fruits from the garden—eggplant, celery, herbs, sour cherry, or plums. A salad and yoghurt with mint and cucumbers rounded out the meal. Father took a glass or two of whisky before dinner—he loved both whisky and iced vodka—and would become quite spirited. Maman prepared small dishes to accompany the pre-dinner drink: slices of cold garlicky lamb, tiny cucumbers with salt, olives, and when a friend from the south visited, dried shrimp. Several nights a week, a bottle of wine would be brought up from the *zir zamin*, and whichever child carried it up was warned not to remove the dust from the bottle. The wine was offered to all of us. I always had a little, even if no one else did, because I had malaria as a child and red wine with dinner was prescribed.

These dinners, sitting in the magic circle in the garden, were exciting. Father recited poems and stories, his own and those of others. He had an unbelievable memory and one epic poem would follow another. He held us spellbound with his deep velvety voice. At times he would act out the stirring tales, becoming in turn Rostam, Zal, Sohrob, Shirin, all the heroes of the historical stories from the *Shah Nameh*. To me, he really became these characters, and I saw the sword in his hand, the horse galloping beneath him. In my mind, the whole garden held its breath while he performed. The frogs, the mice, the beetles, the moths—whatever life breathed in the shadows held its collective breath and thrilled to the great stories of the Persian empire.

Many years later when I was a student at American University in Washington, D.C., I chanced to see, through an open lecture room door, a professor with the same capacity to enthrall. It was Dr. Bradshaw, and he was presenting a lecture on Richard III, standing on the desk, waving his sword and galloping across the field at Bosworth. To my dismay, I discovered it was a graduate level class and that as a sophomore with poor English skills I was not qualified to attend. Undaunted, I went to Dr. Bradshaw's office and begged to be allowed to audit the class. I must have looked desperate because Dr. Bradshaw asked me why I was so determined. My response was, "You remind me of my father." I was permitted to sit in and I learned so much about Shakespeare from this inspired teacher—not because I could read or understand the words in the text, but because he was able to act the parts so brilliantly that it became alive to me, just as the *Shah Nameh* had come alive in our night-time garden twenty-five years earlier.

One evening in the middle of one of our dinner theaters, a thief dared to walk through the garden door. He took several rugs and other items of value from the house and left without us knowing he was there. We realized our loss the next day and Father reported it to the police.

To our great surprise, the thief was apprehended after only a few days. The chief of police brought him before my father. He was a young man, in his late twenties. Father asked him very politely, "Sir, why did you come to my home and rob us?" The thief answered, "The door to the garden was open and I could see that you were very busy reciting poetry to your family, so I just walked in and took what I wanted." He had brought back what he had taken. Before he left, Father reached in his pocket and took out ten *tuman*, quite a lot of money in those days. Handing it to the thief he said, "Sir, you obviously need money, so take this and please, don't come back here again." With a stunned look on his face, promising that he would not return, the thief left with the chief of police.

Mehrdad and I loved to sleep outside and count the stars. We divided the sky between us. I would count the stars in my half and he the other, until we both fell asleep. One day when we were returning with Father from our ritual afternoon walk, we told him that we longed to know more about the stars. He said that if we promised to be quiet we could come to his study while he worked and he would show us a book about the galaxies and known stars. Until then, we never knew that anything else existed other than where we were living, assuming that the earth was the center of everything. The book opened a whole new world to us and our evening entertainment of counting the stars became much more interesting.

While Hushang and Mamak attended the American College, Mali, Mehrdad, and I went to Zoroastrian schools—Mali and I to the girls' school and Mehrdad to the boys' school. They were private schools, and I don't know how my parents could afford the fees. Perhaps they gave us a discount because of my father's position at the university, or his status as a poet. Or maybe as representatives of a persecuted minority, the Zoroastrian schools identified with the difficulties my family faced.

Zoroastrianism is a fascinating religion, thousands of years old, probably the first monotheistic faith. It influenced Judaism, Christianity, and Islam with its beliefs in a cosmic order that included one supreme creator opposed by a force of evil, Heaven and Hell, the day of judgment, the freedom of the individual to choose between good and evil, the immortal soul, and other fundamental ideas proposed by Zarathushtra (in Greek, Zoroaster), who was born in Persia. Zoroastrianism was the state religion of the Persian empire for more than a thousand years, until the Arab invasion in the seventh century A.D. forced Islam upon the population. Zarathushtra relayed God's word to his followers in the form of passionate and complex poetry that was passed on orally for hundreds of years before being written down. Perhaps the love of poetry that is so evident in Iran had its start in the sacred and inspired writings of Zarathushtra.

While we were at school, we three did not participate in the religious classes in Zoroastrianism. It is a closed religion that does not accept converts, but rather acknowledges other religions as paths to salvation and thus sees no need to proselytize. I suppose it was assumed we were Moslems, although my family was not religious.

Actually, in his effort to create a modern, secular society, Reza Shah had banned the teaching of religion in schools and encouraged the teaching of pre-Islamic history and poetry to foster national pride in Iran (in 1935, the name was officially changed from Persia, which is from the Greek, Persis). Iran means "land of the Aryans" whereas the name Persia comes from Pars, a region of Iran where the kings lived. So we studied Ferdowsi's *Shah Nameh* as well as the works of other great poets such as Saadi and Hafez, and were encouraged to write both poetry and prose. The Zoroastrian motto of "Good Thoughts, Good Words, Good Deeds" and the traditions of equality between both the sexes and the races, valuing education to enlighten the mind, condemnation of oppression, and dedication to hard work are a fine basis for children's education. We wore uniforms to school and Hassan drove us in a *doroshkeh*, an open carriage drawn by horses—an improvement over the donkey that used to carry my older brother and sisters when I was small!

There were a couple of years when we had so little money that we could not buy any clothes. For me this meant that there were no hand-me-downs from Mali, the usual source of my clothing. I had outgrown my winter coat, so I had to go without for two winters. I went to school looking very chubby, as Maman dressed me in all the clothes I had under my school uniform to try to keep me warm. I put my hands in Mamak's and Mehrdad's pockets on the journey to and from school because I also had no gloves. Poor Mehrdad was even worse off than I was, as Hushang was so much older that there wasn't much in the way of clothing to hand down to him.

The children at school would make fun of me, but somehow it never hurt me; it just wasn't important to me to be beautifully dressed, which was just as well. Appearance has never seemed to me a useful way of judging another person. By the time my little sister Cherry was older and in school, I was married and able to pay her school fees and make sure she was properly dressed.

Despite our poverty, we were lucky children. We were surrounded at home by love and respect, scholarship and stories, good food and laughter. Our home was an oasis of beauty. Even though my mother could not always pay them, sometimes for over a year, Nani and Asghar were loyal and kind and part of the family. Nani even went into exile with us. Despite all the hardships, my childhood in Paradise was a very happy one.

When winter comes and snow covers the ground outside my small apartment in Washington and I see all the trees covered in white dust, I think of Iran. I look at the stars shining bright in the winter sky and I think of the majestic Alborz Mountains in the north of Tehran with Mount Damavand glowing like a beautiful bride. I recall how Mehrdad and I would gaze at the sky above these mountains in wonderment. I think back to our house and its beautiful garden, to my father, my mother, my brothers and sisters, our kind Nani, and Asghar the gardener. They will always be alive in my soul.

I still hear the sound of children's laughter. I still hear Mamak reading out loud at night from the collection of Nezami's poetry. I think of my father, tall and dignified. He was the one who showed me the road to freedom and positive thinking, and stirred my interest in the world of ideas. I think of my mother who took care of me when I was a child.

I think of Iran, the place that gave me life, the cradle of my birth, where I became who I am. Iran, I have never left you. You will always be with me.

EXILE

THE ADVENT of spring always brings joy, but for me the joy comes with a little barb, one that has its origins in one particular Nowruz that left deep scars on my young heart. Our family was gathered around the *sofra-ye haft sin* that Maman had prepared, the children in a state of high excitement about the gifts we hoped to receive. Just at that moment there was a knock on the garden door. Our gardener Asghar went to see who it was, expecting someone from the family coming to wish us a happy new year. Instead he found several police officers asking to talk to my father.

Father told Asghar to remind the visitors that this was a family occasion and to suggest they come back at another time. Asghar returned in a moment to tell my father that while the gentlemen did not wish to bother the family, they needed to talk to him. My father went to the door but apparently could not convince the policemen to come back later, for they marched past him into the garden and right into his study. They began to go through his things, packing whatever they could find—papers, books, and documents—into large bags. Once they had finished in the study they went into the other rooms in the house, even the children's rooms, and helped themselves to whatever they wanted. Then they told Father that he would have to accompany them to the police station.

The spirit of celebration and joy evaporated. My mother started to weep and we gathered around her, weeping too, even though we had no idea what was happening. We showered poor Maman with silly questions in our effort to make some sense out of our ruined Nowruz. All that day we were in a state of shock and misery. Finally, in the later afternoon, Father called from Shahrbani Prison in downtown Tehran, asking that some clothing and a sleeping bag be sent. The atmosphere in our house plunged into a worse kind of sadness. Later I learned that father had been jailed several times before, but this was the first in my experience. While I was too young to understand, I was keenly aware of the mood of fear and anxiety in our home.

Several months passed without any indication that he would be set free. It was a very hot summer that year. Father was in a cell on the second floor with an open, barred window; between the heat, the mosquitoes and other insects, and the constant noise from the street, he could barely sleep. He was not physically strong and became quite ill, but he endured the harshness of prison proudly and did not bow to his repression.

He wrote one of his most famous epic poems while in jail. It is called *Morghe Shabahang*, or *Bird of the Evening*. In the poem, he talks to the day that never seems to come to alleviate the close darkness of his cell.

Come out and bloom, O chrysanthemum sun, light up the world
Like an unfolding bud that promises a beautiful flower.
When you arrive, you spread your golden glory
As a sparkling tiara adorns a woman's hair.
I am so tired of this oppressive darkness.
The night admits primordial despair.
Try to have a little charity in your tyrannical heart.
Why do you offer only fear and anguish?
Why do you obliterate all things beautiful?
You must have heard how I love the night time—
But not this night. It suffocates the soul.
I love a quiet night
When I can see the moon and the stars.
Through their kind light it seems
The universe speaks gently to the souls below.

In those sad days, our mother's younger brother would visit us every day. We were all afraid without a man in the house to take care of us. Maman suffered tremendously and had no one to help her. She often turned to Hafez's poetry to find answers to our predicament. We were too small to be of help and she had neither money nor resources to feed the five children who had suddenly become her sole responsibility. Almost every night unknown people threw stones at the house, breaking windows and terrorizing us. We told the police but they never came to investigate and might even have been involved. That summer, we could not sleep outside at night for fear of being injured by rocks and breaking glass, so we had to remain indoors and endure the stifling heat.

My father and our family were by no means alone in suffering Reza Shah's persecution. Many intellectuals and liberals and their families were assassinated or imprisoned, some dying in prison. Reza Shah effectively wiped out a whole class of people that he found threatening, reduced the *Majles* to a rubber stamp, and amassed a vast personal fortune. The Pahlavi regime represented a dark time in the history of the country.

While it was awful to have Father in prison, apparently it was not punishment enough. We next heard he was to be sent into exile in Isfahan. It was far from Tehran, particularly in those days of limited transport and poor roads. My mother was informed she had to close up the house and take the children and join her husband in exile. She put all the furniture in one room and bricked up the entrances so that opportunistic thieves could not take everything we owned. While we traveled painfully slowly by bus to Isfahan, my father was driven across the desert into exile in a police vehicle.

We had nowhere to stay. One of Father's friends kindly lent us a house, but within a couple of months the Shah ordered him to turn us all out into the street, an unimaginably petty level of cruelty. Again we had nowhere to go. Maman thought she might sell our house to raise money to find accommodation, but the government would not allow anyone to buy it from us. Instead, my grandmother sold her house and sent the money so that we could rent a place to live. Once we found a little house to rent, we were completely isolated. No one was permitted to visit us there, although my older brother and sisters were allowed to attend school.

Maman returned to Tehran many times to plead for Father's release from exile. I often went with her because I was ill with malaria, but Mehrdad remained in Isfahan with Nani. Poor little Mehrdad. On one such occasion when Maman and I were setting off for Tehran, he sobbed and sobbed. He said that his mother didn't love him and the only thing for him was to commit suicide. He asked for a knife to do the job. Father picked him up and hugged and reassured him, but it was terrible that a child so young could even imagine such a thing.

Father tried hard to alleviate our misery. He would often take us walking to the Si-o-Seh Pol (thirty-three arches) Bridge, a lovely early seventeenth-century bridge that crosses the Zayandeh River just outside Isfahan. There he would sit and write while we played around the foundations, where women washed clothes on the stones just as they had for hundreds of years, and as they do today.

We stayed through the winter. The winter was a harsh one and the muddy streets were frozen. Whenever we left the house, we seemed to be forever falling in the frozen mud and the three who went to school had a real struggle. The house was unheated and we often went hungry. Our clothing was quite inadequate and, in my memory, I was always cold. While I am very glad to have had five siblings, I sometimes wonder why my parents had so many children. With all our upheavals and frequent poverty, it made their lives so difficult. But in those days the choice was not that easy.

With my mother away so much in Tehran trying to find an advocate, Nani had to manage on the very meager amount of money left over from the travel expenses. Somehow she managed, despite too many children and too few means to really take care of us. Maman had sold everything she could to raise money and there was nothing left. Father, despite his great intellect, was totally incapable of grasping the logistics of survival. Into this dismal situation came the news that Reza Shah wanted to send Father even further into exile, to Yazd, far to the southeast and very primitive. It was the Persian equivalent of Siberia, and would have been the end of us.

When spring finally came, there was an historic flood and the water swirled over the bridge and through the streets. I later learned that, during that terrible winter, my father had been very depressed by the situation in which he had placed our family, and by the fact that the Shah could allow such a dreadful punishment for a poet who loved his country. Walking along the river while we children played around the flooded footings of the bridge, he poured out his agony, in extemporary verse, to a friend who had braved official displeasure to accompany him. The friend insisted on writing down the flow of words, which became famous as the poem *Bahar e Isfahan*, and sending it to Prime Minister Mohamamad-Ali Foroughi.

At last my mother's efforts to find a representative paid off. One of Father's close friends, who happened to be Reza Shah's personal physician, finally talked to the Shah and asked him, as a favor, to forgive my father and allow the family to return to Tehran. With the combined pressure from his prime minister, who had been sent the poem *Bahar e Isfahan*, and the personal appeal from his physician, the Shah agreed. Another factor in Father's release was quite fortuitous: The millennium of the great tenth-century poet Ferdowsi was approaching, and Orientalists from around the world were gathering in Mashhad to celebrate. My father was a renowned Ferdowsi scholar and was expected to read his epic poem in homage to Ferdowsi, so his absence from this great occasion would have caused embarrassment at the highest levels. I like to think that Ferdowsi, who also suffered greatly from the cruelty of the authorities, reached out his hand across a thousand years to help a fellow poet.

When Father left for exile in Isfahan, he suggested that Asghar should sell his beloved pigeons and use the proceeds as a small retainer. There were several hundred pigeons in all, a very visible and audible presence in our garden with their coo-cooing, restless movements, and frequent little flurries into the air that caused clouds of soft white down to sift slowly down from the pigeon house.

Many years later Mehrdad wrote a wonderful article about Father's pigeons. He observed that as the birds were flying free and getting smaller and smaller to the eye, one would suddenly leave the flock and begin to sink back toward the garden. The rest would follow like dancers that had been performing in heaven and now fluttered back to earth. These birds were symbols of freedom for my father and he let them out every day. Once they had enough of freedom they would arrive back at the pigeon house crooning their gentle song, their necks puffing proudly as they strutted to the food and water that awaited their return. The females were much faster at pecking up the seed, watching the puffed and prancing males carefully from the corners of their eyes until they were sated. Then the females would croon a love song to the strutting males as they took their turn at the seed.

In his tender homage to the pigeons, "Soroudeh Kabutar" (The Music of Pigeons), Father wrote:

Come my doves, heart's desire, camphor bodies, feet of cinnabar,
Together swirl above the roof, fall around me, gentle snow.
At dawn when the Golden Bird spreads its wings above the eastern stars
You are eager to show yourselves, necks stretching behind the glass doors.
Song of innocence sung low, tail pulled along the ground, a lover's cloak,
On the morning breeze news of love arrives with that murmuring song.
You seem to think the gates of heaven open when I open your cage doors
And suddenly you are angels, wing sewn to wing in the firmament.
Even when you long for water and grain you never cry or raise complaint
Or idle chatter or wasted words—nothing but the same song of love.
Come down my friends from that roof, clapping your hands and dancing
Gracefully to the ground, for there is no man here but me.
Come, my loyal friends, and I shall scatter millet for you.
For in my melancholy I would rather be with you than my fellow men.

Father was absolutely captivated by their innocent beauty. He would sit on a small stool watching for their return, uplifted by their innocent *joie de vivre*. We all knew how important the pigeons were to Father, so when our poor mother ordered Asghar to sell these beloved birds, we understood the burden of sorrow she bore. The topic was never discussed while we were in exile.

When we finally returned to our home after our exile to Isfahan, we arrived early in the morning. Father was subdued. We all were. Paradise was completely empty. He walked into the garden. The only signs of our former life were the water lilies, blooming defiantly on the surface of the pools. Knowing that his birds had been sold, Father nevertheless traced the path to their house at the back of the garden.

All at once he became alert and his pace quickened. He called, "Asghar! Asghar!" Like a mirage, there were the pigeons strutting, coo-cooing, rising and falling in little clouds of white down. Throwing open the door to the coop, my father set them free. The sky immediately filled with their exultant, wheeling bodies.

Then Asghar was there beside him. Father picked him up and hugged and kissed him; Asghar hugged and kissed in return. "But we sold them, Asghar!" The gardener said, "Yes, we sold them. But one by one they returned. And once they returned they refused to leave again."

"But how did you feed them, Asghar? You had so very little money even for yourself." Asghar said that somehow he had managed. "God always looks after us. With the money that I had for my own food, I was able to economize and provide for the pigeons too." The two men clung to each other, tears of joy and relief in their eyes, the one incredulous at what had been preserved, the other content with what he had saved.

IMPRISONMENT

ONE COLD winter morning a year or so after we returned from exile—I could not have been more than six years old—loud noises shocked me out of a sweet sleep. The crash of doors being kicked open and harsh shouting broke the pre-dawn stillness. Little Mehrdad crawled into my bed and we huddled stiffly together, listening to the sounds of violence. Still clutching each other, we crept to the hallway to see what was happening. Even at this early hour, breakfast was prepared and waiting on the hall table. But this morning we saw our fresh-baked *naan*, cheese, boiled eggs, herbs, jam, everything, smashed and scattered on the floor. Only the gleaming copper samovar sat as a squat guardian on the table, its pretty china teapot perched innocently above the murmuring water.

Shivering with cold and too frightened to step through the chaos in the hallway to find our mother, we retreated to our bedroom. Our windows overlooked the courtyard from where all the commotion seemed to be coming. We dragged big pillows under one window and clambered on top to peer over the deep sill.

It was snowing. Tender flakes fell softly into our beautiful courtyard, dancing gaily in the slight breeze in a way that would normally have entranced me. But through the snow I saw a group of strange men, the owners of the harsh voices, moving roughly and shouting coarsely in shocking contrast to the purity of the setting. Our anxious breath fogged the nursery window. We kept wiping away the mist to watch the dreadful scene being played out below. Something—or someone—was being dragged through the courtyard and out towards the street. Suddenly I realized that the person—for it was a person—was my father.

74

Clinging to each other on our unsteady perch, Mehrdad and I were mute, mesmerized. I saw that we were not the only witnesses to the horror. My mother, weeping, was standing on the steps that led down into the courtyard, propped in the arms of our nanny, watching helplessly.

The sight of Maman broke the spell. We scrambled from our perch and ran to her, braving the hallway and the ruined breakfast. Mamak, Mali, and Hushang were there before us, trying to calm her. I broke away from the huddled figures and marched down the stairs into the cold air. Snow was still falling from a gray morning sky. Through the open door wafted the fragrance of brewing tea. I will never forget the jarring contrast between the courtyard, now returned to its normal tranquility, and what I only half understood had just taken place.

I ran through the forgiving snow to my father's study. The lights were on. I would find him at his work. I climbed the few steps, confident that he would be sitting on the carpet. Soon, soon he would be enfolding me in his arms, pulling me onto his lap, laughing at my frightened face. But the room was empty, as part of me already knew. Running back into the courtyard, I saw my family still standing, transfixed, on the steps.

"Where did they take him? What did he do? Will they come back and take us too?" As I joined the huddle of bodies clinging to our mother, shock gave way to fear, and I sobbed and sobbed into the grieving mass that suddenly seemed such a small remnant of my family.

It was several days before we found out that my father had been taken to prison. Amazingly, this was good news. We knew he was still alive. Many others who opposed the regime had not been so fortunate. He himself had narrowly survived assassination not long before at the Majles, when the journalist who resembled him was killed by mistake. But he was too important and public a figure to dispose of lightly.

The suffering he endured in prison was exacerbated by news of the death of one of his friends, a fellow poet, musician, and revolutionary known as Aref (Abolqassem Aref Qazvini). Mourning his friend as the latest example of the passing of the great thinkers and writers over the ages, and lamenting the failure of the government to value Iran's intellectuals, my father wrote an anguished sonnet that speaks of his feelings of abandonment in his prison cell, and hints at his despair at perhaps being the last voice to plead the case for reason and humanism.

Who am I, to feel accomplished and self-satisfied?
I can lay no claim to brilliance; the truly great ones are gone.
I should pack my bags; their last journey awaits me soon enough.
All my heroes—writers and thinkers through the ages—are gone.

Clutching the reins of destiny, we gallop furiously across the dunes of life.
At last each rider fades away; only the dust they raised marks their passage.
Just so did those great geniuses once ride wildly into view, then vanish;
Only their swirling thoughts remind us they once graced the earth.

It grieves me to contemplate the loss of those splendid tellers of tales.
My heart weeps tears of blood for all who evaporated like the spring rain.
The tender hearted tulip, even the blue-green cyprus darken with anguish
When such beautiful and bright faces are plucked from the garden.

Why be shocked when yet another peerless artist joins the ranks
    of the departed?
All of our other giants have already vacated their rooms in the Palace of Art.
But it so saddens me that those who brought us history, poetry, stories,
Are now sleeping, bringing no new insights to the story of humanity.

In the old days, serpents were put in treasure chests to guard against thieves.
Woe to those whose noble hearts poured out glittering gems of thought!
The serpents to whom they entrusted their nation's rich legacy are the thieves,
Appropriating their pearls of wisdom and tarnishing the riches of
    their brilliant minds.

Only one nightingale remains in the garden of knowledge
And the garden, no longer beautiful, is forsaken, forgotten.
Imprisoned in my cell, I sing alone through tears of blood.
I hold close those great ones, vanished into the mists of time.

Months later we were told that he could have the occasional visitor. But there was a catch, a cynical twist to the favor: only the two youngest were allowed to visit him in jail. This meant me and Mehrdad.

One day, we two little pilgrims, accompanied by Hassan, set out to walk to the Shahrbani Prison. We carried an old-fashioned three-layered food container, in which Maman had placed Father's favorite foods: *kashke bademjan*, a rich stew of eggplant and meat, in one layer; *baghali polo*, a rice dish with fava beans and lamb, in another; and for dessert, *yakh dar behesht*, a fragrant "paradise custard."

Mehrdad and I clung to Hassan like two little birds. Our journey took us from the northern part of the city where we lived, through the fashionable center of Tehran, all the way to the southern section where the prison lay. Two very small children filled with anxiety and foreboding, we carried the love of a whole family on our shoulders. I had no idea what a prison was, but the very name, Maidan'e Toupkhaneh (Cannon Square), filled me with fear. What would happen to us there? Could we be dragged away too? Kept there? Shot by a cannon?

The square was huge. In the middle, an imposing pool and fountain would, in other circumstances, have caught my delighted attention. Now they loomed, large and dangerous within a surrounding guard of trees. The stern buildings around the square, with the exception of the prison on the eastern side, housed government offices. As we approached the prison, my heart was hammering and I heard my breath rasping in my throat. With my small fingers, I clutched frantically at Baba Hassan's coattails and pressed against his leg, trying to become one with the only person standing between me and the awful fear. I knew that on the other side little Mehrdad was also hanging on for dear life. Hassan meanwhile, making difficult progress with the pot of food in his hands and two desperate little birds clutching at his sides, tried to reassure us that we would be quite safe, that we had nothing to fear, that soon we would see our father.

The prison, a two-story building, faced us with the blind eyes of many bricked-up windows. On the second floor, the few remaining windows were barred. As we crept through the tall green doors we saw many large, uniformed policemen standing around. We were taken into a room in which many more policemen stood or sat about; intimidating in their blue uniforms. In the middle of the room stood a big table. We were told to place the lunch container on it. A policeman whose arrogance indicated he was in charge opened the container and, to my horror, ran his thick fingers through the lovingly prepared food. I suppose he was looking for evidence that my father was receiving some sort of communication from outside the prison.

I opened my mouth in protest at this disgusting act, but Hassan's quick squeeze of my hand told me to be quiet and do as I was told if I wanted to see Father. Licking his fingers slowly, one at a time, and staring at us with mocking eyes, the officer asked which prisoner we had come to see. "These are the children of Bahar. They have come to see their father," Hassan told him.

We were told to take off our shoes, and our small bodies were patted all over by coarse, dirty hands to see if we were concealing anything. The menacing guards who did this clearly took pleasure in our discomfort and humiliation, exercising their petty power as paid tormentors with leering relish. Standing there on the cold stone floor in my short socks, I shivered at the unexpected violation. Mehrdad stood meekly beside me, his head hung low.

After this inspection, another policeman took us to a courtyard a few steps away. As we gingerly made our way across the gray, muddy ground, my foot slipped and I fell flat. Maman had prepared me so carefully in a white dress and shiny black shoes to lift my father's spirits. My courage failed me as I fell towards that thick gray mud. I had been so proud of myself in my beautiful dress, imagining Father's expression when he saw me. For a second I forgot why I was there and felt that my heart had been torn from my body. Then I remembered: my dress was not why I had come. I had another, far more important mission that, young as I was, gave me the courage to go on.

Dirty green water partly filled a small pool in the middle of the courtyard, reflecting the grim walls. We passed a few forlorn, hunched prisoners in shabby prison garb and entered a gloomy hallway. Stale, humid air hung heavily above a muddy floor, rank with the smell of unwashed and frightened bodies. Our guide led us to the end of the corridor. Signaling to another guard seated outside a steel door, he announced us as Bahar's children, come to visit their father.

The guard stood up. The large bunch of keys at his waist jangled dangerously in the ominous quiet. Taking his time, watching us as we shivered with fear and cold, he selected the key to Father's cell. The door opened, but we saw only a dark square. No light came from that stinking, airless place. A candle stood on the corridor side of the door hatch. I later learned that the candle was never lit in the daytime, being reserved as a special torment for the night. With day and night reversed, my father wrote at night, knowing that the dawn would bring a return to darkness.

As my eyes became accustomed to the dark, I saw on the dirt floor a small piece of grimy carpet. Seated on it was my father, wrapped in his *aba*, a large woolen cape. He took us in his arms and drew us, as he always did, onto his lap. He was so happy to see us. A great sense of security flowed from his arms and into my trembling heart, washing away the hideous policemen, the defiled food, the mud, the squalor, and the fear. Here, again, was the father I knew and adored. I was safe.

All the words I had been burning to pour out to him were stuck in my throat. He understood. He gently eased the way. He asked about Maman, about Hushang and our sisters. He wanted to luxuriate in the details, begging us to tell everything slowly, slowly, so that he could drink in the atmosphere of our home and savor each image.

He was in high spirits and his shining eyes and tight arms made us feel at ease despite the surroundings. I saw that his dark cell was smaller than Reba's kennel in our garden. His cruel conditions were much worse than any animal would be made to endure. It was a tiny area in which he could just stretch out to sleep, with a reeking hole for a toilet, and a faucet from which a trickle of water emerged for drinking and bathing.

Even in this state of extreme deprivation, my father produced miracles. By the light of the nighttime candle high in the door, he penned many beautiful poems. At the beginning, he was given paper but no pen, and he wrote using spent matches (he was allowed cigarettes). In a magnificent epic, *Morghe Shabahang* (Bird of the Evening), Father talks to the nightingale (a metaphor for himself as a caged poet), whose song was the only thing of beauty that he could experience in his dark cell:

Fly down. Be my companion.
Come and sit next to me
And we can sing a song together.
Come, bird of the night,
From your perch high in a tree,
Be my friend for this one night.
If you want to relieve my sorrow
Come down and sing the truth.
Answer me! "Truth! Truth! Truth!"

Sing, sing from your cage
You sad nightingale.
Listening to your sorrow
Fills my heart with dazzling pain.
Hearing of your agony
Illuminates my own experience.
Sing more, heartless bird
Of the grief of separation from my beloved.
Make it shorter, shorter, shorter.

As we sat wrapped with him in his woolen mantle, Father questioned us closely about the garden he so loved, asking whether this or that plant was flowering, whether certain seeds had sprouted where he had pressed them into the earth. Carried along by the joy and warmth of his being, we lost our fear, telling happy stories of the work nature had wrought in the spring and summer that had been stolen from him. Though his body was trapped in a man-made cage, through our eyes and voices we transported him far away; his unbroken spirit flying freely, like his beloved pigeons, to a place of beauty.

In the first verse of *Zendan* (Prison) written at that time, he says:

I ask not that you open my cage,
But please, hang it in the garden.
The season of flowers is passing me by.

For God's sake, sit in the garden and remember me.

The flowers must all be blooming.

Stand up! Celebrate the coming of spring!

And birds, when you sing among the blossoms

Just remember—one of you is in a cage.

To those who keep a captive bird in their house,

Please, for my sake

Take it outside and set it free.

If *my* home has been consumed by fire,

Think what will happen to the hunter's home!

If the candle burns out, think not about the candle—

Think about the moth that has been circling the light.

Tyranny and oppression shorten the lives of our children.

And you officials, for God's sake, give the people justice!

If you crush the house of a gnat,

How can you enjoy your own palace?

It is my lot to be cornered in a prison

But you who are outside, appreciate your freedom.

The image of paradise created in that small, dank place that day has stayed with me all my life. The knowledge that, whatever evil confronted me, I was free to follow my father to a place of beauty and calm sustains me. When I saw that his soul could never be imprisoned, that his response to even the worst torments inflicted on his body was powerful and beautiful poetry, I was inspired to follow his magnificent example. I knew that no matter what defeat pulled me down, I was free to rise and walk again. The little girl who crept quivering, sullied by mud and cruelty, into that sad place emerged proud and triumphant as a queen. In *Morghe Shabahang*, Father also extolled his children to carry high the torch of freedom for the country.

I am so sad that my youth has gone;

I wasted it trying to change this country.

I am the villager who takes water from the spring

And spreads it in the desert to keep things green.

Remember when you sleep in your comfortable beds, my children,

Remember how your father's life ebbed away in jail.

Remember, my wonderful sons,

The malicious ruffians who crushed me underfoot.

Remember my humiliation and be proud to be my heirs.

Remember, my daughters, go to school and become wise

So that you understand those who killed your father.

Remember, in the future, all my misery and grief

And take revenge on these thieves and oppressors.

Don't be afraid of death.

Put on its shroud in defiance,

Walk proudly in front of your oppressed countrymen,

Put one foot in front of the other and lead them.

On the Day of Judgment you will see

Those who inflicted cruelty are the losers

And you will all be free.

Don't ever forgive those who ruined your country.

If you accommodate them,

You will be in a prison of your own making.

On Judgment Day, those who hold the scales of justice

Know well which are the criminals.

As Mehrdad and I left with Hassan, our arms swung freely by our sides and there was a defiant skip in our walk. We carried a sense of that great mantle of strength, given as a precious gift by our father, not only back to our waiting family but also into our adult lives. I only have to close my eyes to recapture that thrilling feeling. When everything else fades in my last moments on this earth, it will be this that illuminates my mind.

MARRIAGE

I HAD JUST turned sixteen when I married. My husband was twenty years older. I had never heard of him until his family approached mine. I saw him only twice before the marriage, on both occasions in the company of family members.

My two older sisters, Mamak and Mali, were already married. Mamak wed at eighteen to one of our father's students, also a poet. Mali married at seventeen to a much older, well-established man. Mamak lived with her husband in our household while he finished his studies at the University of Tehran, where my father taught.

Girls in Iran married young in those days, and the prettiest ones married as soon as they reached the legal age of sixteen. Very few girls finished high school and only a tiny number ever went to college. After the revolution in 1979, the marriageable age for women dropped to twelve and yet today women are now the majority presence in higher education. While I was familiar with discrimination against women in my own country, the inequality of women and minorities in the United States when I arrived in the early 1950s surprised me.

Sixteen is very young to marry. I knew nothing other than school, my home, and my family at that age. While I knew there were rich and powerful people in Iran—big landowners, the former aristocracy from the Qajar dynasty, the people surrounding the Shah—I never came in contact with them. Most people were poor, as were we, at least in terms of having money. We never went to other people's houses, other than the homes of my grandmother, who lived with my aunt and uncle, or Father's brother. Most people were afraid to associate with us; we were ostracized, virtual political prisoners in our home. Even at school, many children had been warned not to play with us. Out of school, we had no friends other than each other. Perhaps this is why Mehrdad and I were so close. I think this is why family has always been central to my existence. It was all I had growing up; this close group of people who cared deeply for each other. So even for an Iranian girl, I was young and unworldly as I approached my sixteenth birthday.

Nevertheless it was the duty of parents, even enlightened ones like mine, to choose husbands for their daughters, and it was now my turn. One night Mali's husband, Mojdehi, came to our house and he and Maman huddled together for a long time, talking. Mojdehi had come on behalf of his friend Ghafary to ask permission for his family to visit our family. The oldest son of the respected Ghafary family, Moez, was interested in marrying me.

The Ghafary family was unusual. They were very sophisticated and well-educated, more European than Iranian. The father had accompanied the young Crown Prince Ahmad to Europe as his teacher and companion. The whole family lived in Europe for many years. The children grew up speaking French rather than Persian.

Moez was thirty-five years old when he paid court to me. Starting with the hushed conversation between my mother and brother-in-law, and throughout the courting process ending with the proposal of marriage, I was not consulted. I was not even asked if I wished to marry. My acquaintance with men extended only to my immediate family, and I was totally naïve.

One summer afternoon at five o'clock, a beautiful tableau was created in our garden. Ashgar arranged the chairs and tables under the grape arbor, which hung heavily with great bunches of green grapes. In the welcome shade cast by the large leaves, Hassan placed four small round tables, with about a dozen dainty metal chairs arranged in a circle around them. Colorful flowered tablecloths were thrown over the tables. Tiny cookies fragrant with cinnamon and cardamom were piled in a pyramid on one table. On a second table, a large silver platter, glinting in the filtered sunlight, offered a glowing profusion of summer fruits—peaches, apricots, figs, cherries, and grapes, all from our garden. A third table held two crystal bowls, one filled to overflowing with bright orange dried apricots, golden mulberries, soft fawn almonds, green pistachios, pale golden chickpeas, and other sweet dried fruits and nuts. The second bowl held salted pistachios, watermelon seeds, and almonds. On the fourth table, pretty china plates, fruit knives and forks, and a pile of starched napkins waited ready for serving.

On summer afternoons, Asghar, carried in buckets of water from the *jube* to revive the garden. This particular day he took extra care, knowing guests were coming to ask for my hand in marriage. Everything glowed. The garden was cool and fragrant, a magic place.

Asghar never showed his emotions, verbally or physically, but his affection for every one of us shone through his deeds. He and the garden joined forces that day to produce a setting fit for this momentous occasion. Wallflowers and geraniums filled the beds with splashes of red, white, pink, and purple. Water lilies danced on the ornamental pools. Father's roses never looked so wonderful—a joyful chorus amid a fresh green oasis of leaves and trees, of dappled light and shade. It was enchanting. I felt like an observer to a storybook pageant.

At five o'clock, the guests arrived. My mother and father, joined by Mojdehi, went forward to greet them. First came the parents of the prospective groom, then the groom's sister and her husband. Last came Moez himself. He was good looking and wore a stylish gray suit with a red silk tie. I was struck by his kind eyes. I felt relief when he appeared younger than I expected.

What an elegant, smiling party his family made. They were all dressed beautifully in chic European style and appeared totally at ease. I had never seen such people before. The women had coiffed hair, makeup, perfume. No one I knew ever looked like this. Maman cut our hair and we dressed simply. We never wore makeup and none of us had ever owned a bottle of perfume.

Mojdehi made the introductions and my parents led the party through the garden. We sat down and Nani handed around tall crystal glasses of *sekanjebin* from a large silver tray. Sekanjebin is a refreshing summer drink of water, vinegar, sugar, and mint, a sweet-and-sour treat served on hot afternoons. Its very appearance offers relief from the heat—a pale golden glow, glimpsed through the condensation on a faceted crystal glass with deep green mint leaves trapped among the cubes of ice. Vinegar is known to cool the body, so this is the first thing offered to guests who have traveled through the afternoon sun to pay a visit.

At first the conversation revolved around the weather, the rising cost of living and other inconsequential chitchat. At last they got to the point. Mrs. Ghafary thanked my parents profusely, in the flowery language of formal occasions so favored by Persians, for allowing them to come that day. She asked permission to talk about her son, who was sitting quietly. I also was sitting quietly, mesmerized by what was happening around me.

Moez, it transpired, had many good qualities. Mrs. Ghafary proceeded to enumerate them. "My son has studied in Europe, receiving two BAs, one in French language, the other in German. When he returned from Europe, he studied Persian in Tehran, and now has an important job in the Ministry of the Interior. He is a very religious man, believing in God, and has never hurt anybody in his life. Now, if Parvaneh-*khanoum* accepts our offer, we would be honored."

After this speech, it was time for my mother to talk about me. I was wondering what she would offer to match these fine credentials. Could she talk about all the foreign languages I didn't know? What *could* she say? Could she talk about all the education I hadn't had in Europe? She caught my eye, and I was thinking, "Maman, please don't tell them that I don't listen to what you tell me. Don't tell them about those ugly gray uniforms, so long and embarrassing, that you make me wear to school. Don't tell them that I spend half my life sitting in the top of a tree with Mehrdad. Please don't tell them about our wrestling matches or that I sneak all the sweets set out on the table for New Year." For what else could she say about a mere schoolgirl, and one who was a tomboy at that? As far as I could tell, my only qualification was that I was pretty—and I could hardly take credit for my looks.

While in this anxious reverie, I heard my mother's voice begin to extol my virtues. "Parvaneh is really only a child. She has just finished the ninth grade. She has no knowledge of cooking, cleaning, or any other household duties." And that was all she said. I was so relieved that she hadn't spilled the beans about my negative qualities that I barely noticed the faint praise she had bestowed on me.

Mrs. Ghafary took the next step in this elaborate dance of custom. "We love Parvaneh-*khanoum* just the way she is. She does not need any other qualifications. If she likes our son, we see no problem in this marriage."

Now that I think about it, what on earth could a man like Moez, thirty-five years old, well-educated and elegant, sitting so passively while our two mothers talked about us, have wanted with an ignorant and unworldly child of fifteen? And I, perched silently on my chair, I felt as though I were being offered at auction in the bazaar. Willing my legs not to swing and clenching my hands in my lap to prevent me from biting nervously at my nails, I wondered, since Moez did not grow up speaking Persian, how we could communicate.

At last my future husband began to talk. He spoke passable Persian, with a French accent and liberally sprinkled with French words. Fortunately, I had studied French in junior high school, mostly to please my father, who had always said that if any of us studied French, he would give that person his complete set of the Larousse encyclopedia. It was compulsory for Persian children to learn either French or English in junior high school and I had chosen French, hoping to lay claim to the encyclopedia. One of Father's students came twice a week to our house to tutor me, so I could understand the language fairly well although I spoke it like the schoolgirl I was.

Moez talked about himself, self-promotion I suppose. No one asked me whether I had anything to say. Even if they had asked, what could I have said?

The guests left about at about six thirty. Moez shook hands with me as he departed and was very polite. After they left Maman asked me, "Did you like him?" How could I know? I had no one with whom to compare him, other than my family.

I was thinking to myself, "What is marriage to me?" Marriage, I decided, was freedom: freedom not to go to school in my horrible uniform; freedom to choose my own clothing; freedom to get away from my very strict mother and her demands. Marriage meant having money to go to the movies, to buy ice cream and candy. What a magnificent world this seemed! Who would not want to get married when there were so many benefits?

I looked at my mother and said that whatever decision she made, I would accept. If she liked this family, then I liked them too.

Shortly afterwards, Moez's older sister invited us all to her home for *asraneh*, afternoon tea. This time, both my older sisters and their husbands, my younger brother Mehrdad, my parents, and my aunt were invited.

Maman ordered a dress in a light pistachio crepe de chine for me from our dressmaker, whom we called Mademoiselle, and paid twice the usual fee to have it ready in time. The dress was beautiful, transforming me from the little girl of yesterday into a young woman. We bought white shoes and bag to complete the outfit and I pulled my long, thick hair into a ponytail, with a pin on either side. I wore no makeup, but still managed to look older than my fifteen years.

Mehrdad made fun of me relentlessly, laughing and saying, "That poor, poor man! He doesn't know what he's getting. If he only knew, he would escape to Europe!" I chased him and tried to hit him on the head, but he managed to dodge my blows.

The day of the tea party was soon upon us. We went in three *doroshkeh*, each drawn by two horses. Mali and her husband came in their car, a rarity in those days.

The whole Ghafary family came to the door to greet us very pleasantly. We were taken into their big garden where large wooden chairs were set out around the tables. This was the second time that Moez and I met.

My mother told his family that I accepted the offer of marriage from their son. Once more, nobody talked to me. I am not sure why. Perhaps it was because I was such an unimportant part of the process. By the end of the party, they arranged that when I reached the age of sixteen the following month, the Islamic ceremony of *aghd* would take place. *Aghd* is somewhat like an engagement, although legal marriage documents are signed and if the man decides he does not want to go ahead with the marriage, he can simply divorce the woman—even by sending the papers to her through the mail if he so chooses. The man also has the right to refuse a divorce should the woman not wish to continue with the marriage. In this case, a woman can remain in the marriage without living with her husband or enjoying any of the financial or social benefits of being a wife for the rest of her life. He has no responsibility towards her and can go on and marry someone else, but the poor woman is in limbo.

During the period of *aghd*, I would not live with my husband but we could spend time together. We could even go out in public and get to know each other before the actual wedding night, the *arousi*. While this may seem draconian, it was more liberal than the custom in my parents' day, when they could not even see each other during *aghd*.

Now that I think back, I wonder why my parents were in such a hurry to get their daughters married, especially me. I was a child, a tomboy, very immature. Several years later, when I visited Mehrdad in London where he was studying, I put this question to him. He reminded me that it was considered a great honor to have a proposal from a prominent family, that many girls were married at sixteen, and that it was the norm. I suppose my parents thought they were doing the best thing they could to ensure me against the vagaries of our family's fortunes.

The day of the *aghd* ceremony arrived. It was summer, a week or two after my sixteenth birthday in July. My long wedding dress was ready. Nani and Hassan went to pick it up from Mademoiselle on Istanbul Street in old Tehran near to where my mother grew up. When the old houses on Istanbul and Lalehzar Streets were torn down to make way for a business precinct, the small mall that replaced my grandmother's house was named after her—"Gohar Taj." It always amused my family that our very dignified grandmother had been transformed into a shopping mall. While Nani picked up my dress, Mamak and Mali and I went to the beauty salon run by Madame Pessian on Avenue Reza Shah in the north side of the city. The whole fourth floor of the building was her salon—one of the best in Tehran—with the latest facilities for makeup, hair styling, manicures, and pedicures. Like most of the beauticians, Mme. Pessian was a Christian Armenian.

First, Mme. Pessian washed my long dark hair. Then I sat under the dryer with curlers all over my head while a manicurist attended to my nails. I chose dark red enamel, feeling very daring. Madame then turned her attention to my sisters and soon we were all sitting in a row under the big silver dryers.

I emerged from the dryer after about an hour and Mme. Pessian sat me in front of a mirror in a reclining chair. Pushing the chair almost horizontal, she began on my face. She plucked, tweezed, moisturized, tinted, and powdered, finishing with an application of dark red lipstick. In those days, brides were as heavily made up as if they were playing a part in a movie.

When she raised my seat and I looked in the mirror, I could not believe it was me! I even turned around, to look for the beautiful woman standing behind me. I had never had so much as lipstick on my young face and was amazed to see this glorious, mature person staring back. I worried that Moez would not recognize me but it was too late to change anything.

Just then, Nani walked into the beauty salon with my wedding dress. We went behind a screen to exchange my modest girlish dress for my beautiful gown. Nani fastened the long row of covered buttons and I emerged in all my glory. The simple chiffon dress was long-sleeved and high-necked. It skimmed my body and then flared out, ankle length at the front but spreading to a long, heavy train at the back. My mother lent me her pearl drop earrings to complement my elaborate hairdo. Madame fastened a white flower on one side of my face and attached a short tulle veil at the back of my head.

Once more I gazed at my reflection. My God! I was so beautiful! It was such a shame to have to go and get married—I wanted to just sit there and have everyone come and admire me!

My sisters were ready and had changed into their dresses too. In Iran, we don't really have bridesmaids in the Western sense, but my sisters were there to lend support and accompany me.

Clambering down the four flights in my white satin high heels, with Nani and my sisters holding the heavy train up behind me, I was relieved to see Hassan waiting outside with the open carriage. Hassan, on the other hand, was clearly stunned to see me heading for the carriage; I think he only finally recognized me when he caught sight of Nani bringing up the rear. We climbed in. Hassan sat up front with the driver. Passing through the streets with everyone looking at us in all our finery made me feel like a princess in a story. I was happy and excited, smiling regally and waving as we made our procession home.

We reached home in about twenty minutes. I was sad the trip ended so soon. One of the servants greeted me with the *mangal*, a copper pot with a burning coal inside, on which pieces of *esfand* root smoked, scenting the air and bringing good luck to the bride. Nani gave me a coin to give to the servant, as tradition demanded.

With my sisters again holding the heavy train, I mounted the stairs and walked to my parents' room. The ceremonial setting was already prepared. It is a very beautiful ceremony.

Two low chairs sat against the wall in my parents' bedroom. I sat on one, holding the Koran, surrounded by all the women in both families. My sisters held a long piece of white silk over my head, making a canopy above the chairs. As I watched in the big mirror set up on the opposite wall, one cousin performed the ritual of stitching a colored thread onto the canopy, symbolizing the happiness of the bride and groom being joined in their new life. This rite also suggests that relatives, particularly the mother of the groom, should keep their mouths sewn shut and not interfere in the new couple's affairs. A second cousin ground two big pieces of sugar together above the canopy, creating a gentle rain of sweetness in the hopes of sweetening our union.

I felt so dignified and mature that I was shocked to overhear someone asking Mrs. Ghafary, "How old is she? She looks so *young!*" My mother-in-law answered proudly, "She has just turned sixteen." Both women nodded knowingly.

In the adjoining room, all the men were gathered in silence in the company of an *imam*, a high-ranking clergyman. The *imam* began to recite in Arabic. I had no idea what he was saying but all of a sudden I heard him ask me, in Persian, if I would like to marry this man. I was glad I had been paying attention. My mother had instructed me not to answer until the *imam* had asked the question three times. When I finally responded with "Yes," everyone started clapping and congratulating each other and offering sweets. Moez walked through into the room and sat on the chair next to me. He kissed my cheek.

Father walked through too, and kissed me on the cheek. He did not look very happy. Then my mother invited all the guests to go into the garden. The door closed. For the first time I was alone with my husband. We looked at each other. It was silent in the room. Thoughts were racing though my head. What will we talk about? I don't know this man. He will think me a foolish child. I stared in disbelief at our reflections in the mirror. I was *married* to this stranger!

Fortunately Moez started talking. He held my hand and looked into my eyes. I panicked—perhaps he didn't recognize me in all this finery and makeup? But he said my name, so he must know it is, after all, me I thought. He said, "Parvaneh-*joon*, we must *tu-toyer.*" I didn't know what he was talking about. Could it be some strange demand he would make? I sat there, staring at him like a goat, round-eyed, blank-faced, my dark red lips pursed. He started to laugh and explained that his mixture of French and Persian meant, "We need to address each other with the informal pronoun, *tu* in French, or *to* in Persian, instead of the formal *vous* or *shoma.*" Still I sat there, mute, staring, goat-like. It was all very well to be informal, but what would I talk about?

I longed for Mehrdad, with whom the pool of conversation was bottomless. If he were only there, we could have been talking about the ceremony, making fun of everybody—and eating. All those goodies around me and I couldn't touch any of them!

I became so quiet that my husband took pity and began to talk about his experiences in the West, describing how women in Europe talk and act. I was overwhelmed—he was a Don Juan. He had so much experience with women. And he was the first man with whom I had ever been alone.

I was saved by the appearance of my mother, suggesting we come out to the garden to meet the guests. Moez helped me to rise from the low chair and held my train so that we could walk to the garden. As we appeared at the top of the stairs into the garden all the guests began to clap. We descended slowly into their midst. On this July evening, the garden was magnificent. All the roses were in bloom and the trees and flowers seemed to be singing a chorus of congratulation to the newlyweds.

I noticed Father standing with the *imam* and Moez's father. Our eyes met and I walked towards him. He said wistfully, "Parvaneh-*joon*, you look so beautiful." He kissed my cheek once more, then cupped my chin in his long-fingered hand, tilting my face this way and that and looking into my eyes in an almost puzzled way. Perhaps he barely recognized his young daughter in this made-up, coiffed, and resplendent bride.

That night, so involved was I with my own magically transformed appearance and the tension and excitement of my performance, everything seemed like theater, not real. When Mehrdad and I were younger, our sisters had loved to dress us up and play weddings. They would seat the two of us behind a curtain, me with flowers in my hair and Mehrdad wearing a tie, and act out the ceremony. Then the curtain would be whipped away and Mehrdad and I had to walk about as the bride and groom. That was exactly how I felt that evening. Perhaps this was still play-acting, just at a more sophisticated level? I half wished it was Mehrdad who held my arm and walked about among the guests with me, although our "weddings" had usually ended with a chase though the garden or even a wrestling match, to the utter annoyance of our sisters.

At some point, Moez came to me and kissed my hand, saying that he would come the next evening to take me out to dinner. Then I realized—I'm not in a theater. I am really married. The period of getting acquainted was about to begin. Quite soon, I would have to leave my home and family and never again, really, enjoy the easy intimacy and companionship that had been my life until now.

During the evening I noticed Mehrdad standing alone in a corner, looking miserable. I saw that he had been crying. When I asked him what was wrong he answered gruffly that now that I was married, he would have to call me *Khanoom*, which is a respectful form of address rather like Madam. It was only decades later, that same day when we were together in the Mayo Clinic after he was told that his condition was incurable, that he told me the real reason for his tears. During the wedding he too had realized that he had lost his playmate, his other self. That the friend who had shared almost every moment with him for fifteen years was lost to him. That this time, the wedding was not make-believe, an interlude in an otherwise active, companionable day spent playing in the garden. That soon I would join my husband's household and our lifetime of loving proximity would end. And he was heartbroken.

From July to October, Moez came to visit once or twice a week. We often went out to dinner or to a movie. During all this time he never extended our intimacy beyond holding my hand or kissing my cheek. I who knew so little of the world thought that this was normal. No one had talked to me about marriage. I knew vaguely that "something" happened, but nothing more.

In October, the second ceremony took place. It was held at the home of Moez's sister, who was married to a general and had a big house. Because of the cooler season, the event took place indoors. Again I visited Mme. Pessian and emerged with heavy makeup, stylish hair, and a manicure. The same wedding gown was brought out, and a similar flower was placed behind my ear. But this time I was not so stunned by my appearance and this time Moez and one of his brothers came to pick me up in a car.

There was no religious ceremony, but the wedding reception, held on the second floor of the grand house, was very lovely. The rooms were full of flowers and very elegant. Again the two families and some friends were invited for the dinner. At the end of the evening Moez and I went to his family home, which was to be our home too. We had our own room but meals and general life were shared. I found myself thrown into an environment in which I knew no one, not even my husband.

The house was on Avenue Bahar, only two or three blocks from my own home. It was very large, three floors, on the north side of the street. On the first floor were the kitchen, hallway, living room, dining room, and a single room in which Moez's unmarried brother lived. On the second floor, Moez's mother and his young sister shared a room. Moez and I had a room on this floor, and Moez's married brother, his wife, and two children had two rooms there. Each floor had a shower and a toilet. A large room on the top floor, really an attic, belonged to Moez's father. From my own secure, decidedly Eastern world, I was transported into a group of complete strangers who were thoroughly Westernized.

The house had an internal courtyard but this held few plants and was nothing like our lush oasis. The family was very civilized and kind. They adored Mrs. Ghafary and were supportive and helpful to one another. I was lucky to be part of such an educated and genteel family, for I could have found myself in a very different situation. Moez's mother was very affectionate towards me. I called her Mama, like everyone else, and she treated me like a daughter.

I was the youngest member of the household apart from Moez's sister, the baby of the family, who was then about nine or ten. She became my playmate, and we spent hours together in the courtyard, playing and singing songs. In many more ways than one, I was playing at being married.

DIVORCE

I LIVED IN the Ghafary household for about twelve months before I talked to Moez's mother about the situation between Moez and me. Our marriage remained unconsummated. Mama did not seem surprised. She told me that the family was preparing to send us to Europe to see a specialist. I was glad, because whereas Moez had originally been affable and easy to get on with, he was becoming increasingly agitated and bad tempered, and we were both suffering the effects of his insomnia and headaches. In all that time, I never once talked to my family about the problem in my marriage. I did not want them to be unhappy or hurt on my behalf; and anyway, not being sure how a normal marriage was conducted, I didn't really know how unusual mine was.

At the end of 1945 Moez and I left for Europe on a two-engine plane. Both families came to the airport to say good-bye, loading us up with gifts, cookies, nuts, and sweets in the time-honored Persian tradition. Leaving Tehran by air was quite an occasion in those days. There were very few flights—perhaps one a month. The plane made several refueling landings en route, the first in Baghdad. I was quite scared looking out the window at the matchbox world below, and relieved to get out in Baghdad, where we spent a couple of hours before flying on to Egypt.

In the early morning light of our arrival, Cairo looked beautiful. It was very busy, the streets crammed with people. To me it was all very modern and amazing, especially our hotel. The first floor dining room where we went to have lunch was set with beautiful china and silverware on pink tablecloths. The waiters all wore red and black Egyptian costumes and red-tasseled fezzes on their heads.

That afternoon we walked through the streets and I just loved it. After dinner that evening, I followed the sound of music coming from one of the public rooms and saw elegant men and women dancing cheek to cheek. I completely forgot my fatigue and wanted to join the happy crowd; but Moez was too possessive and jealous to risk another man dancing with me, so we went to our room. As we drove through the streets of Cairo on the way to the airport the next morning, I promised myself that I would come back one day to this enchanting city.

From Cairo we flew to Benghazi, an Italianate city in Libya on the Mediterranean. We were taken downtown by bus to spend the night in a hotel. The windows from our small room opened onto a street thronged with people on their way from the *Souq*, and I could see evidence of the bomb damage the city had recently suffered during WWII. It seemed a shame to be merely passing through such an interesting place but again, Moez showed no inclination to explore. I felt lost. I had never left Iran and nothing seemed familiar. Tired and dispirited, I fell asleep as soon as I lay down. Moez, who could not sleep in even the quietest of places, sat up all night.

The next stop—finally—was Paris. I was terribly excited to see the "bride of cities" as it was known in Iran, but in the end I was sadly disappointed. It was mid-winter. The sky was gray and cloudy and I felt the cold right through to my bones. The airport was crowded and no one smiled. Passengers were left to fend for themselves and we helped each other through immigration and on to the baggage claim area. One of Moez's relatives was waiting for us; that made me feel better. He took us in a taxi to our hotel.

The look of the city after the long years of war surprised me. A depressed atmosphere seemed to hang over everything. Although our hotel was immense, there were few lights and no heat in the hallways and the air was damp and freezing. As we registered, we were told there was no heat in the rooms at night, hot water was scarce, and the elevators had been stopped in an effort to conserve energy. Breakfast would be provided if we gave half an hour's notice.

Our room was at the end of a hallway. It was large, with a big brown bed and dresser, heavy green curtains, and dim lighting. Moez's cousin took his leave, promising to pick us up the next day.

I was drawn to the enormous claw-footed tub in the bathroom. I undressed and sat in the bath and turned on the tap. Luxury—warm water! But almost immediately the trickle of warm water turned cold. Leaping from the bath into the frigid air, I dried myself on a thick, white towel—the only luxury left, it seemed—dressed, and went to the bedroom. Moez was already in bed and sound asleep. I got into bed fully dressed. Even with the covers pulled up my body was shaking with cold. I was thinking, "Is this the Paris I have heard so much about?" With the strangeness of the trip, the fatigue, and the homesickness, the emotions I had kept squeezed inside me surged up. Tears began to seep from my eyes. How lonely I was.

The next morning, we ordered our breakfast by telephone—not that there was any choice. Everything we asked for seemed to be unavailable. Eventually a tray was sent up. Tea—no coffee was available—and two pieces of hard bread. No butter, no jam, just a little honey. It might still have been wartime.

Moez's cousin came to get us and we set off to see Paris. It was as though the city had not seen sun for a long time. It was grim. Most of the shops were closed and those that opened did so for just a few hours a day. The people's clothing looked old and worn and I saw women wearing *sabots*, the wooden shoes of peasants. Food was scarce and rationed. I had never seen the effects of war.

We experienced some rationing in Tehran while Iran was occupied by the British, Americans, and Russians, but we still ate quite well as our garden provided so much of our food. I had never felt deprived or hungry. We read about the war and there were radio broadcasts, including some from Germany telling us how the Germans were winning and would unite with us as their Aryan brothers (they were hoping to get our oil). But I was very young and ignorant. Nothing prepared me for this level of devastation.

The cold weather and the obvious misery of the people had a strong effect on me. I cried constantly. I kept wondering why people had to fight. Why couldn't people understand each other? I missed Tehran. I missed the beautiful sunshine. I missed my family. I hated Paris! What a relief that we would be going to Switzerland the next day.

When Moez's cousin took us to the train the next morning, he assured us that Switzerland would be more to our liking. As our train passed through the

French countryside, we were further saddened by the terrible destruction. So much lay in ruins.

It took four hours to reach Geneva. The first thing I noticed as we left the train was the sun. It felt so good. The sky was blue and the air was crisp. I felt as though I had moved from the dark to the light. Behind the reception desk at our hotel, two well-dressed, elegant men smiled in welcome. After my gloomy Parisian introduction to Europe it was reassuring to find at least one place where people could smile and be kind to each other, look prosperous, and generally seem more like what I had expected. I realized the difference was war and peace: The French, who had just emerged from a devastating war, had little reason to smile or be welcoming, whereas the neutral Swiss had seen no fighting.

We had a large room on the fourth floor with two beds, a dresser, and a big wardrobe. The bellboy brought in our luggage and opened up the curtains. Light flooded into the room. A crowd of pigeons perched on the red tiles of the next building, enjoying the sun just as I did. In the distance the sunlight played over lush green trees. It was exhilarating after the grayness of Paris. I instantly fell in love with Switzerland.

As Moez prepared for dinner, I decided to bathe. Apart from the terrible trickle in Paris, I had not had a bath since leaving Tehran. I asked Moez whether hot water was rationed here, too. He laughed and said I could use as much hot water as I wanted. Standing under the shower, I reflected that I had never appreciated the luxury of getting clean in comfort until my miserable experience with cold water in a cold room in Paris.

The hotel suggested a good restaurant within walking distance for dinner. An immaculate waiter politely ushered us to a table set with crisp white linen and shining silverware. The china was so clean I could see my face reflected in it. We ordered a meal of steak, French fries, salad, bread, and—O joy—butter. What a contrast to our sad little breakfast in Paris. I felt so good being in this cozy place.

The hotel was our home for three days until we found a pensionne in the north of Geneva. It was a wonderful place. From both sides of our ground-floor room, windows opened onto the garden. Everyone in the building got together for three meals a day, which were included in the rent.

The Iranian government organized a job for Moez at the International Labor Organization. One of my father's friends, the great Persian writer Jamalzadeh, was also working at the ILO. Moez and I became friends with him. He and his German wife Gaby became very important in my life. They had no children and Mr. Jamalzadeh took on the role of the loving father I so missed.

Moez went to Professor Beckel, a famous internist, to get medical help for his problem. I looked for a French teacher and was lucky to find a professor, not too far from the pensionne, with whom I could study for a couple of hours a day. Soon I was able to manage my everyday life in French. Fortunately, I was never shy about trying out my new language and started a conversation with anyone in the pensionne who would talk to me. Everyone was very amused by my enthusiastic efforts, but at the end of the six months we spent there my French had improved greatly. I was so eager to learn more, Moez decided that from then on we would speak only French to one another.

We moved into an apartment on Avenue de Roches. It was much more spacious with two bedrooms, a living room, a dining room, and a kitchen. From the larger bedroom, which we took for ourselves, a spacious balcony presented a beautiful view of the city.

Feeling quite established, I registered at the International School of Geneva to resume my high school education. My days were divided between going to school, taking care of the apartment, and learning to cook. In the evenings we listened to classical music. Moez would explain the music to me as we listened to it at home, and every week we went to a concert. On the weekends we visited museums. Moez was a very good teacher and taught me a great deal about music and art. Before this I had known only Persian culture; I will always be grateful to him for the time he took to introduce me to things that have brought me much pleasure.

We had been in our apartment for a couple of months when my father came to Switzerland seeking treatment for tuberculosis, and stayed in the smaller bedroom for a few days before he moved to the sanatorium in the mountains in Leysin.

About a year after our arrival in Geneva, I realized that Moez was becoming increasingly agitated. He walked all night around the apartment and acted in a very jealous way if I talked to another man. He even started to follow me to school to see what I was doing and would get into arguments at restaurants with friends who showed any interest in me.

One day when my husband was out, the phone rang. It was Dr. Beckel's receptionist. She told me that the doctor would like me to come into his office to talk about my husband, and suggested that I not mention this appointment to Moez.

The following day I walked to Dr. Beckel's office, which was on the third floor in a large medical building. His receptionist ushered me into an elegant room. Dr. Beckel wore a white coat and was a good-looking man in his fifties.

"Good morning," he said graciously and led me to a sofa. Pulling his own chair close to me, he turned it with its back towards me and straddled the seat, leaning on the back and looking intently into my eyes. He asked, "How old are you?" I was rather taken aback, but told him I had just turned eighteen. He asked, "How long have you been married?"

"Two years."

He thought for a minute, his head bowed. Looking up, he queried, "You probably love your husband?"

"Of course," I said, automatically. But as I said the words, I realized that I had never considered the question.

Then he told me that his duty was to inform me about my husband's medical condition. He said that Moez had been born with equivocal gender, a condition for which at that time there was no effective surgery or treatment. He and his colleagues had tried their best, but were unable to improve the situation. Again he looked at me intently. "You are very young. I am sure that you want to have a normal life. I am sure that you want to have children. Isn't that true?"

I replied, "We have been hoping that you could cure him."

With obvious pain he said, "No, he is not going to be cured. He will never be able to function fully as a man. My advice is to leave your husband. I have already talked to him about that and if he loves you, he will let you go."

A cold chill ran over my body. I rose and Dr. Beckel guided me toward the door. I left quickly, rode down in the elevator, and found myself walking around the streets, no destination in mind. As I tried to grapple with what I had just heard, I realized that this was a problem I had to solve for myself. I had no one to consult, no one to go to.

My steps eventually took me towards our apartment. I was just eighteen. I was facing a divorce. Moez was waiting for me. I told him about my visit to Dr. Beckel's office. He was silent for quite a while but seemed to descend into a great sadness. Finally he said, "I think we had better go back to Iran. You pack the suitcases and I will notify the landlord." We never discussed his diagnosis. It was so painful for both of us that discussion seemed futile.

My father was at the tuberculosis sanatorium in Leysin and Moez and I had been visiting him every weekend. I knew that I would have to tell him we were returning to Iran. But I did not have the heart to add to his burdens by telling him about Moez's condition. So I said nothing about it.

At the end of the month, when our lease on the apartment was up, we went to Leysin to say goodbye. My father held me and said, "Oh Pari-*joon*, I feel as if my soul is being taken away!" I started to cry. Not only was I leaving my father in Switzerland alone and unable to converse in French, but I also had to go back to Tehran and face divorce. I sobbed all the way from Leysin to Geneva. Moez withdrew into himself.

The next day, we left on the Setebelo, a luxury train that used to run between Geneva and Milan. It was near sunset when we left Geneva, heading towards the Italian section of Switzerland. A running commentary on the places we passed came over the loudspeaker in English, French, and Italian and despite my misery, I was fascinated. It was like watching a movie or sitting in a history class. We learned the names and history of the villages and towns we passed, as well as the history of Switzerland. We had dinner on the train. Our compartment had two beds and after a comfortable night, I woke up as we were coming into Milan.

Our hotel there was in the old section of town and our room on the tenth floor. The window was flung open as we entered and I went to look out. I felt as though I had gone back to the Middle Ages. The buildings, all of which seemed to be host to many birds, were interesting and old. When he saw me completely lost in the view, Moez suggested that if I were not too tired, we could have breakfast and explore the city. Tired! How could I be too tired when I was only eighteen? And breakfast could wait.

So we went out and started to walk towards the great Milan Cathedral. On the way, we stopped at the Galleria, a pedestrians-only section of the city filled with cafés and shops and people enjoying themselves. The weather was absolutely lovely so we sat at an outdoor café and ordered coffee and biscuits.

I was amazed that even at this early hour, the streets were full of people. Groups of men and women were talking at full speed to each other. It seemed very different from Switzerland, where people were dry and withdrawn. Here it seemed everybody knew everybody else. I had the feeling that the Italians were always in motion. The language sounded very beautiful, and I caught many French words too. Most of the people I encountered were smiling and very charming, especially when it came to coaxing us out of our money.

After about an hour of people-watching, we headed for the cathedral once more. The cathedral was so poetic. Built in glorious white marble with a sweeping, high ceiling and tall columns, it looked to me like a beautiful forest. As I stood in the body of this great church gazing about, the majesty and peace of the place seemed to drain me of pain. I was overwhelmed by a sense of spirituality, and a profound silence and stillness took over my body and my mind. Somehow the pressure of my problems seemed less important. The cathedral was built with the intention of focusing people's attention on the power and majesty of God. It was obviously successful, for here was I, centuries later, rooted to the ground in awe at the divinity I felt around me.

The next day we walked around the city, lunching again at the Galleria. Somehow our hotel managed to get two tickets to La Scala for that evening to see La Bohème, by the Italian composer Puccini. I had never seen an opera or even listened to operatic music. Moez told me the story, and I waited with great anticipation for this new and exciting experience.

La Scala is situated in the middle of Milan. I could hardly believe that the opera house had been devastated during the war but was again presenting opera. An usher with a black suit and a golden necklace showed us to our seats. I looked around at all the beautiful boxes, newly renovated in red, with gold edging glittering beneath impressive chandeliers. I saw the beautifully dressed people, and felt extraordinarily happy.

The stage was huge, with the musicians beneath stage level. When the curtain went up, the whole opera house went silent and seemed transformed into a great cathedral. As the music began below, I thought of my father and yearned for him to be in good health and be there with me. He always loved something new. I remember once in Tehran, when I was about fourteen years old, I went with my father to a concert. They were playing Chopin. We were sitting in the first row and I watched my father almost drowning in the music. As we went home I asked him if he liked the concert. "Oh, it was magnificent," he answered dreamily, still lost in its spell.

I knew that I would be seeing more opera. A seed had been planted in my soul. Moez suggested we visit the tomb of Verdi, one of the great Italian composers of opera. I imagined he would be buried in one of the churches, but we took a taxi to the Piazza Buonarotti. To one side was a big garden, in the middle of which was a large building that had been Verdi's home. With no children, Verdi had left his home in trust to musicians in need and it now housed a hundred musicians. I thought he must have been a good man.

Verdi's tomb and that of his beloved second wife were down a narrow path at the end of the garden. On Verdi's tomb was inscribed, "He shed tears for everyone, and everyone loved him." As we went back along the path, I imagined all the musicians who had lived in his house since he had died. None of them had been blessed with his genius or his luck, but all had benefited from his generosity.

The following day we took the train to Rome. We had to wait nearly a month there before the next flight left for Iran. I was excited, having heard all the stories of Rome's greatness, its history and art, its churches, museums, beautiful fountains, statues. I could hardly wait. Moez had visited Rome many times while he was growing up in Europe, and as we journeyed there he organized a program for our stay. We visited first the Vatican and St. Peter's Basilica. I had never been exposed to such magnificent paintings as I saw at the Sistine Chapel. And the library! I could have spent months just there.

I was quite intimidated—even scared—when we went to see the Coliseum. The screams of innocent people echoed in my ears and I found it hideous. I much preferred to walk in the streets and hear the laughter of the living.

Then bad luck intervened. After just a week, when we were returning from a meal in a charming little restaurant, a man held a gun to Moez's back and we were forced into an alley and robbed of all our money. We had been warned against leaving valuables in our hotel room, so Moez was carrying everything we had. Rome—and most of Europe—had huge numbers of people left destitute by the war. Street crime was very common. After leaving us penniless, the thief distracted us by crying, "Police!" and ran off.

So there we were, nearly three weeks to wait and no money. We didn't know what to do. We had a room and until we left, the hotel would not demand payment. But we had no money for food. Moez seemed to have no plan at all. We tried to continue our sightseeing, but kept interrupting it to conserve energy by spending as much time asleep as possible.

After a few days of virtual starvation, I became quite desperate. Vendors sold spaghetti and bread to working class people in the city squares. I watched the way the system worked before making my move. Once a customer had paid for his meal, he held out a plate and the vendor scooped out hot spaghetti and added a bread roll from a basket. I chose my moment as the spaghetti was being served, when both the customer and the vendor were distracted, and snatched two bread rolls and scurried away. Moez and I shared quite a few such stolen meals before help unexpectedly arrived.

Our savior was the mother of one of my former classmates. I spotted her on the Via Veneto one day. Rushing into her arms, I sobbed out our pitiful story. Before I had even finished, she led us into a restaurant. After eating like two starving *jube* dogs, we finished the story, and this kind woman lent us a sum of money to pay our hotel bill and buy food for the rest of our stay. I don't know what we would have done if not for this serendipitous meeting. We had already decided to slip out of the hotel without paying, but my continued stealing would probably have landed me in jail before that time.

We resumed our sightseeing and I enjoyed seeing Rome with Moez as my guide. Soon, however, reality intervened and we had to leave for Iran. The enchanting pause in our miserable situation was over and I had to face my destiny.

It was almost morning when we reached Tehran. The plane circled three times around Mehrabad Airport before landing and the city looked so beautiful. All the lights were on and it reminded me of the nights my brother and I had peered through our mosquito nets at the stars. A bus came right to the plane to pick up the passengers. I was not very happy to return. I had left my father alone in Switzerland and the weight of the impending divorce pressed upon me.

As we came through the exit doors we saw a crowd of relatives waiting for us. I had missed my mother very much and saw the strain of my father's illness and absence in her face. I hugged her first, then my youngest sister, Cherry, my two older sisters, then Mehrdad. Hushang was studying in India at that time. My husband's family was there, too. I felt very sad, as I loved them all and would soon leave them. Moez's youngest sister looked much older than she had when we left. I could hardly believe that she had been my playmate after my marriage. Now I felt so old.

While we were away, Moez's family had moved to a much larger, more central home and we drove there in my father-in-law's car. Moez and I were allocated a big attic room.

My family came for lunch and stayed all day. I was wearing a simple but very beautiful green dress that I had bought in Rome—it was a time when travelers dressed quite formally. Moez's family was delighted by my newly acquired language abilities and we all spoke in French. My sister Mali, who has always been very humorous, asked me, "Now that you come from Europe and look so elegant, will you drink water with a fork?" This is a Persian joke about people who had become Westernized and everybody laughed, including me. But inside, I felt far from laughter. The secret knowledge of what was to come seemed to create a barrier between me and my family, as though I were watching their joy and merriment from an adjoining room.

A month passed. Every day members of our families came, singly or in groups, to greet us after our return. I had not talked about our situation to anyone, but one morning I woke up convinced that I could no longer put off the inevitable. I would face it that day. I dressed and started downstairs. The door to my mother-in-law's room was half open and I heard her call out, "Parvaneh-joon? Is it you? Do

you want to see me?" I told her, "Mama, I am going out. Do you need anything?"
This was something we always said in that family. She looked at me closely and
said, "No, my dear, I don't need anything. But where are you going?"

"I am going to see my mother."

"Please give my love to her."

Closing her door, I went down to the first floor and walked into the courtyard.
No one was there. I walked through the gate and into the street. I looked back
at the house, thinking, "Two years have passed." A huge burden suddenly seem
lifted from my shoulders. Yes, two years. I would terminate this artificial marriage.
A cab took me straight to my parent's house.

The gate was half open. Walking in, I saw Nani cleaning the green vegetables
in the courtyard. She jumped up and came towards me. "Oh, it's you! My sweet
Parvaneh-*joon*." I asked her how she was and she replied, "Oh Parvaneh! I am
always better when I see you. But what are you doing here?" Before I could answer,
my mother, who had heard my voice, came out to join us.

Her concerned face seemed to unleash my feelings, so long kept tightly in
check. I said, "Maman, Maman!" and started crying. The tears rolled down my
face. She was very upset.

"What in the world has happened? Why are you crying?"

Nani stopped cleaning the vegetables and came over to me. "Parvaneh. Please
tell us what is wrong."

I told my mother, "I don't know how to explain. But I am here to stay. I am
not going to be with my husband anymore."

We walked into my mother's room. Maman was stunned, speechless. She
looked at me with curious, waiting eyes. Hesitantly at first, but gaining momen-
tum as the truth finally tumbled out, I told her about Moez and the reason we
had gone so suddenly to Europe. One by one, I went through the things that
the doctor had told me.

Without a word, Maman got up and went to the telephone in the hallway. She
dialed Moez's house and asked to talk to his mother. I heard her say that Moez's
family had known of his condition and yet had sacrificed her daughter to him.
She spoke with great courtesy but said, "Parvaneh will not return. Tomorrow I
will send someone to pick up her clothing and other belongings."

When Maman came back into the room she looked very agitated. She asked me, "Why didn't you tell me this before? You should have left that marriage in the first year, not have waited all this time." I was crying with grief and relief.

"But what am I to do?" I sobbed. My mother said that she was going to ask Father's great friend Mr. Assar to come immediately to talk to us. He was a very spiritual man who had been a huge support to our family, especially in my father's absences. She sent Hassan to ask him if he could come on an urgent matter.

Hassan returned with the message that Mr. Assar would come that afternoon. Nani was preparing the table for lunch and muttering to herself darkly. I found that I couldn't eat at all. I was confused and tired. I had not slept the night before. In fact I had not slept properly for a long time. Unburdened at last, I lay down on my mother's bed and fell instantly asleep.

Around five o'clock Maman came to wake me. "Parvaneh, get up," she urged. "Mr. Assar is waiting for you in the garden." After washing my face and smoothing my clothing, I walked out to the garden. Mr. Assar came towards me and hugged me. "Thank you so much for coming," I said, to which he replied, "Your mother has told me everything. You do not need a divorce. Under the Islamic law, a marriage that is not consummated within a year can be annulled. Any gifts you have received should be returned."

With relief mixed with sorrow I asked him if he could tell me what I needed to do. He immediately said, "Yes, of course. You are like my daughter. I will organize the procedure. Don't worry any more. Give me two days."

As Mr. Assar left the telephone started to ring. It was Moez, who wanted to talk to me. When I picked up the receiver all I could hear was weeping. I was crying also. I told him, "Moez, this would have ended sooner or later. We have no other choice." The next day Nani and Hassan went in a taxi to pick up my things, mainly clothing.

In our house there was a room off the hallway that had been occupied by various people over time. It had been Mamak's room for a time and then servant's quarters, but was currently unoccupied. A door and a window opened onto the courtyard and a second door opened onto the street. My mother cleaned it up and designated it as my room.

Two weeks later, Mr. Assar made an appointment for us in the Family Court.

Moez and I were each to be accompanied by a witness. Mr. Assar was my witness and Moez's brother was his witness. The day arrived. It was an extremely difficult one for me. I didn't know how I would confront my husband. I had not slept the night before and got up very early. Thinking I might feel better if I walked, I wandered the streets for several hours before we left for the hearing.

Family Court was in a very old, grim house in an old section of Tehran. When we knocked, we were first taken into a small courtyard then directed upstairs into a gloomy waiting room that had a big table in the center and many chairs arranged around the edge of the room. It felt like a funeral. Moez and his brother were already there. Moez walked towards me, crying. Taking my hands, he asked me to forgive him. He said that if I did not, God would never forgive him.

We went through into the hearing room. The judge asked us many questions. We both answered carefully and truthfully. He recited those verses from the Koran that annul a marriage and asked us to sign a paper. My eyes were red from crying and I put on my sunglasses to hide them. I walked away with Mr. Assar, saying good-bye to my husband of two years and to his brother. I was still only eighteen years old.

Maman wrote to Father, telling him everything. She received a telegram that he must have sent right away, saying, "Now that Parvaneh is free, you should send her back to Switzerland. I need her."

He followed this up with a letter that I read only after Maman had died, when I was collecting his papers for the Archives. Even now, as I reread this letter, it makes me weep for the loss of this dear man, whose view of women was so modern and whose love for me was so strong. He wrote:

> Now, I would like to talk to you about my dear Parvaneh. It is a shame that this young woman was married to someone who was wrong for her. She has tried everything in her power to make me happy. Next only to you, I can trust her with my life. Parvaneh understands far more than her age would imply. She must have complete freedom to express her feelings. If she can come back to Switzerland, it would be very, very good for me; I miss her greatly.
>
> I know that Parvaneh has many suitors—she had many in Switzerland too,

but she gave herself to none of them. You can tell all these suitors that they can wait, and wait. Whoever she chooses will be rewarded with a magnificent wife. Encourage her not to be shy. Allow her to go out twice a week to the movies. She should be allowed to invite all her friends home, or go to their parties. She needs more social life. Men only know what they see with their own eyes, so she should not hide inside the house but be out in society. Try to give parties for her.

But on the other hand, I think she should come to Switzerland right away. I need her more than anyone else.

I love you, my darling companion, and I still kiss both of your hands and thank God that you are my wife.

SOJOURN WITH FATHER
IN SWITZERLAND

IT WAS when Moez and I were in Geneva, seeking treatment for his condition, that Maman wrote me that Father had tuberculosis and was coming to Switzerland for treatment. She sold part of our garden and some land she had inherited in northern Tehran to pay for his trip.

Although I was saddened by the news, I awaited Father with great anticipation. Moez and I went to meet him at Geneva airport. Father's cousin, Dr. Mehdi Bahar, accompanied him. As I hugged Father I saw that in the year I had been away, he had become thinner and lacked energy. His face seemed sad. He had a fever and had no patience to deal with the formalities of airport arrival, even though this did not involve the crowds that we experience today.

The four of us took a taxi to our little apartment. Father was unusually quiet and there was scant conversation. As soon as we had settled him into the bedroom I had prepared for him, he lay down and closed his eyes, seeming not even to notice the flowers I had arranged to cheer him. I covered him with a blanket and closed the door behind me.

Dr. Bahar—who had suggested this trip to Switzerland—filled us in on the illness, no doubt brought on by the years spent in jail. He had arranged for Father to be treated at a sanatorium in Leysin, high in the Bernese Alps. After three days' rest, when my father felt less fatigued, we went with him to the sanatorium. From Geneva we took a train to Lausanne, then on to Montreux and the old section, or Vielleville, of Aigle. Father was quite revived by the beauty of the landscapes we passed, pointing out sights with great enthusiasm. For much of the trip, we travelled alongside Lac Léman (Lake Geneva), and the pretty towns and villages, the reflection of the magnificent mountains in the famously cerulean blue waters fed by the Rhône Glacier, the castles, churches, and picturesque farms and vineyards kept us enthralled. The last leg was the funicular (cable railway) up the mountain to the village of Leysin. It was my first time in a funicular and I was amazed at finding myself in a little room high up in the air, dangling over the majestic landscape for half an hour.

It was early afternoon when we arrived. A polite young man from Hotel Belvedere, the sanatorium Dr. Bahar had chosen, met us and helped with the luggage. After seeing Father safely installed, Dr. Bahar left us to go to Paris to seek further training in tuberculosis, which became his specialty.

Hotel Belvedere, a large white building situated on the top of the mountain, was one of dozens of clinics that had been set up in Leysin in the late nineteenth and early twentieth centuries when high-altitude heliotherapy was the favored treatment for a number of illnesses, particularly tuberculosis. Many of the dozens of sanatoriums in Leysin were called "hotels" and some were quite luxurious.

By the time Father was settled in, the afternoon was almost over. His room was on the second floor and, like all the patients' rooms, faced the sun and had a big balcony. The other side of the building was allocated to administrative and medical functions. My impression of the accommodation was that it was nothing like a hospital. Each high-ceilinged room had its own bathroom and was decorated in white with a little touch of green, giving it a fresh, clean appearance. Next to the large bed was a table with a lamp on it. Near the wide glass doors to the balcony, a sofa, two chairs, and a low table looked inviting.

The view was gorgeous, looking out over mountains and forest to Mont Blanc and down the Rhône Valley. My father walked straight to the balcony doors and threw them open. He looked like a man who was breathing for the first time in ages. As I hung up his clothes and put other things away in drawers, Father changed into pajamas and went to bed. About half an hour later dinner was brought, and I waited until he had eaten before I left.

Father generally ate like a bird. Even when we were at home, Maman would send me to his study to announce that lunch was ready as the rice was being put on to steam. We knew that food held little interest for him compared with his work, so we always gave him a good forty-five minutes to finally join us at the table. I remember one day when I went to call him for lunch he told me, "I wish one day they would create pills, one for lunch and one for dinner. Then I could be over with it in a second!"

Leysin is really two villages, one on top of the mountain, the other lower down, separated by forest. The funicular stops at both sections of the village. Between the two sections, steps descend through the forest—a pleasant walk which I often preferred to take rather than waiting for the funicular.

I took a room in a small pensionne near the hospital for a couple of weeks to be close to Father. Visiting hours were ten in the morning to one in the afternoon, and four to eight in the evening, and I spent every available minute with him. Rest, pure air, and hours of sunshine were the cure, so, after lunch, Father would be covered up warmly and his bed rolled out onto the balcony. Hotel Belvedere was well-managed and professionally staffed. There were a few other Iranians there for company, all much younger than Father. During that summer, quite a few Iranian students made the pilgrimage to Leysin to study with him. Their respect and kindness made his stay much more pleasant.

Tragically, at the Belvedere Father was diagnosed not only with tuberculosis of both lungs but also of his bones, which at that time was considered an incurable illness. We heard of a new antibiotic treatment created in the United States that held promise of slowing the illness. It was very expensive but we were able to procure it. Father's temperature went down and he began to put on a little weight, so the doctors allowed him to start taking short walks with me. His improvement meant he could sit more comfortably in his bed and have enough energy to do some work; encouraging signs.

While Moez and I were still in Geneva, we visited my father every weekend. We stayed in the same pensionne near the sanatorium. We would take the train on Friday afternoon after Moez finished work and return Sunday evening. Within three or four months after Father's arrival, however, Moez and I returned to Iran to formalize our separation.

Just a couple of months after my divorce, I set off once more for Switzerland.

This time I traveled alone. To pay for my trip, my mother sold many possessions, including jewelry, antiques, and other items that came from her family. At the Geneva airport, Gabi, the wife of Jamalzadeh, was waiting for me and took me to stay at their apartment. The next day she took me to the railroad station, where I took the train and then the funicular to Leysin.

I had again arranged to stay at the now familiar pensionne in the upper village. As I signed in, the manager asked me how long I would stay this time. I told her that it would depend on when the doctors said Father was able to leave the sanatorium. I took my suitcase to the second floor, to the room that was to be my home for the next three months: a small, simple room with windows that opened onto a forest. Without even unpacking, I walked to the Belvedere. It was late afternoon and I knew that dinner was about to be served.

My father was still in the same room, so I went straight to it. When I knocked on the door, I heard his familiar voice say, "Yes?" I opened the door. I will never forget that moment, when my father saw me there. The dinner tray sat as yet untouched before him. The light was on and although the windows were closed, the view of the mountains and forest was still visible in the fading sunset. Such happiness shone through Father's eyes as he said, "You are here, now." He quickly wrote a poem:

With your love
I have no fear
Even were the whole universe to turn against me.

As I hugged my father, I thought how wonderful this man was, what a kind father he was, what a magnificent poet he was. Tears gathered in our eyes, but they were tears of happiness, not of sadness.

Unfortunately, after three months we had to accept the fact that both the sanatorium and my pensionne were too expensive for us. We found a cheaper clinic in the lower village of Leysin directed by a young Iranian doctor, Dr. Shaghaghi, whom Father liked immediately. It also helped that he spoke Persian. I found a cheaper pensionne nearby. Most of these boarding houses catered to convalescents who were no longer contagious but needed some extra rest and mountain air before going home; a much smaller number of friends and relatives of the patients at the various clinics rounded out the population.

Another group in the village consisted of doctors and nurses and their families. It was a lively and interesting assortment of people, mostly young and from all over the world, and we formed a close community. The recognition of death was a tangible presence that lent a mood of almost reckless celebration, a sense of borrowed time, to many of these young lives—an atmosphere of revelry unmatched by anything I could have imagined. Later I recognized this same desperate, tragic, uninhibited carousing during the time of the Black Death as described in Boccaccio's *Decameron*. With one nostril you could smell the fear of death, with the other, the glory of life. From time to time we would hear of patients who had left the sanatoriums and hanged themselves in the forest or plunged from a mountain ledge.

Perhaps a better analogy for my time in Leysin would be Thomas Mann's *The Magic Mountain*, set in a similar sanatorium town. Like young, naïve Hans Castorp, I had left the "flatlands" of Iran and gone to the rarefied Alpine atmosphere of Leysin to be with a tubercular relative. Between visits, I had unexpected freedom and learned a great deal about life and love, emerging as a much more mature person than the girl I had been at the beginning. My father was like Settembrini—an enlightened humanist who even in ill health wrote feverishly of democracy and human rights

It was a strange period for me, living in two different worlds. I was either with my father in the clinic, where it was hard not to feel sad surrounded by so much physical and emotional suffering, or caught up in the gaiety of the village life. My father wrote a poem called "The Beggar Girl" that explores this theme, although he did not write it at that time or with me in mind.

I saw a little girl, out begging in the street.
She wore a flimsy dress, shabby and sadly torn.
Though dressed in rags with nothing on her feet
Her natural grace shone through those ragged clothes.
She looked at me through tears of great distress.

I handed her some coins and went on my way,
But all day I was haunted by the pitiful sight.
That night, when I went to the river to walk
I saw her again, now wreathed in smiles.
Approaching this graceful child I asked:
"Was it not you who was crying this morning,
Scorching the heart of all who passed?
Now tell me, how were you then so forlorn
And now so happy and bright?"
She looked in my eyes, saying, "This is my story:
My mother and father are crippled and worn.
My tears this morning were for their plight,
My smiles this evening are for myself
In gratitude for my youthful glory."

Since there were no cars on the mountain, everyone traveled on foot or by sled or horse, making it easy to meet people. In my year and a half there, I became familiar with many of the patients. I made a habit of visiting the younger ones to read and talk to them, particularly those whose bones had been infected with tuberculosis and were thus immobilized.

I was quite popular, as I was young and pretty and healthy and exotic. Several nights a week I would be invited to parties in people's rooms where there was much eating, drinking, dancing, storytelling, and hilarity. I discovered that I loved fondue, which was fortunate because we ate a lot of it. It was a natural meal for these gatherings, as fondue is communal and cheap to prepare.

In the lower village, there was a community center where a dance was held every Saturday night. Three or four times a year there would be a big party—a masked ball, a casino night—organized by the villagers who would sell tickets to the events.

I had been studying English twice a week with a young black American convalescent who was very beautiful and charming. One day he asked if I was going to the masked ball that Saturday. I said I was and he asked if I would reserve a dance for him. When I said, "Of course," he said, "But I want you to promise. In fact I want you to sign that you will dance with me." I asked him why I would need to do that, since I would like to dance with him, but he insisted that I sign an oath.

I had very little money and there was only one dressmaker in the whole of Leysin, but I decided to have a new dress for the ball. I bought some light green taffeta and had her make a dress with a great big bow at the back. That evening I added a small mask and set off excitedly for the community center. As the guests arrived, they walked down a long curving flight of stairs into the ballroom. To my horror, I suddenly saw my American friend standing theatrically at the top of the stairs—completely naked! Not even a mask! He walked slowly down into the ballroom, dramatically waving his piece of paper with my signature on it, shouting, "Where is she? Where is Parvaneh? I am here to redeem her promise."

I was frightened and embarrassed. I might have been married for almost two years, but I was still an innocent and had never seen a man naked. I tried to hide behind people, but somehow no one allowed it—perhaps they were all in on the joke. I had no choice but to dance with him. There was no way I could have lived in that village if I failed to honor my pledge. Everyone formed a circle and watched us dance. I thought it would never end. I was scared to death and felt ashamed as he held me close—I was after all, a sheltered Persian girl.

As soon as the dance finished, I grabbed my coat—it was the middle of winter—and ran back to my pensionne. Of course I cancelled my English lessons. Even though my father was the most tolerant person in the world, this was one experience I definitely did not share with him. Now I can laugh at the image, even be glad that such a wild and crazy thing happened to me. But at the time . . .

There were a few Persian doctors in Leysin and I knew all of them and their wives. One evening, one of the doctors, Dr. Birjandi, invited me to join their group at a dance for the medical professionals. I wore my fateful green dress again and a string of lovely pearls. Two white roses caught my long hair behind one ear. After we had found our table by the dance floor, I went with Dr. Birjandi to carry back some drinks. We were standing by the bar when he smiled at someone over my shoulder and said, "I would like to introduce you to someone." I turned to see who was approaching and there before me was the most handsome young man

I had ever seen—tall, slim, blond, with big green eyes. He shook my hand and spoke to me in French. His name was Franco Micchetti. I will never forget that moment. I don't know how long we stood there with my hand in his, looking into each other's eyes. Time stood absolutely still just like in a romantic movie. Everything but this young god melted away. I felt as if we were both bathed in brilliant light.

Franco, I discovered, was a third year medical student at the University of Lausanne. Even before the drinks arrived, he asked if I would dance with him. Without a moment's hesitation I said "Yes." We went straight to the dance floor. We never went back for our drinks. We danced all night together. We danced and danced and danced without stopping until most people had left. Finally, at four in the morning, the police came to close the place and we had to let each other go. It was as if nothing existed in the world except the two of us. We were young, shy, and inexperienced, but the attraction between us was so instantaneous, so strong that it didn't matter. I had no idea how the hours had passed. It was the first time in my life that I had experienced romantic love and the first time I had been attracted to a man. It was heavenly.

Franco walked me back to my pensionne and left. The next day he invited me to his home for a meal, after which I went with his parents to watch him play hockey. I sat right by the rink and every time he swished past he would look straight at me. In fact he would take quite unnecessary turns around the rink just so that he could catch my eye. I was breathless. He was magnificent. I have always been prone to feeling the cold, but even though we were out in the open in the middle of winter, I did not feel it at all. After that, I went to all his games and I was so filled with happiness and the fire of love that never once did I notice the cold.

We met every weekend. Franco picked me up at my pensionne and we would walk to different cafés, or go to upper Leysin by funicular to have tea. Then we would go for dinner with his parents and he would take me back. In all that time, even though we both knew we were head over heels in love, we never mentioned the word love.

One day, we decided that I would go to visit him in Lausanne in the middle of the week to see Laurence Olivier's new film, *Hamlet*. I asked permission from my father, who gave it willingly. I took the funicular down, then the train to Lausanne where Franco was waiting for me at the station. We fell into each other's arms and hugged and kissed, right there on the platform. It was my first real kiss, ever. It was wonderful.

We went by tram to his university, a beautiful place. The students there sported big felt hats and the custom was that good friends would write messages inside. He asked me to write something and I wrote, in Persian, "*Man doostet daram.*" He wanted to know what I had written and I whispered shyly, "I love you."

Father's room at the clinic in lower Leysin was smaller than at the Belvedere, but adequate and clean. It was arranged in the same way with a sunny balcony in front of which was a ski slope, where the action was quite diverting. The treatment was the same and it was affordable, and soon Father began to look better.

I was thrilled to see a smile returning to his face. I stayed with him every day during the twice-daily visiting hours and we had long conversations about everything under the sun. At the time, this seemed the natural thing to do. It never occurred to me that I was making any kind of sacrifice by devoting my life to my father when he needed me. It is only now that I am older that I can see how important it is for children to show this kind of love for their parents, particularly when the parent is ill. I was too young to see beyond Father's pleasure in my company to understand how deeply he appreciated my being there, even though he composed a beautiful poem, expressing his love and gratitude, and read it to me on one of my thousands of visits. Now when I read this tribute, I can catch a glimpse of his powerful emotions.

My dear daughter. My beautiful Parvaneh.
You are my happiness in life and the right arm in my sleeve.
You left your mother in Iran and came here to be my companion
Because you saw that I am in pain.
Because of your love you came and stayed with me.
You are trying very hard to relieve the sorrow of my heart.

Although you are still very young
I still can see the greatness in you.

With your intelligence, depth, and beauty,

You are my child, my daughter, and you will succeed me.

I ask God to give you the best of life, my dear Parvaneh.

When I saw Father so much improved, I wrote to his friend in Nice, Mr. Shirazi, who invited us to visit him. I asked Dr. Shaghaghi if he thought a trip would be a good idea and he consulted the doctors at Belvedere. Everyone felt that it was quite manageable. I began to plan our travels, choosing easy distances and sufficient time for Father to recover between stops. The first part of the trip was to be an exploration of the various parts of Switzerland, traveling by train. It was a roundabout, sometimes criss-crossing route based on places I thought he would enjoy, the availability of people whom he would like to see, and a few events such as a conference in Geneva he had been invited to attend.

I have to admit, I was never very good with maps. I was, however, very enthusiastic (and at eighteen, very young and inexperienced) and chose destinations based on reports of the beauty of places I read about or heard about from returning travelers. Details have never been my strong suit. But the distances were short and the train travel was pleasant and scenic, so it really mattered little that the itinerary was inefficient. It was wonderful to be together on the train, watching the glorious landscape roll by. Following our forays into Switzerland, we were to head via Paris to the Mediterranean and Nice.

From Leysin, we headed first to Lucerne. It was cold, the middle of winter, and the lake was frozen. Each morning we walked around different parts of the city, returning for lunch and heading out again in the afternoon after a rest. We often went to movies in the evening and I translated the dialogue if the film was in French. One evening we saw an Edward G. Robinson movie, and Father was so inspired by the acting that he asked to see it again the next night. Sitting in the dark, side by side, we entered the drama and romance of the characters on the screen, a sweet respite from our own story.

From Lucerne we traveled to German-speaking Zurich, where a friend of Father's, an Iranian businessman, met us. He was so handsome that I think I might have fallen in love with him if I were not already in love with Franco, but he paid me no attention at all. He was an honorable man who respected us both.

Every evening we were his guests; during the day he sent us his car and driver so that we could sightsee and visit museums and galleries.

One day he came to have lunch with us. After the meal, Father went for his rest and his friend invited me to see his home. It was a magnificent house, beautifully furnished and obviously the residence of a rich man with great taste and a love of Persian literature. He was about forty years old, more than double my age, very good-looking and, I believe, attracted to me despite his reserve. But after showing me the house and having tea served by the butler in the elegant living room, this principled man took me back to the hotel. Father was already up and dressed and I know he saw us come from the car together. But he never made mention of it. I so admired him for that restraint, quite unusual for the Persian father of a young daughter. I never determined whether it was more that he trusted both me and his friend, or that he felt it was none of his business, or both; but he had so much respect for me and my freedom that it was never spoken of. My mother would have pounced on me with a shower of denunciation as I walked in. But not my father.

It was hard for me to say good-bye to this glamorous, intellectual man, but after a few days he saw us onto the train to Bern where we were to stay for two days. The Iranian Ambassador and the members of the embassy came to see us, inviting us for a dinner at the embassy that night. We both enjoyed the company of Persians and the freedom that speaking our own language afforded us. And the food was delicious.

We next traveled south to the Italian-speaking part of Switzerland, to Lugarno and Locarno, which I knew my father would enjoy. These two cities were beautiful and full of flowers, the people warm and vivacious and filling the restaurants and streets with laughter and music. My father was fascinated by the Italian influence in this part of Switzerland, a marked contrast to the German-speaking part. One afternoon as we took tea outside at a tearoom, Father talked for a long time about the influence of culture on the way people live, making completely different environments out of places only a few miles apart in the same country. I began to look at the places we visited with newly opened eyes. When we moved on to French-speaking Switzerland, I watched for these differences.

In Geneva, a conference had been organized in honor of my father. Father's friend, Mr. Jamalzadeh, the famous Persian novelist was also invited. That evening, Father addressed the mainly young Iranian men and women who were students attending the conference. He spoke of the succession of cultural and military invasions that marked the history of Iran, and reminded the audience that the one thing that stood between colonization and independence was the language and literary heritage of Iran, binding the citizens together through a unique mix of pride and nationality that enables them to resist being dominated from outside. He also gently urged his listeners to return and use their skills and knowledge to serve Iran when they finished their studies abroad, noting that in any other country they would always be foreigners.

Father and Mr. Jamalzadeh enjoyed each other's company for the week we stayed in Geneva. I was delighted to be in the presence of these two great intellects, drinking in their discussions and debates about poetry, politics, civilization, history, and language. It was quite an education!

We traveled on by train from Geneva to Paris. Father's cousin, Dr. Bahar, had booked two rooms for us near the Etoile. It was Father's first time in Paris, and he loved it at first sight. I got a much better impression of the city than on my first miserable acquaintance. We stayed a full month. Every day we explored, enjoying the beauty of the city.

One day Father gave me the telephone number of Professor Masset, an Orientalist at the Sorbonne, who had lived in Iran for many years and specialized in Persian literature and history. I set up a rendezvous at the Champs Elysées metro station and walked to meet this famous scholar. In my mind he was a giant of a man, so I was stunned when a little man approached me and asked in flawless, unaccented Persian if I were Mademoiselle Bahar. After the initial shock of reconciling my image with reality, I led Professor Masset back to the hotel and left the two men to talk. When I returned about six hours later they were still talking, eagerly leaning towards each other in animated discussion. Such meetings and conversations were like a tonic to my father, who was starved for the kind of intellectual stimulation that had been a daily part of his life at home. It was the best medicine he could have had.

I took care of my father throughout our European trip. He had no notion of the costs, as Maman sent money each month to a bank under my name. Once in Paris when we lunched with a friend, he said with a flourish at the end of the meal, "Today we are Parvaneh's guests!" He walked behind me or at my side, indicative of his great respect for women in general and for me in particular that is evidenced in much of his poetry. At every turn he encouraged me to think for myself. He passionately believed that only when a country has an educated female populace can it achieve real progress.

In the month we were in Paris we visited many palaces and museums. We went back often to the Louvre, of which we never seemed to get enough. When we stood on the balcony looking down on Napoleon's tomb at Les Invalides, Father turned to me and said, "Parvaneh, there is only one democracy and that is death. Even Napoleon died."

I convinced my father to travel to Nice by plane as train travel tired him. We arrived during the carnival of flowers. Our hotel was on the Promenade des Anglais, with a wonderful view. The sight of all those beautiful flowers lifted Father's spirits immeasurably. Mr. Shirazi, the Iranian businessman who invited us to Nice, had lived there a long time in his lovely home, which he called "Villa Gholestan," or Flower Garden, in the hills above the town. We were his guests at the hotel throughout our stay. Every day he would come down to the hotel, taking lunch with us and walking and talking with my father.

One night as we dined in the hotel restaurant, a man from another table approached us, asking Father in French, "Are you Malek o'Shoara Bahar?" He was an Egyptian scholar. I was amazed that he had recognized my father. He began to speak in Arabic and, to my great surprise, Father replied in the same language and they started a conversation. I didn't know that Father could speak such good Arabic. It transpired that they had long maintained a correspondence, and the man had recognized my father from a picture.

After a month in beautiful Nice and the generous company of Mr. and Mrs. Shirazi, it was time to return to Switzerland. It was a sad day when the old friends said good-bye for what they must have known was the last time. Back in Leysin, the doctors said that Father's good health was temporary. I saw that the days of his life were slipping away even as the cooler fall days got shorter. One day he told me that he was tired of this expatriate life. He wanted to return to Iran so he could be buried in his own country.

I could see how the long exile, voluntary though it was, had taken a toll on my father. He had spent his whole life trying to effect change through his words and actions and longed to be home. He wrote a long epic poem, *Leysinieh: Beh Yadeh Vatan* (In Leysin: Remembering my Country), while he was in the sanatorium. Sitting on his balcony, he watched as a dense fog poured over the mountains behind Leysin and obliterated the landscape, likening it to the poisonous miasma of corruption and greed that had enveloped Iran. In one small fragment, he says:

I saw majestic forested peaks and ravines all vanquished.
Then the anguish in my heart returned threefold
As I contemplated the glorious past of my country
Overtaken by the fog of folly.
Please, God, take care of the people.
With splendid peaks of history behind them,
They deserve better than this.

In April of 2001, for the fiftieth anniversary of my father's death, I attended a celebration of my father's work at the Sorbonne in Paris, and *Remembering My Country* was read. In 2007, the head of the Department of Persian Literature at the University of Maryland, Dr. Ahmad Karimi-Hakkak, chose this poem to read on a "Voice of America" program to celebrate the 120th anniversary of Father's birth.

I arranged for our departure from Leysin with a heavy heart, not only because of Father's decline but also because I was leaving Franco behind. I was sure that marrying him was my destiny. It was almost impossible to leave Switzerland. I was completely torn between my duty to Father and my family on the one hand, and my desire to live my own life with Franco on the other. Father and I stayed in Geneva for a couple of weeks after we left Leysin, while I made final arrangements for the return to Iran.

The proximity to the love of my life was too strong a pull to resist: Every morning, I would get up around five o'clock and take the train to Lausanne to have breakfast with Franco. Then I would take the train back so that I was ready when

Father appeared at around eight o'clock for his breakfast. I just never told him. It was too complicated. It would have hurt him to see me in pain, and anyway, I was sure he would have preferred me not to marry a European. I thought it could be resolved, however, for Franco's parents liked me very much and it was clear that they and their two other sons approved of me as a future wife.

Franco had seven more years of medical school, so there was no way we could marry at that time. Our plan was for me to go back to Iran, apply to Ecole La Source, a nursing school in Lausanne, and return to Switzerland to get a nursing diploma. The school would pay for my tuition, but I would need enough money to pay for my board and food. Meanwhile, Franco would finish medical school. It seemed a workable plan and sustained us with hope as we separated.

But life is rarely what you expect. Destiny had quite a different plan for me. When one is healthy and young, it seems that everything can be controlled. But this is not how life is. Back in Iran, events overtook me. I struggled to find the money for Father's medication. I could not afford to go back to Lausanne. Franco and I wrote to each other for a while. Eventually I had to accept that there was no hope. I never saw him, or Switzerland, again.

When I first went back to Leysin after my divorce, my father asked me to sit down and tell him all about what had happened between me and Moez. I recall that I insisted he first eat his dinner; only then would I talk. Later, he told me that I must write down these experiences, things that no one has ever written before. This was the secret of his own brilliance: the originality and personal message conveyed in all of his work. It has taken me over half a century to do as he suggested.

Top: My father as a young man in Mashhad, around 1906, and my mother, Soodabeh Qajar.

Below: A faded photgraph showing my family when we were in exile in Isfahan. Maman always insisted on keeping a record of our experiences. Here she has hung a bedcover as a dignified background to our suffering.

Top: The Bahar children in 1932, after we returned from exile in Isfahan. From left, standing: Mamak, Hushang and Mali; seated, Parvaneh and Mehrdad.

Below: My father as Minister of Education in the formal attire worn for royal audiences, 1947. My mother in 1945.

Top: Sitting with father while he took his heliotherapy treatment for tuberculosis on his balcony at Hotel Belvedere. My father towards the end of his life, in his bed, writing.

Below: My marriage to Ali Akbar Khosropur, September 1950. At a party soon after I married Moez. I was sixteen years old.

Leo Rosenthal, NY

Top: With Eugene Black, President of the World Bank 1949–62 (left) and my husband, Dr. Ali Akbar Khosropur, at the United Nations, April 7, 1955.

Below left: Reading part of my father's tribute to Pakistani philosopher-poet, Mohammed Iqbal, at the Iqbal Day commemoration at American University, April 1959.

Below right: With my daughter, Sudi, the day I graduated from American University, June 1961.

Top: Invitations to the Eisenhower and Kennedy White House.

Below: Parvaneh and Iranian Ambassador Zahedi at the Iranian embassy, Washington, D.C., in the mid-1960s.

Top: With King Faisal Ibn Abdul Aziz Al Saud, when he visited Washington, D.C., in 1966. Apparently no one warned me about wearing such a daring dress!

Below: A poster for the International Colloquium at the Sorbonne celebrating the 50th anniversary of my father's death.

The statue of Malek o'Shoara Bahar in Mashhad

FATHER'S LEGACY

IT WAS the spring of 1949 when my father and I returned to Iran. On the morning of our last day in Geneva, I laid out his clothes ready for the trip. I had got into the habit of performing this small service for him, continuing what my mother had always done. I set out his suit, his shirt, one of his beautiful silk ties, his socks and shoes, and a clean handkerchief on the table next to his bed. I lovingly put his glasses and his signature cane within easy reach. He was an elegant man and I enjoyed helping him to maintain his appearance. This particular morning my preparations felt like a sacred rite. At nine o'clock Mr. Jamalzadeh joined us for a final breakfast together and again I had the sense of a religious observance being performed, of a chapter closing. Not just a chapter, but a whole book.

The weather that day was clear and bright and we sat next to a window that opened onto the garden. Father had his usual breakfast—a boiled egg, two pieces of toast, and tea. Mr. Jamalzadeh ordered the same breakfast. After a quick coffee and a piece of bread and butter for myself, I left the two friends to talk as I arranged to have our bags brought to the lobby. At eleven, the three of us left together in a cab.

The springtime parks were bursting with new life as we rode though the city for the last time. I was overtaken by melancholy at the contrast between all this vitality and my father's waning strength, but he was enchanted by the beauty of Geneva. While I knew he was happy to return to Iran, it pained me to think that people would assume his departure from Leysin indicated that he had been cured of his illness. I anticipated a stream of visitors asking Father to do all sorts of things that he would not be able to do. His students were very anxious for his return, too. During his time in Switzerland, his room was often thronged during the weekends with students and intellectuals who had made the pilgrimage to see him.

As we arrived at the airport, my mind swirled in anticipation of what awaited us in Iran. A big crowd of well-wishers met us. All the Iranians who lived in Geneva, plus many students studying in France, gathered at the airport to see us off. A large bouquet of deep red roses was presented to Father. He handed it to me to carry; he was too weak to manage anything more than his cane, really. I sometimes even wore his hat while carrying his coat and briefcase, so the bouquet was quite beyond his strength. Father shook hands with everyone. He reminded the students again and again to please return to Iran after they finished their education, emphasizing that in Europe they would not be able to retain their identity. Finally, Father and Mr. Jamalzadeh embraced affectionately, both aware that this was a final good-bye.

I had purchased tickets on Swiss Air—a first class ticket for Father and a coach class seat for myself right behind the first class section, so that I could watch out for Father during the flight. We went via Istanbul, stopping only for an hour before we took off again for Tehran. When we started our descent early in the morning, I went to help Father prepare for landing. I found him overwhelmed with emotion, tears in his eyes. It was two years since he had seen Iran. As we made our way to the door after landing, I took his hat and coat and briefcase. In those days, visitors could come right to the plane to greet arriving passengers, and a large crowd had gathered on the tarmac. As we emerged onto the stairs, cheers and cries of welcome erupted from the family, friends, colleagues, and students below.

Father went first to our family, hugging each person, then turned to his friends and students. Only Hushang was not there from the family. Two years earlier, he had left for the United States for his university education. Father's sojourn in Switzerland ate up all of our resources. The family was no longer able to support his studies, but he managed to find a job and remain in school. It was only years later, when I visited him in Montana where he had done his B.A., that I learned how very difficult it had been for him. He worked every night until midnight, attending classes and studying all day. But he did well and went on to the University of Michigan to earn his master's degree in sociology and anthropology.

In 1970, I attended Hushang's inauguration as the founding president of Tompkins Cortland Community College—known as TC3—in Groton, New York. He was appointed in the spring of 1968 and, largely as a result of his enormous energy and an almost missionary zeal for the concept of the community college, the school opened on time in September—a mere six months later. Until TC3 moved to its permanent site in Dryden, New York, in 1974, the school was housed in an old typewriter company office building and, for a time, Hushang's office furniture consisted of an orange crate. To his delight, he was once mistaken for the janitor when he was found sweeping the floor; when the visitor asked if he could please show him to the president's office, Hushang led him down the hall and through a curtain that served as a wall, sat on his orange crate and said, "May I help you?" Apart from two years in the early 1980s, when he was invited to Lesotho to assist in developing their education system, Hushang led TC3 until his retirement in 1986.

By the time of the inauguration I was a librarian, so I was all decked out in the Library Science lemon hood over my academic gown. How I wished that the rest of my family could have been present as Hushang, our household god, our handsome and intelligent *Dadash*, accepted this honor. My brother always seemed to me like a hurricane, sweeping in, full of energy, a masterful speaker, and he certainly looked presidential as he formally assumed the leadership of the college. But I also saw a young boy bent over his books in his room, Reba at his feet, persevering through all of our family's trials. I imagined the lonely years away from home, the willpower it took to get to this point when, rather than supporting a brilliant young scholar, our country's determination to crush the Bahar family sent him into permanent exile. I was proud of him.

Mehrdad at that time attended the University of Tehran. Mamak and her husband and son had moved out from the family home into an apartment, as had Mali and her husband and their daughter. Cherry was only eleven years old. The only child who was alone, yet not a real child, was me. I had no husband and was back living at home. But the two years I was privileged to share with my father in Switzerland had made a great impact on me. I grew intellectually and emotionally, and experienced a freedom that most Iranian women never enjoyed.

For the first year back in Tehran, I accompanied Father to every occasion to which he was invited—conferences, lectures, meetings with foreign Orientalists and writers. It was quite an education. Father was well enough to carry on a busy schedule, even teaching several classes at the university, which brought in some much needed income. Sometimes he received his students at home. At the request of the government of Pakistan, he chaired a big conference in Tehran to commemorate the great Pakistani poet Iqbal Lahouri, a friend and long-time correspondent who had just died. Father wrote a beautiful poem in honor of Iqbal, and I sat up front with Pakistan's ambassador to Iran, quite lost in the magic of the recitation.

That first summer was harsh for Father after the cool air of Switzerland. Concerned that the fierce heat of Tehran might be too much for him, one of his friends, Mr. Zahedi, offered the use of his garden on the cool slopes of the Alborz Mountains. Many wealthy people had these summer retreats, planted with flowers and fruit trees for shade and graced with an ornamental pool, and had built second homes where their families gathered during the summer. The lower part of Mr. Zahedi's property was a beautiful garden in which he set up tents for our family. Father stayed for the whole summer, while we came and went.

Walking in the garden one day, my father came across a family group having a picnic. The garden had no walls and they had wandered in and set up their meal beneath some trees. Father approached them, telling them that they had picked a poor spot for their picnic. He offered to lead them to a much nicer one next to a quiet pool. The delighted group followed him to the chosen spot and settled happily down for the day. Later, Father came and asked if they wanted tea and had some sent to them. The family assumed that this humble man was the gardener.

As they were leaving they sought him out and were surprised to find him installed in a beautiful tent. Pressing a few coins into my father's hand, they thanked him for his kindness. Father realized what had happened and refused the coins, telling them that he was not the gardener. They asked him who he was. "Malek o'Shoara Bahar," he replied. They recognized the name at once and were amazed that this unassuming man was the famous poet.

By the second summer, Father was coughing badly and losing strength. Moreover, we were almost at the end of our money again. One day, Father asked me to take a letter to the president of the Central Bank of Iran, asking if they would accept our house and garden as collateral for a loan of 10,000 tuman. I called the bank early the next morning and with great difficulty arranged a meeting two days later. I had tried very hard to make it sooner, but to no avail.

The day of the appointment came, and I walked to the Central Bank. I was a bit early and the secretary asked me to wait until the appointed time, eleven o'clock. After what seemed an age, I was ushered into a large room. The president of the Central Bank rose from his chair, shook my hand coldly, and asked me the purpose of my visit. I handed him the letter, saying that I had come on behalf of my father. After reading the letter, he stood up and angrily told me that he could do nothing for me. I explained that we did not want a handout; that we were willing to put up everything we owned to secure the loan. He reiterated his statement, more coldly and angrily than before.

As I rose to leave, he said good-bye, but I did not even turn my head. I knew if I caught his stony eye, I would start to scream. I raced down the steps and into the street and stumbled towards Maidane Ferdowsi, the square named for the great poet. I was drawn to the statue of Ferdowsi, sitting with such dignity with his book opened before him in the middle of the square. I gazed at it for a long time, thinking how cruelly this magnificent man was treated in his time nearly a thousand years earlier, and how the same treatment had been meted out to my father.

Once when I was at my girls' school and about twelve years old, I had volunteered to give a speech about Ferdowsi in the weekly assembly. I asked Father to tell me all about him. He told me the story of how the ill and struggling poet wrote his magnificent epic, Shah Nameh, and sent it to the king, Shah Ghaznavi. The ignorant king sent him a trifling amount of money in return, not realizing the treasure that he had been given. By the time the shah came to his senses and sent a fitting tribute, his emissary arrived in Khorasan just as the funeral procession for the impoverished and broken-hearted Ferdowsi left the city.

I thought of that story as I gazed at the gentle face of the pride of our nation and thought of Father, how he too had been broken in body by all the small and large cruelties heaped upon him. I felt so much pain, an old pain, the pain of imprisonment, the pain of exile, the pain of seeing my mother's tears as our lives were uprooted again and again. I felt dizzy at the images I had of my father's life's work, so powerful and so unappreciated by the Pahlavi regime, of his terrible wasting disease, the legacy of the state rewarding his talent by condemning him to prison and poverty.

Finally tearing myself away from the statue, I turned towards home, lost in my grief and my disappointment at having failed in my mission, reluctant to bear the bad news to my family. Someone called me from behind. "Parvaneh! Parvaneh!"

Turning, I saw my friend Tazi Namdar. He ran up, anxiously demanding what had happened to make me so sad. I said I had neither the time nor the energy to tell him, but he insisted that we have a coffee. Just nearby was a small café that sold ice cream and coffee, so I agreed to sit awhile and talk. Tazi asked, "Do you want café Turk or café Français?" I was beyond caring. He came back to the table with two cafés Françaises. I told him about the letter and the president's refusal to help our family. Tazi asked me, "Is the president of the Central Bank an enemy of your father, that he wouldn't help?" I told him, "No. He is supposed to be a friend. That is why his refusal to help is so hurtful."

Tazi suggested I ask the National Insurance Company of Iran if we could take out a loan. I had no knowledge of this place, but my friend told me he worked there and would arrange an appointment with the president. I asked him who this president was, and he told me, "Dr. Ali Akbar Khosropur." "Oh! I remember him! I met him last year at a big party at Moghadam's place. He talked to me and recited some of Father's recent poetry. But of course, he won't remember me." Tazi assured me that he wouldn't have forgotten me, but he added, "What does it matter anyway? You are putting your property as collateral. We do it all the time."

As I left the coffee shop, I anxiously asked Tazi to call me if he could make an appointment, and he assured me he would call me back with good news. I walked slowly home, delaying the time when I would have to disappoint my mother with the news of my failed mission. But when I walked into my mother's room she saw right away that I had not succeeded. Urging Maman not to tell Father yet, I explained there was the possibility of a loan from the insurance company.

It was a hot day, and we went to the *zir zamin* in search of cooler air and the possibility of relaxation and perhaps even sleep. But it was no use. After a tense couple of hours, I heard the telephone ring and ran straight out onto the searing stones of the courtyard, not taking time to put on my slippers. I grabbed the receiver, urgently saying, "Hello? Hello?" until I heard Tazi's voice. He told me that he had made the appointment for eleven o'clock the next day and that I should come a few minutes early so that he could escort me personally.

When I returned to the *zir zamin*, Maman was sitting waiting. "Who was calling at this hour?" she asked. I told her about the appointment and a tiny smiled flicked at the corners of her mouth, so often sad these days.

That night I couldn't sleep at all. The next morning I set off for the city. In my anxiety, I was far too early and there was so much time to kill that even gazing in every window of every shop until I had memorized its contents was insufficient to fill the time. When I ran out of shops I went back and started again, revisiting the windows, crisscrossing the street, the sun blazing down on me. Finally, mercifully, it was ten thirty and I found myself climbing the stairs to the insurance company.

It was a big building with an impressive reception area. A man with two telephones on his desk looked me up and down suspiciously. "Yes?" he said slowly. "What can I do for you?" I told him that I had an appointment with Mr. Namdah. But he needed to check with his office. Soon Tazi appeared. "Why are you here so early?" he asked. "I couldn't sleep. I had nowhere to go. So I came here." I didn't tell him about all the time I had spent in the street.

Tazi invited me wait in his office until the appointed time. He asked me why I was so nervous, and I told him that I had no hope. If this man also threw me out of his office, I had nowhere else to turn.

After an eternity of waiting, we went to a very large office on the fourth floor. Chairs lined the room and a solemn secretary sat at a desk. Tazi introduced me, and the secretary rose from his chair and went to the door to announce my arrival. A voice from within invited me in, and Tazi and I entered a large and elegantly decorated room. A few armchairs rested on beautiful Persian carpets, beyond which the smiling man I remembered from the party sat behind an imposing desk on which several telephones clustered importantly.

As Tazi began his introductions, Mr. Khosropur said, "No, no! She needs no introduction." Turning to me, he graciously invited me to be seated and told Tazi he could go. Mr. Khosropur asked me what I needed and I told him about Father's medical needs and expenses and our desire to borrow 10,000 tuman, using the house as collateral. Picking up one of his phones, he told his secretary to call Mr. Namdah to come back to the office. My heart sank. I thought perhaps he was about to throw me out. But no, he told Tazi to go that very day with an engineer and an appraiser to measure and value our property and report back to him the following day.

Turning to me, he said with a smile, "Your check will be ready by the end of the week." I rose with shaking knees and told him I didn't know how to thank him. He brushed this aside, saying the company would do the same for anyone else. "But in this case," he added, "there is the bonus that I will get the chance to meet the great man, Bahar." Barely taking the time for civilities, I raced away from the building and took a taxi straight to the garden in Shemran, where I knew Father would be.

Almost before the taxi had stopped, I leapt out and ran to the tent where Father was resting while Cherry read him news of the Korean War. "Father! I was able to borrow the money from the insurance company!" My mother hugged and kissed me, delighted and relieved by the good news. I told them that I had to go back to the house to be there for the appraisal, but that I just couldn't wait to tell them that we had been saved.

Two weeks after he had arranged the loan, Mr. Ali Akbar Khosropur called me and asked for an appointment to see my father. He arrived with a big bouquet of flowers for Father and they sat and talked for about an hour. A few days later, he invited me for dinner at the home of one of his friends.

Every day after that dinner, a big bouquet of flowers was delivered to our house by his chauffeur. The house soon became a veritable *gholestan*—a flower garden. Since we didn't usually have cut flowers in the house, we soon ran out of vases and containers, and still more flowers arrived. Every room was filled with flowers, even the kitchen. Khosropur had heard that I especially loved the heavenly-scented *maryam*, or tuberose, and this was a feature of all the bouquets.

Perhaps because of the dry air, perhaps because they are bred more for their taste and scent than for looks, fruit and flowers smell much stronger in Tehran than in many other places. Persians love fruit and typically place a large selection of seasonal fruit and small cucumbers on the table in their sitting rooms: the distinctive aromas of strawberries, melons, apples, quinces, and other fruits greet you well before you see them. Flowers likewise fill the air with their fragrance, almost shouting, "We are roses! We are lilies!" The pots of hyacinths that most households have on their tables in spring almost make one swoon. I remember too the enticing smell of rice steaming, especially the fragrant varieties that come from the Caspian area. I have rarely experienced these sensory delights in Washington. The flowers and fruits, while usually plump and magnificent and available year round, have very little aroma and don't speak of the sun and soil the way their often smaller, but more intense, Iranian cousins do. Iranians look forward to the seasons for particular fruit that are picked at their peak. To sit down to a plate of Persian melon in the summer is to taste heaven.

After the very difficult life I had been experiencing, all this cherishing by a suitor was like a gift from heaven. Father was deteriorating by the day and could barely walk in the garden in Shemran, but my mother kept him abreast of the situation and I often took some of the flowers up to his tent when I visited.

One day my father told me that he had heard of the daily shower of flowers and invitations to attend parties. He said that Khosropur seemed a kind and gentle man, but that he was much older than I was. "Very soon, he will ask to marry you. Have you thought about his age? He is more than twice as old as you. Don't forget he has been a bachelor for forty-five years." I told him it was something that had never been discussed. Father said he didn't know the man, so it was up to me to decide, should he ask me to marry him.

The parties and dinners continued throughout the summer until one day, Khosropur did ask me to marry him. I accepted right away. From a contemporary perspective, it may seem a questionable decision. But at the time, this marriage was a godsend. My father was dying, the family was in debt, and I was exhausted. The previous three years had been a huge struggle, and I longed for someone to take over a portion of my burden. Here was a good man whom I loved, who could offer me security, who lavished attention upon me during the courtship, and who saw it as an honor to be part of my family.

The wedding celebration was held in our garden in September of 1950. It was quite a contrast to my first wedding. For one thing, I was eager to get married, and I knew Khosropur because we had been going out together for several months. While it was the same ceremony, I was now twenty-one, with a taste for independence and knowledge of the world, a very different person from the little red-lipped doll who had been so passive and confused at her first wedding. I wore a stunning creation in guipure lace decorated with satin roses that swept down the skirt to the hem. I had invited a number of my French, Russian, and Swiss friends, and wanted the ceremony to be as authentic as possible so that they could experience our old traditions.

Khosropur spared no expense. The garden was decorated with thousands of little lights and an elaborate dinner was served. A live band played all evening and there was dancing and much laughter. I was very happy. The only thing to mar my pure delight was that Father was too ill to attend, and remained in his room.

We drove to a luxurious hotel on the Caspian Sea for our honeymoon. It was a wonderful week of swimming and dancing and romance. Since the Revolution, these sorts of vacations are a thing of the past. The beaches are segregated and women must cover themselves even while swimming. But in 1950 it was very different and I wore attractive little swimsuits and pretty dresses. My life had changed utterly and I rejoiced in my release from responsibility and financial insecurity and loneliness. I anticipated a happy life of love and sharing with my Prince Charming, who was wealthy, successful, and generous. Khosropur, who became vice-president of the Central Bank soon after our marriage, was delighted when I soon became pregnant.

I visited Father every day, sometimes helping him into the car in his pajamas for a drive to the Shemran hills for a change of scenery. One day, I encountered a crowd of young people who had come from all over Iran to ask Father to be the head of Anjomaneh Solh, the peace movement in Iran. It was part of a big peace movement that was springing up all around the world after the horrors of World War II. Father loved freedom and hated war and dictatorship, so he

accepted. He wrote his last great epic poem, *Jokhd Jang* (The Owl of War), to
commemorate the peace movement, finishing it within a week despite his illness.
A big gathering was organized and, with enormous difficulty, Father attended.
Leaning on the podium for support, his body weak but his voice ringing out
passionately, he read his anti-war epic to the crowd. This is just an excerpt:

> I curse you, shrieking owl of war!
> May your voice be stifled for eternity.
> May your wings be severed and your legs crushed.
> You snatched away my friends and family,
> May you forever be denied friends and admirers.
> There is nothing more savage and painful than war
> And no one can escape its cruel clutches.
> Its wine is the blood of the working class,
> And their bones are the food on its table.
> The language of the owl is death and destruction
> From which no one escapes unharmed.
> The world has become a ceaseless mill,
> Grinding out guns and bombs,
> Powered by rivers of blood from the innocent.
> The owl of war is a furious dragon,
> Slithering through the world,
> Hunting simple, ordinary people,
> Plucking the hearts from all he meets.

+   +   +

> I don't want him!
> No matter what gains a war might bring,
> I want nothing from that owl.
> I will hurl his bounty back in his face.
> I reject his friendship and his arrogance—
> Through both he plots to take innocent life.

+   +   +

Where are the days of peace and security?
Where is the blooming garden of truth and humanity,
Where the light of love glows like a beacon?
Where is the age of friendship and equality?
When I speak in praise of peace
My whole existence bursts into flower.

I wept with pride and sorrow as I watched this great performance. Father's passion and conviction remained undaunted, his poetic gifts were never more powerful, his sense of urgency as he called for freedom and peace filled the audience with strength even as his own body failed him. It was his last great act. The feverish week of writing and then the performance sapped the last of his resources.

One afternoon when my husband and I went to visit Father we found him lying on the floor unconscious. Khosropur immediately drove to get help, not wanting to wait for an ambulance. He came back with a couple of doctors equipped with an oxygen tank and Father was revived. I had been sitting on the floor next to him, holding his head in my lap. As soon as he opened his eyes he asked, "Why? Why did you want to bring me back? Please, don't do that again." It was plain that my father did not want to suffer any longer, that he wanted to die.

Over the next two weeks Father declined markedly. Then one day Nani called me, urging me to come at once. I called Khosropur and he quickly came from the office to drive me to my parents' home. I jumped out as the car stopped in front of the courtyard, where a large group of people had gathered. I talked to no one, running to Father's study. I experienced the same anxiety and fear I had felt sixteen years before when I ran to the study that morning the police dragged him away to prison. I was five years old again.

I was thinking, "He will be there. He'll be so happy to see me." My heart hammered as I entered the room. Maman stepped out of the study, her eyes awash with tears. I said, "Maman?" She took me in her arms and we both wept. Again I said, "Maman? Father?"

"Yes," she said. "Your father is gone."

"I must see him," I sobbed, but Maman held me tight, saying, "You are pregnant. It will upset you too much. They will be taking his remains away soon."

"Remains?" I asked. "That is all that is left? All that knowledge and education and passion? It has all gone? How can that be?"

Apart from my grandmother who had died when I was very young, this was the first death I had really experienced. I was only twenty-one, and seven months pregnant. I tried to comfort myself with the knowledge that they hadn't taken him to jail this time. But he was really gone. Forever. I walked outside. I passed through the courtyard. I did not acknowledge the growing crowd of people there. I got into the car. The driver looked at me questioningly. "My father has died," I told him. I could speak no more. He drove me home.

The Pakistani ambassador later told me that on the day Father died, he visited him with a request that he again chair the conference to commemorate the poet Iqbal Lahouri. Father told him that he was not well enough and moreover was unable to write. The ambassador picked up pen and paper and said, "Why don't you send a message?" My father smiled and said, "This time, I will take the message to him myself." He rose to see the ambassador out, shaking his hand. It was April 25, 1951. My father died later that day.

Father's body was taken to the great Sepahsalar Mosque near the Majles in the center of old Tehran. The next day at four o'clock, despite the government's declaration discouraging people from attending the funeral, the mosque and the streets filled with mourners. The bazaar closed in his honor and students did not attend classes. Father's own students carried his body from the mosque on their shoulders. They were supposed to take him from the mosque to the Majles where he was to be put in a hearse. Unwilling to let go so soon, the students carried his body for mile after mile towards the Zahir Doleh cemetery, named for the Sufi master Zahir Doleh, in the foothills of the Alborz mountains. This cemetery, cared for by Sufis and reserved for poets, writers, and artists, has become a national heritage site. Finally the students were forced by the police to relinquish his body, and the hearse transported him to his final resting place. The enormous crowd followed his body to the cemetery.

I looked at my father as he was put into the grave. He was so small, shrunken from his illness. What had made him great, the huge spirit that had made him seem larger than life, had departed, leaving this empty little husk behind. I thought of my strong young body, the temporary resting place for the baby that my father would never see, and realized that Bahar's physical being had been but a resting places for his great poetic soul. I hoped—I knew—that his words would still inspire people hundreds of years into the future, just as those of Ferdowsi and Hafez are still powerful centuries after they were written. His body had been washed at the morgue by *mordehshur*, professionals who wash the dead in the traditional way of Shia Islam.

My brothers and some of the students took his body, now wrapped in a plain white cloth, to the burial place prepared for him. In Islam, the body is returned to the earth just as it came into the world. There is no coffin, just a simple grave dug into the earth; the body lies on its right side and the head faces Mecca. After the grave was filled in, a flat stone inscribed with his name was placed over the top. It is a humble and yet very dignified departure from this earth, devoid of pomp and ceremony and the same for everyone, no matter what their station in life.

Later, an impressive memorial was built over his grave. Although the cemetery has been closed for many decades, people get permission to visit their beloved writers and artists, especially at anniversaries. At each anniversary of my father's death, many students visit his grave, taking flowers, singing his songs, and celebrating his life and work.

As I watched these last rites, I knew that my father was indeed gone. At that moment, I felt I had lost everything. From my earliest memory of him, it seemed his life had been a struggle—a struggle for freedom and people's rights, a struggle for democracy, a struggle to be heard, to stay out of jail, to protect his family and provide for us all. And then his last struggle with tuberculosis. He never complained; he just went on living his life. And now he was gone. He had, especially over the last years of our being so much together, become my closest friend.

It was ironic that he died on the anniversary of his friend and fellow poet Iqbal. Perhaps Father was right. This time he would carry the message himself.

My mother's financial situation was now perilous. Although Father had created the College of Literature at Tehran University and had written all of the textbooks for the courses—many of them are still being used today—he was never given a permanent position and so received no pension. His salary was stopped on his death, which meant that no money was coming into the household. Maman had already sold off almost everything she could sell. She was reluctant to follow my brother-in-law's suggestion that she petition the government for a pension, but she eventually had to request it. The Senate passed a dedicated bill that authorized a tiny pension for her. Even for that small amount, there were senators who disagreed with the bill. The allowance was 500 tuman a month, a pittance that she was ashamed to collect. This was the reward for all of my father's contributions to the country in literature, politics, and education: that his widow should exist in penury and be grateful for it.

My mother sold off another part of the garden to raise money to renovate the house, which she rented to a French family. She and Cherry, now fourteen, rented a small house in the center of Tehran. It was so hard for Maman to finally give up her home. The home in which she had raised her children. The home filled with happiness and hardship, where she had lived for so many years at the side of my father. Our Paradise.

Why could not the government have bought the house, to preserve it and the gardens as a museum for the following generations and make his library a public library? I can never forgive the Pahlavi regime. They allowed this treasure to be destroyed because they were afraid of the power of Father's words, a treasure that belonged to all Iranians, present and future.

I never knew why my new husband did not offer to help my family. The generosity he showered on me during the courtship and the lavishness of our wedding did not seem to follow through into our married life. Certainly he was pleased to see me well-dressed and our home well-appointed, as befitted his status. But I quickly learned that I would not enjoy the financial responsibility that I experienced in my own family. Perhaps I was too distracted by my father's death and the new responsibilities of wife and mother to really pay attention. Or perhaps I was already becoming intimidated by my husband and reluctant to ask for help for my mother and Cherry. Or could it have been that, once my famous father was gone, the glow of association with the Bahar family began to dim?

My son Babak was born two months after my father's death. Father had chosen this name should the baby be a boy, and Taraneh if I had a daughter. My sister Mali, who was pregnant too, had a daughter and called her Taraneh.

I decided after Babak's birth that I had to collect all of the work of Malek o'Shoara Bahar and have it published. Somehow it seemed the only thing to do. Father had tried to publish a collection of his poetry during his lifetime, but Mohammad Reza Shah seized the books from the publishing house before they could reach the public. Gathering his work for publication was a task of value that I could undertake, a much greater tribute to my father than sitting around mourning.

It was a huge undertaking in which I was helped greatly by the poet Mohamad Ghahraman, a cousin of my sister's husband. This generous and dedicated man, with no expectation of compensation but a powerful desire to preserve Bahar's writings, worked side by side with me for a year and a half. One of his invaluable suggestions, as we were setting out, was that we go through every book and manuscript in the library and look for any poems that Father might have written on the backs or in the margins of his books, or on pieces of paper interleaved among the pages and forgotten. We found numerous pieces of his work that way. Persians love to write in the margins of their books, and Father was no exception. Of course, much of his handwritten poetry and writings were collected in his many notebooks, but not everything was thus preserved.

Mr. Ghahraman's second excellent suggestion was that we look at all the newspapers and periodicals that we could lay hands on for published work. For this we needed the permission of the Majles to use the parliamentary library—which we obtained. We also scoured the public library. In those pre-computer—indeed, even pre-microfiche—days this meant going through every publication, page by page.

A third really good suggestion was that we advertise in all the major newspapers in Iran, requesting that anyone for whom my father had personally written poems, something he often did, send us a copy for the collection.

Once we had completed our research, I asked Maman to give me the manuscripts that she had. With all the available poems together, we hired a typist to transcribe the work. Every day, from one in the afternoon to seven in the evening, the three of us worked on the collection, typing, editing, correcting, and retyping.

After about a year of this, the collection finally was ready to go to the printers. My father's brother agreed to supervise the first publication of the collected works of Bahar. But it was not the complete works that came out. The Pahlavi regime censored the poems that dealt with the injustices of their rule.

It is interesting to note that after the Islamic revolution, the mullahs also censored Bahar's collection. They reinstated those poems that criticized the Pahlavis, but they removed those in praise of the freedom of women or critical of religious fundamentalism and the clergy.

There are several editions of the collected works of Bahar, each one revealing the view of the moment about which of my father's ideas and words were too dangerous to be made public. I have copies of each edition, and it would make an interesting political and sociological study to compare them.

How sad it is that in a country where the people love and revere poetry, where poetry has been the medium for the expression of the highest aspirations and the transmission of the stories of greatness of a culture with over two and a half thousand years of continuous identity, successive governments have sought to control, edit, and expunge the words of poets. A country where poets are allowed to starve, where poets are thrown into jail and their families are persecuted, is a country with a government that fears the truth that poets write.

GOING TO AMERICA

O VER THE first two years of marriage, the full import of my father's warning about my husband's age and long bachelorhood gradually became apparent. Far from doting on me, he seemed less and less involved in my daily life. Almost from the beginning, I noticed small, confusing signs. For instance, he never kissed me when he returned home, very unusual in the Persian culture. When I raised the issue, he answered, "I only start to do those things that I wish to continue, so I won't kiss you."

We had a busy social life, but he began to spend more time playing poker with his male friends, who were much older than I was. When I accompanied him to these card evenings, nobody seemed to notice me and I often fell asleep on a sofa until Khosropur awoke me to go home at around two in the morning. It was as though he were able to separate himself completely from me, mentally placing me on a shelf and then taking me out and dusting me off when it suited him to have a "wife."

If it weren't for my family, I would have been quite miserable. Having survived one very untraditional marriage, I now found myself in a very traditional one in which the balance of power was shifting rapidly away from equality. I was used to the model of a strong partnership between my parents. Moreover, I had exercised considerable responsibility in my family. It was hard to be relegated to the role of ornament.

After an otherwise uneventful pregnancy, I unexpectedly went into early and long labor—over twenty-four hours—before a caesarian section was performed.

Babak was premature, tiny, and had to be kept in an incubator for several weeks. Khosropur was delighted to have a son to carry on his name, but the baby soon joined me in the "family" compartment of his father's life.

I had reason to believe that he was not faithful to me, and I felt even more isolated from him. Despite his admiration for my father, he showed little interest in the work I was doing to preserve Bahar's legacy. We hired a Russian nanny, an older woman who was capable and kind, and I resumed my social duties, accompanying my husband to parties at court, at embassies, and in government circles. One of the highlights was attending the wedding of Mohammad Reza Shah and Princess Soraya at the Gholestan Palace, a lavish affair attended by heads of state and celebrities from all over the world. I can still see the gown I wore, black lace over yellow satin with a swoop of yellow satin roses down the skirt.

In the middle of 1953 a rumor was circulating in Tehran that Khosropur was to be made head of the Agricultural Bank. Nine years earlier, in July of 1944, the Bretton Woods Conference had established the International Monetary Fund and the International Bank for Reconstruction and Development (commonly known as the World Bank). These institutions began operations in 1946. In the summer before the 1953 annual meetings of the World Bank and IMF in Washington, D.C., the government of Iran was asked to send a new representative to Washington to replace the outgoing Executive Director for the Middle East and North Africa. A young economist was chosen, with the Shah's approval, and his name forwarded to the Bank so that travel arrangements could be made. He was to travel via London to pick up his wife, who was there for medical treatment. In those days the trip from Tehran to Washington took three days; the first stop was Hamburg, Germany, where the traveler would spend the night. As the man went back to the airport to join the flight to London, his taxi was involved in an accident and he was killed.

That same day, my husband was called to the Palace to be introduced by the prime minister to Mohammad Reza Shah as the new head of the Agricultural Bank. While they were waiting for their audience, the Shah received the news that his representative to the IMF and the World Bank had died. When the prime minister and my husband were ushered in, the Shah told them that he wanted Khosropur to leave immediately for Washington as the new representative. At that time, the Executive Director for the Middle East and North Africa represented fourteen countries, including Iran, Iraq, Pakistan, Saudi Arabia, Sudan, Algeria, Morocco, and seven others.

My husband called me from the Central Bank and told me that we had to be in the United States by the end of November. I was stunned, but as I thought more about it, it seemed like a huge adventure and I became excited. The United States was so far away in those days. I asked Khosropur how long we would be gone; he told me two years, the period for which the representative was appointed.

I called Maman to tell her the news, adding that I would bring all my things to her house while we were away since it was for just a short time. My mother-in-law and Mehri, her young orphaned niece, were living with us. Rather than interrupt Mehri's studies—she was about to start high school—we decided to get a small house for them while we were gone. Within the week, we were packed and ready to go, spending our last two nights at my mother's house.

On November 21, 1953, all our friends and family gathered in the afternoon at Maman's house to say good-bye. Everyone was there except my two brothers; Hushang was still studying in the United States and Mehrdad was in jail, among the thousands arrested for participating in the opposition movement. The Shah had only recently returned to Iran after the joint U.S. and British sponsored coup removed Prime Minister Mossadeq and with him, any hope for a democratic Iran. I was very sad that I could not say good-bye to Mehrdad, and it was several years before I saw him again. He was by then exiled to London and in despair; he wanted to finish his studies at the University of London but had exhausted the meager supply of money that the family had scraped together for him. When he wrote to me, asking if I could help him, I asked my mother to send him my savings, put aside from the housekeeping Khosropur gave me to run our household and invested cleverly by my mother. It was only a few thousand dollars, but it saw him through to graduation.

The story of Mehrdad's exile is an odd one. Just before I left for Washington, I went to a dentist in Tehran for a dental problem that I did not want to ignore until I was in the United States, mainly because I spoke no English. In the waiting room I ran into Asdollah Alam, who was at that time *Vazire Darbar* (Minister of the Royal Court.) Our fathers had been very close friends and he used to visit our family with his father. He was older than I was, but I had known him for most of my life. I immediately told him how desperate and anxious my mother and I were about Mehrdad, that he was in jail and we didn't even know which jail he was in. There was a telephone on the wall of the dentist's office and I asked him to call my mother to reassure her. I even dialed the number and handed him the receiver. He spoke to Maman for quite a while and promised her that he would find Mehrdad and take care of everything.

Many years later, this wonderful man came to Washington for a visit and I was able to thank him for Mehrdad's freedom. It was only then that I learned that Mehrdad had actually been slated for execution. Our friend, who was close to the Shah, had asked as a personal favor that Mehrdad be spared and the Shah had relented, but ordered that he be exiled outside of Iran.

The same big group came out to the airport with us to say a final good-bye. At seven that evening we took our first class seats aboard a Scandinavian Airlines plane. I strained to catch a last glimpse of my family and friends as the plane moved away and we took off for Hamburg, a ten-hour flight. To our surprise, a driver met us there in a limousine sent by the World Bank. It seemed this time they didn't want to take any chances with their new executive director.

We spent our first day and night in a lovely old hotel in central Hamburg. Windows opened onto a pretty park. It was the beginning of winter but very beautiful. Khosropur went out to see something of the city, while little Babak and I stayed in the room and slept. I was exhausted by the rushed preparations for our departure and by the trip itself. I had received no help at all from my husband, who had looked scandalized when I begged him to look after his son for an hour on the flight from Iran so that I could take a nap. The limousine took us back to the airport after an early breakfast and we flew to Edinburgh in Scotland, changing planes after a couple of hours in the airport to fly on to New York.

The first class section on the trans-Atlantic flight was divided into two areas: one for socializing and one for travel and sleeping. Beds, each screened by a curtain, were stored in the ceiling above the seats and lowered by the cabin staff on request. Babak and I slept in one bed, Khosropur in another. In the morning, we went to the dining section for breakfast. When we returned, the beds had disappeared. It was a thrill to hear the captain announce around noon that we were approaching

New York. Our plane circled over the city and, despite everything I had heard and seen about New York, I was totally unprepared for its size and grandeur.

Once more a limousine awaited us as we left Customs and Immigration. The driver took us to an enormous hotel near Penn Station and gave us train tickets for the next day to Washington, D.C. It was November 23, 1953; I have never forgotten the day I arrived in the United States.

It was close to evening when we left the hotel in New York to have dinner. In the street I had the sensation that I was in Europe but a huge Europe, one that had somehow been enlarged. Everything was enormous, and seemed a little odd. I was acutely aware of being in a foreign country in which I didn't know how things worked and, unlike my husband, I lacked the language to communicate.

When we went into a restaurant, the waiter immediately produced a high chair for Babak. As soon as we were seated, we were each brought a big glass of iced water—on a very cold winter evening. We were surprised to learn that in America, no matter what the season, this is the first thing that happens in a restaurant. The meal that arrived also seemed huge and unfamiliar.

We took a short walk after dinner, and even the fruit in the street-vendors' stands seemed outsized. When we looked up, we could barely see the sky beyond the skyscrapers. I was a bit intimidated by it all and felt I could not live in a city where I couldn't see the sky. Tehran was, at that time, a low city, an old city with human proportions. Here I felt like an ant—a mute and foreign one at that.

The train we took the next day was another source of wonders. I was amazed at the beautiful big blue swivel seats, the cleanliness of it all, the immaculate waiters—all black—in our first class carriage. The train pulled into Washington's Union Station at ten in the evening. It was not as cold as New York but a light drizzle was falling. After the hugeness of New York, Washington looked comfortably proportioned, with lovely buildings and an abundance of trees. We were booked into a suite at the Statler, a quality hotel with many shops and several restaurants close to the World Bank.

The next morning, when Khosropur left for work, I found myself on my own with an active little boy and no English. If we stayed in the room I felt suffocated. If we left the room I had to chase Babak through the halls and into the restaurants and shops. This situation lasted a whole month, with Khosropur leaving quite

early in the morning and not returning until six or seven in the evening. I spoke
to no one other than my husband and son.

There were many days when I felt quite sorry that I had come to the United
States. My only joy was in the letters that came from Iran. In what seemed like
an endlessly repetitive cycle, morning became noon and noon became evening and
then it was the next day again. On a couple of occasions we hired a baby-sitter
and went to a movie, but even that was not particularly enjoyable because I did
not understand the dialogue. It was a lonely time with neither friends nor family
to talk to, nor any source of escape from the routine. Khosropur seemed totally
indifferent to the difficulty of my situation. It was as though, when he shut the
door as he left for work, Babak and I ceased to exist until he brought us back to
life by coming home again.

Eventually the Bank helped us to find an apartment in northwest Washington.
Khosropur bought a car and we chose some furniture—at least, Khosropur did
because I was too busy running through the store after Babak. Having the car
gave us the freedom to see the city. We would study the map to find different
places to visit on the weekend.

When spring came, my spirits lifted with Washington's transformation by
the annual explosion of cherry blossoms, apple blossoms, azaleas, dogwoods,
tulips—so much beauty was almost painful to me. I wrote to my mother that if
she ever visited us in spring she would have no need to go to heaven.

My father always delighted in the coming of spring and walked about the
garden, seeking the first signs that it would soon be emerging from winter's deathly
grip. He wrote about this in "The Splendor of Nature," a poem written in 1929 in
answer to another poet, Seyed Ahmad Pishavari, who had expressed very negative
thoughts about the world, concluding bitterly: "in this beautiful garden, there is
not one flower without a thorn." My father, by contrast, gloried in the beauty of
Nature, and his response to his fellow poet exhorts him to open his eyes and
really look at the gift of creation.

If God created the world in his own image,
How can you constantly complain about it?

It is magnificent, glorious, sublime,

Worthy of worship like a pagan idol!

Before we were told there was but one God

People rightly worshipped the earth as divine.

Look! This beautiful, celestial umbrella of a sky!

Underneath, everything is glittering light.

Not even one small shred of darkness.

The colors keep changing—

Sometimes you think it is dark

But it is just less light, an intense turquoise.

Look at that small hill;

A small cloud kisses its crown but the rest is bright.

Look at the top of that mountain!

Still wearing a mantle of flashing snow.

It is spring; go outside,

Celebrate the magnificent dance of nature.

Oh! You are bored with the seasons?

Come, just look at the universe!

No architect could ever create such beauty.

Sit down on the lush green grass.

Open your eyes! Rejoice! Rejoice!

If you cannot respond to this glory,

You cannot see the divine in Nature.

Open your eyes and see these tiny rosebuds.

Don't see the thorn, see the million flowers.

Marvel at this beautiful spring!

The warbling water so clear it looks like tears.

Just look at that little bird

Chattering and singing its heart out.

It never complains; it is filled with joy.

Each element in harmony to sing the beauty of this world

Look at that sun! See how high it rides in the sky.

You think that is just happenstance?

Everything fits together to celebrate creation.

Look at this beautiful flower in spring!

So joyous, purer than any friend you could have.

Smell the gorgeous fruits ripening in the tree.

With the warmer spring weather, I took Babak to a nearby park each afternoon to play with other children and, I hoped, to learn a little English. I tried to talk to the other young mothers, but they were impatient with my tortured efforts to communicate. I found more sympathetic companions among the elderly, retired, or widowed women who also frequented the park. It was pleasant there amidst the trees and flowers, glorious and luxuriant compared to Tehran's dusty dryness. Sitting under the blossom-laden cherry trees reminded me of our garden and the tree under which Reba was buried.

I missed my mother, sisters, and brothers terribly and daydreamed about a hole in the immense wall between Iran and Washington through which I could easily pass to visit my family. As I watched my little boy running and laughing around me, I let the memories of Paradise float gently into my mind like soft pink petals. I began to think that I just might enjoy my two years in the United States, if only I could learn the language, make some friends, and find out what the city had to offer. As it turned out, more than half a century has passed and the Washington area is still my home.

MY EDUCATION IN AMERICA

Now comfortably settled into an apartment, I was keen to employ a housekeeper to help with cooking and housework and the care of little Babak. It did not occur to me that this might be seen by many as a luxury. In Iran, even families like mine without much to spare had household help; indeed, the social structure depended on it.

One day Khosropur called from his office to say that one of the other executive directors no longer needed his Jamaican housekeeper, employed on a special visa for foreign domestic workers arranged by the World Bank. I asked Khosropur to arrange an appointment with her and begged him to be at home when she came so that I could communicate with her.

The next Monday morning, the doorbell rang at eight and I opened the door to a tall black woman, a little chubby in her long black coat. She had a jaunty red hat and bag, and said a cheerful "Good morning! I am Blanche," in a lovely, lilting voice. When I motioned her to come in, a smile lit up her face. Khosropur was still shaving, but soon appeared and negotiated Blanche's working conditions—$50 a week, five days a week from nine to five, with two weeks' paid vacation. Fishing her passport from her big red bag, Blanche handed it to Khosropur to have it stamped by the World Bank for her visa.

She took off her hat and coat and hung them in the hall closet. Pulling an apron from her bag, she approached me with hand outstretched, saying, "I am going to call you Mrs. K." Khosropur left for work. Neither Babak nor I could communicate with this new member of our household, and Babak hid behind me, peering shyly around my skirts. Blanche immediately laughed and said, "Pretty boy!" Babak parroted her words coyly and, grasping her hand, took Blanche to his room to show her his toys. I was relieved. I saw that they would like each other.

Blanche arrived promptly each morning to clean and wash and iron and play with Babak. Sometimes she cooked a meal for us or took Babak out for a walk in his stroller. If we needed a baby-sitter, she was happy to earn a little extra. It suited us all very well. After a week of this new routine I began to think that I might just be able to learn English now. I longed to be less dependent on my husband, and learning English was clearly the necessary first step.

In fact, Blanche was my first English teacher. She would point out everything around the house and tell me the name in English, repeating it until I understood and could say it too. One indispensable tool in our growing communication was the Persian-English dictionary. Sometimes when Blanche had finished her work she would take a book out of her bag and sit in an armchair and read. It puzzled me. I wondered, who is this woman? An educated woman who was poor in her country and needed to come to the United States to send money back to her family? There was a nobility and grace about Blanche—what was her story? But I couldn't communicate such complicated thoughts.

At least two or three times a week we were invited to parties by people at the World Bank or the International Monetary Fund, or at the embassies of the various countries that my husband represented. If I found someone with whom I could converse in French, I enjoyed these functions. Otherwise I felt quite isolated, a situation painful to me as I love to talk to people and learn things about other cultures. Other than these parties, I had no social contact and felt very lonely.

A month passed and though Babak and Blanche really liked each other and I knew I could leave them together, I still had no idea how to start on my project to learn English. Luckily for me, Mr. Namazi, a wealthy businessman involved in trade between Iran and China, invited us to dinner at his Bethesda, Maryland, home one evening. He had gathered all the Iranians in the Washington area— some embassy people, doctors, and businessmen, not a large number, perhaps twenty in all. It was wonderful to be able to speak Persian and interact with a whole roomful of people.

That night I met Mr. Ansari, a doctoral student at American University and also a diplomat at the Iranian embassy. I told him how dreadful it was to know no English, how lonely and frightening to be unable to exchange even a few words with others. He knew of a wonderful teacher, a colleague of his at the university, and promised to ask her if she would accept a private student.

I told him that I would be eternally grateful and gave him some examples of how handicapped I felt. One day, I said, I had a headache. I went to the drugstore to buy some aspirin. I told the pharmacist I wanted "as-pereen," but he shook his head. Next I tried the French pronunciation, "os-pe'rine," but again he looked puzzled. Finally I beat the side of my head and frowned and made a sad face—now he understood! I had a headache. I said, "The only word I know is okay, and now everyone at the World Bank calls me Okay!"

Mr. Ansari laughed but he was sympathetic. I asked him why Americans didn't speak any language other than English, whereas in Europe almost anywhere you went, people could speak French in addition to their own language. He suggested that Americans were made lazy by the fact that everyone else was willing to learn English.

Another story I shared with Mr. Ansari was about the time I wanted to buy a stroller for Babak when he got too big to be held all the time. Khosropur had told me to take a taxi to the Hecht Company, which was then on 7th Street NW in Washington's still vibrant downtown shopping area. He even wrote the name down. I took a taxi and showed the driver the piece of paper. But having successfully got myself to the store, I could not find a single stroller anywhere. I approached every sales clerk I could find, but no one could understand me. Finally, exhausted, I found a sales clerk who spoke a little French and she took me to the fifth floor where there were ranks of strollers, more than I could ever have imagined under one roof.

Mr. Ansari asked if I had any Iranian friends in Washington. No, I said, I didn't know anyone. At that moment his wife, a beautiful young woman with black hair and a smile on her lovely red lips, joined us. I was so happy to meet her and told her so. I said that I felt I was in a cage, longing for a family member or friend to talk to until I learned that darned English.

As we drove home, I told Khosropur about the possibility of English lessons and he was pleased. He said it would be a big help to him if I knew English because then we could entertain. I wondered why he had not made some inquiries himself if he was so enamored of the idea. When Mr. Ansari called me a few days later to tell me that his colleague had agreed to take me on, I was so delighted that I jumped around the house like Babak.

The teacher who was to have an enormous impact on my life was Dr. Ella Harllee. She taught English at American University and also had an office at the Federation of Churches, where she prepared her acclaimed television program on religion and art. This was the office where she suggested we meet, and Mr. Ansari offered to take me there for the first time. We stopped in front of an old walled building on N Street NW. I was worried that I wouldn't be able to talk to my teacher, but Mr. Ansari put my fears to rest by saying that she spoke some French.

As we walked through the open gate in the tall, ivy-covered wall, we entered a wild and untended garden surrounding the building. Inside the building, we found ourselves in a large paneled hall with dim overhead lights. It felt a bit like an old Italian church. Winding my way up a curving stairway to the second floor, I saw a blonde, blue-eyed woman in her fifties standing at the top, waiting for us. Dr. Harllee took my hand and held it, saying, "I am very happy to meet you."

Mr. Ansari left and we went into Dr. Harllee's office. It was a big room, every wall covered with bookcases crammed with books of religious art. A big television occupied the table in the center of the room. The professor led me to a small table with two chairs by the window. In French she said that we would call each other by our first names and invited me to call her Ella. This was strange to me, because in Iran and Europe people address only their family and very close friends by their first name. Well, I thought, I am in America now.

Ella Harllee was the daughter of a general who had died several years before. She came from a prominent, highly educated, and politically connected Southern family. Ella's mother was politically and socially active and her brother, also a general in the U.S. Army, later became an aide to President Kennedy. They lived in a beautiful old house in the then very chic Mount Pleasant neighborhood. I generally went there for my thrice-weekly lessons, because it was close to our 16th Street apartment. Afterwards I would go home and practice with Blanche.

With the help of Ella, Blanche, and our television set, little by little the fog of separation that divided me from America lifted.

I became quite close to Ella. Khosropur and I were often invited to her family home. Ella had no children and never married, so in a way I was almost adopted into her family. She was my first American friend. She taught me so much more than English; through her I learned about the history, politics, and culture of the United States.

Over two days in 1954, she took me to the Capitol to watch the Senate in session. It was the McCarthy era. I had no idea who Senator McCarthy was, but she knew that these hearings were history in the making and wanted to share it with me. As I sat in the balcony and watched the proceedings, it became apparent to me that there were two kinds of political systems. Here were people who held different points of view but were able to discuss them together. In Iran only officially sanctioned ideas could be expressed and opposition was crushed with imprisonment or death.

Another day, Ella took me to the White House. I could hardly believe that the president's house was so modest and open to the public and that it belonged, ultimately, to the people. How different it was from the guarded palaces of the Shah. I could hardly believe we were able to walk through the rooms and see that, in most respects, the president and his family lived very much like everyone else.

I had been studying with Ella for a year and a half when one day she said, "Parvaneh, you must go to college." I was taken aback, telling her that I had only studied to the ninth grade in Iran and for one year in Geneva. I had never managed to get a high school diploma. Ella told me that American University had classes for adults who for one reason or another had not finished high school. She talked to the admissions office and helped me sign up for two years of intensive preparation for college.

That evening when I talked to my husband, I found him unenthusiastic. He asked, "Don't you think your duty is to your family, rather than going to school? What do you need an education for, anyway?" I didn't answer these questions. I fiercely wanted to go to university and become an educated woman who could stand on her own two feet. If I let this opportunity slip by, when would another one come along?

When I first met Khosropur, I was an independent young woman with her own bank account, and in charge of her family's finances. I had an active social life and, since I belonged to both the Iran-France and the Iran-Soviet Union clubs, a circle of friends that included a number of foreigners with whom I could discuss the latest books in French and Persian. Khosropur admired me for these qualities yet, after our marriage, sought to crush them. While we lived in Iran, he was quite generous and I maintained my support system; but once we were in the United States, I was essentially dependent on my husband's whims.

Many women in Iran like to get married because of the new freedoms they experience away from their family. In my case, the situation was reversed. Suddenly I had no money of my own and had to ask permission for everything I wanted to do. All the household expenses, including Blanche's salary, were under Khosropur's control and he wielded the power of the purse strings like a despot. I had no money other than what he chose to give me in cash for housekeeping. I found it humiliating to ask for money, but if I did not ask it was never volunteered. If I charged something to his credit card, I was questioned closely when the bill arrived at his office. A couple of weeks after I took Ella to lunch at a restaurant called The Birdcage, for example, I received a very irate phone call. "Why have you spent all this money on a stupid birdcage?" he sputtered. "We don't even have a bird!" On another occasion, when we were in Paris on the way to Iran, I mentioned that I needed some white shoes. Khosropur did not even respond. A few days later, I raised it again. "I have not yet decided whether you need white shoes," he said. I never did get the shoes.

Like many immigrant women, especially mothers with little or no English whose legal status is linked with their husbands' visas, I had little control over my situation. Unlike my father's beloved pigeons that were free to fly up to heaven every afternoon, I was a caged bird with clipped wings. I think that is why I invested so much hope in my education. It was the one thing I could do for myself.

We had been in the United States for two years and my husband had recently been re-elected to his position for two more years. I mulled it over all night and into the next day. Even if we returned to Iran my educational efforts would not be wasted. I could enroll at the university in Tehran. Why shouldn't I do it? I *would* do it! I made a plan. That evening I promised Khosropur that I would never ignore my duty to him or to Babak.

In September 1956, I started my high school classes at American University. Ella Harllee accompanied me to class on the first day. It took a frustrating two months before I could properly understand what the teachers were talking about. The professors who taught the classes were very encouraging, and the students were highly motivated. With the help of Blanche and the support of Ella, I finished my high school education in 1958.

I immediately sent off my diploma, together with my ninth-grade diploma from Iran and the certificate from my year in Geneva, to American University as part of my application for a Bachelor of Arts degree. Within three weeks I received a conditional acceptance: I must finish my first three courses with a B average. I took the letter to Ella and confided that I was really frightened I might not be able to maintain this standard. I thought perhaps my husband was right—I was not clever enough to get a university education.

Ella told me very firmly that a lack of confidence was the worst thing in the world. Had she not seen that I was capable of gaining a degree, she would never have suggested it. She breathed strength into my heart and I felt enormous gratitude for all she had done for me. With renewed courage, I approached Khosropur—who again said I was not "university stock." He went further. He said I should restrict myself to the classes with Ella because he was concerned that if I tried for more, I might lose my mind. But I knew that if I backed down now, I would never forgive myself. In fact, the more my husband ridiculed my ambitions, the more stubborn and determined I became. Stubbornness and determination were the attributes that had kept my mother going and I was very much her daughter.

So on September 15, 1958, Ella and I went to the basketball gym where students signed up for classes and I registered for three courses at American University. It was a hot day, as September days can be in Washington. The sky was blue and cloudless, which seemed a good omen. I was extremely excited. To me the university was a holy place, the only place that touches your soul, your mind, and your heart because it will open the whole world to you. Despite the conditions and obstacles, I felt free and happy.

Classes commenced on September 25. My first class was English Composition and Ella came with me. I was the only foreign student in the class and only the second Iranian student at the university. The other students were very kind to me. If I had questions, they would help me; and before I handed in my papers, they would offer to read and correct them with me. I was most impressed by the generosity of my classmates.

My other two classes were World History and World Literature. Sometimes Ella would slip into the room during class to see how I was doing. With all the help I received, I finished these first three classes on time in January. The first week of vacation was probably the longest of my life. I must have gone twenty times a day to check the mailbox. I couldn't sleep at night, torn between my husband's put-downs and Ella's encouragement. One morning Ella called to see if I had received my report card. I told her, "No, and I am very worried." She started laughing on the other end of the phone. She told me that I would get the results that day or the next and asked if I had chosen my next three classes. "Classes?" I whimpered. "What classes? I don't feel at all optimistic."

Ella suggested I come over at two the next afternoon so that she could help me with course selection. She seemed to be allowing no possibility of failure and I let a tiny ray of hope slip into my heart. The next day I asked Blanche if she could pick up Babak, who by then was attending nursery school, so that I could meet Ella. As I passed the shops in the tram, I decided that I would buy a new dress on the way home. I had been so involved in other things that I had paid no attention at all to fashion, which in those days changed from season to season. I felt like a peasant in front of Garfinkel's as I gazed at window displays of elegant models in the latest empire-line dresses, and one or two of the outrageous new "sack" dresses that had startled Paris when the spring collection was shown. My own clothing seemed instantly unwearable.

With Ella's guidance, I decided on four courses for the next semester, although I still had faint hope of being allowed to continue. I got home at about four, my new dress in a bag over my arm, and went straight to the mailbox. It disgorged a pile of letters onto the floor. With my heart pounding and my knees weak, I stooped to the ground and shuffled through the mail. Yes. There was a white envelope with the university address on it. I couldn't open it. Even in the elevator on the way up to our apartment, I clutched it to my chest and couldn't bring myself to look inside.

Blanche heard me as I came in. She called out very loudly, "Mrs. K? Did you get your letter?" I told her yes, but I was too scared to open it. Blanche pried it from my fingers and went to the kitchen to get a knife. I heard her slitting the envelope. She laughed, very loudly, and started to sing, "Mrs. K! Mrs. K! You passed! You passed!" I ran to the kitchen and took the open letter from Blanche's waving hand. English Composition: B. World Literature: B. World History: B. I sank into a chair. Tears started pouring from my eyes. This was the first, the sweetest achievement of my life.

Babak held onto my clothes, anxiously asking, "Mommy! Mommy! Why are you crying?" Blanche took me into her arms, saying "Mrs. K! I knew you would pass!" We all clung together as the realization washed through my mind and body. Then I went to the phone and called Ella. She was not at all surprised.

Two years went by. I attended classes all year round because I felt I was so behind and could not waste a minute. Babak was now going to school and attending camp in summer while I was in class. My advisor called me in to discuss choosing my major. I was very interested in literature. English or American, he asked me. I chose English literature. That evening when I told Khosropur that I wanted to pursue English literature, he scoffed at me. "Why do you want to do that? Unless you want to read Shakespeare all your life!"

All of this time, my husband had been unaware of how hard I was studying. He had agreed that I take an English course here and there. I believe he saw it as a kind of distraction or a hobby that would make me a better hostess. I had no independent financial resources, depending on the money that he gave me for housekeeping. To keep Khosropur in the dark—for I was convinced that he would throw barriers in my way if he knew—I had scrimped and saved on my housekeeping money so that I could secretly pay for two courses for every one that he paid for. Only in this way was I was able to finish all my requirements and get to the point of choosing my major.

Given the enormous effort that I had to make, essentially fulfilling the demands of two lives, I was always somewhat envious of the other students, most of whom were English-speaking teenagers whose parents were paying their fees. They seemed to live lives of great freedom to me, with no responsibilities other than to themselves. One day, for example, the professor was late for a World History class. The students began to get restless, and after about ten minutes, they all decided to leave. Everyone seemed to be really happy not to have to attend the class and went out laughing and cheering. Soon I was the only one left in the lecture hall, feeling terribly disappointed. I was really looking forward to this class, the big lecture given once a week to the whole class of about 350 students by the head of the department. I had left Babak with a babysitter and taken two buses to get to the university.

A few minutes later the professor rushed in. Surprised, he looked around the empty hall and then noticed me. "Where is everybody?" he asked. I told him that everyone else had left because they assumed he was not coming. "They didn't even wait for the announcement from my secretary?" He looked quizzically at me. "Why didn't you leave?" I told him that I had come such a long way and felt sad at the thought of going back home without having heard the lecture. He smiled at me. "Then stay where you are. I will give the lecture." And he did, just for me. When the results came out for that grading period, I had an A. Everyone else had an F.

I finished my junior year. But as I started on my senior year, my enormous energy and enthusiasm suddenly deserted me. I could hardly get out of bed in the morning. I felt sick and often had a headache. I called my physician, Dr. Walsh, who had me come in for blood work and an examination. A few days later the doctor called. He asked me how I felt and I told him that I had not improved at all. I asked him what was wrong with me and he laughed. "Nothing," he said. "You are pregnant. Congratulations!"

Disaster! All of my dreams would evaporate. I returned home and sat like a stone in my chair. Babak was now in school all day, leaving me time to really study as well as keep up with our busy social life. And now, a new child. I could never do it. And if we had to return to Iran, it would be out of the question to finish my degree. Tears of frustration and self-pity and disappointment coursed down my face. I must have sat there for an hour, my mind in turmoil. "What can I do?" I groaned. I heard a quiet voice within myself, answering: What is wrong with being pregnant? It is not a disease. It is a healthy state. Why shouldn't I continue going to school? I can still follow my chosen path. I have a son already—perhaps this time I will have a daughter.

I got up from the chair and went outside. It was springtime and the bulbs were out. The trees were misted with the pale pistachio color of tender buds. Magnolias were pink with promise. Beautiful, beautiful Washington spring. I walked towards Connecticut Avenue, an inner dialogue humming in my head. "I will not allow pregnancy to finish my dream of education."

That night I told Khosropur I was pregnant. He immediately exclaimed, "Now is the time to finish this education nonsense! You must not compromise your health. You must stay home and take care of yourself and the baby." But I insisted that we see the doctor together to let the expert say whether education was damaging to the health of a pregnant woman. To my immense delight, Dr. Walsh told my husband that not only was it not harmful to continue with my studies, but just the opposite was true—that the nine months would pass quickly if I were engaged and happy.

I could have leaped over the desk and embraced that wonderful Dr. Walsh. With Khosropur's objections dismissed, I raced to school and asked for a special exemption to study six classes in the fall. I wanted to make sure that I could finish almost everything before my baby arrived.

By this time I had made many friends at American University and they were all very kind to me. Plodding up and down the stairs many times a day made me increasingly hot, even in winter. A place by the window was always left open for me even if it meant the others had to keep their coats on, and there was always someone to carry my books.

I spent my pregnancy either at home with my husband and son, or at the university. My mother came from Iran in December to be with me for the birth. I was busy and she had no English, so she suffered the same helpless dependence that had so oppressed me. My required reading was huge and I began to think my child would have to be a writer after absorbing so much of the written word.

In January, as I sat in my last examination in Nineteenth Century English Literature, I became aware that the slight and periodic pain I had experienced all day was getting more noticeable. My professor was watching me, noting that I looked uncomfortable as I perched sideways on my chair so that I could fit behind the desk. He came over and suggested that if I were not feeling well, his secretary could take me home or even to the hospital.

One by one, the students finished their examinations, took their blue books up to Professor Clark, and left. I was determined to finish. When I asked if I could make a phone call and return to the room to complete my paper, the professor told me to go next door to his office. His secretary, Kathy, hovered nervously as I called my doctor and was advised to go immediately to the hospital when the pains came every five minutes. I told the anxious secretary that it was not time, since it was all of fifteen minutes between contractions. Professor Clark was amazed when I returned and, with great difficulty, finished my examination. I was almost the last student left.

The contractions were now coming every ten minutes. Kathy brought her car right to the door and drove me home. My suitcase was already packed and I asked Khosropur to take me straight to the hospital. Before we left I called my next-door neighbor and friend Alice to collect Babak. Then, having slain all my dragons, I finally set off to have my baby.

My daughter was born that day, on January 29, 1960. I called her Soodabeh after my mother. Not only did my studying not damage little Sudi, it put us both in the best of health. And I was triumphant. I had done it!

We were now a family of five. After the death of Khosropur's mother, we had brought Mehri from Tehran to live with us and finish her education. Mehri was my first child really—we had supported her since she was eleven and I loved her like a daughter. Sudi was a very difficult baby, crying inconsolably with colic, and Mehri was a great help to me.

My husband, on the other hand, was no help at all with the children and became impatient if they cried or kept him awake. He saw them as completely my responsibility, which was ironic since he expressed no confidence in my ability or intelligence. One morning, tired after getting up several times during the night to attend to Sudi, I complained that he never helped me. He looked at me in astonishment. "I married a young woman to look after my children!" he sputtered.

The next day, still feeling the sting of his chauvinism, I went to Garfinkel's, which in those days was the most elegant department store in the downtown shopping area. I found a beautiful black alligator handbag, the height of luxury and fashion, and charged it to his credit card. A week or so later when he received the bill, he called from his office, angry that I had been so extravagant. He told me that I must return the bag immediately. With tremendous satisfaction, sweetened by my anticipation of this moment, I purred, "My dear. I married an old man to pay my bills."

Nearly forty years later, I was in Paris with my sister, who had come from Iran. As we walked down the Champs Elysees, I saw a gorgeous black alligator bag in a shop window. We went in and I asked the price. It seemed very reasonable for such a beautiful bag, so I decided to splurge. My sister and I were talking nonstop—we had not seen each other for some time—and I put my credit card down on the counter. It was a most elegant shop but even so, I was impressed by the care with which the purse was wrapped in tissue paper, placed in a soft velvet bag, then more tissue paper, and finally a pretty box with ribbons. The whole creation was handed to me in a smart carry-bag with even more tissue paper. It was only after I received my credit card bill on my return to Washington that I saw the reason for all the fuss. The price that I had quickly converted to $300 in my mind from the French franc price was actually $3,000! I could just imagine my husband's glee if he were only alive to see my face as I realized my mistake. I unearthed the old bag and had it refurbished since it suddenly seemed so valuable. Now I have two black alligator purses. I paid dearly for both of them.

That spring semester, I completed the two classes I needed to graduate, and in June of 1961 I received my BA in English Literature. I felt as though I had climbed Mount Everest, triumphant but exhausted.

Until Sudi was three years old, I stayed home as a full-time mother, then I registered her in a cooperative morning program and worked there once a week. I desperately wanted to continue my education but I didn't know what field I wanted to pursue. Sadly, this was an era where it was difficult for women to enter certain professions.

I was interested in law but most schools had a quota for women. American University, for example, which was my top choice because it was close enough for me to fulfill my duties at home as well as study, accepted only ten women into law school each year. I was so determined to be one of those women that the effort almost killed me: I barely slept or ate for months, studying for the entrance exam while also running the household and caring for my two children. While I equipped myself well—American University sent me a letter congratulating me on my results—as the eleventh woman, I did not get a place.

This was the first time I was personally confronted with discrimination against women in the United States. I could not see why, since I had passed the test, I was passed over for a male candidate. The injustice left a big scar on my soul. It brought home to me a realization that there are barriers to achievement in this country for many people.

Now that my mornings were free, I spent a lot of time at the Library of Congress. I researched many areas, partly because I wanted to find a field that interested me and partly for the sheer joy of being in that magnificent library. An area that attracted me a great deal was Orientalia, as it was called in those days; now it is Middle Eastern Studies.

One person I saw and talked to a lot was Mr. Poorhadi, the head of the Department of Orientalia at the Library of Congress. When I confessed to him that I was confused over my career choices, he suggested I get a master's degree in Library Science from Catholic University and then, if I were interested, I could come and work for him. The library had a huge collection of books in Persian and Cyrillic that were largely uncatalogued. My language skills would be in demand in libraries almost anywhere in the world, he told me.

At that time, by a stroke of good luck, my brother Mehrdad sent some money to repay what I had given him for his university education in London. I had forgotten all about it, but he insisted I take it now that he was on his feet and finished with his studies. The sudden windfall of $5,000 meant that I could go to graduate school. My husband would not have given me the money, but suddenly I had this opportunity.

I applied to Catholic University and arranged for an interview with the head of the department before we left for Iran that summer. On our return, I found I had been accepted. Fortunately I had just learned to drive, so I could leave Sudi at kindergarten in the morning and pick her up at twelve thirty.

I tried to arrange my classes for the morning, but sometimes I had to bring Sudi to an afternoon class. She would sit quietly in the classroom, painting pictures of the teachers and students that she would proudly present to her subjects as she left. No one ever objected to her presence. There were several different libraries at Catholic University for training purposes, including a small library for children where I often entertained my daughter. When it was hot, I took Sudi to the university's pool and taught her to swim between classes.

I found the first year, with its technical focus, quite difficult. Like most people, my experience of libraries was of calm and order with a librarian sitting behind a desk. Despite my extensive use of libraries, I had no idea how much work and expertise lay behind that silence. In those days before computers, librarians were trained to be walking encyclopedias. In addition to the technical areas, we also studied the history of books and bookmaking. Fortunately, since it was an important part of the job, I already had three languages.

After passing the comprehensive examinations in my second year, I began on my thesis. The topic I chose was the translation of Persian poetry into English from the Arab invasion until the present. It took me six months, during which the Library of Congress gave me a desk on the "deck" (the stacks) and special access to the collection. On my first day at my little desk in the Orientalia section, I looked down upon the thousands of books stretching out on either side and below me and I felt less important than a pinprick among all that knowledge.

Much as I loved it, I could not sit in the stacks for more than a couple of hours at a time. It was claustrophobic and the odor of old books could become overpowering. I would go out for some fresh air for about fifteen minutes and then plunge back into my research.

Finally, I handed in my thesis and waited for the results. Just as I had suffered through the wait for my first results at American University, I found the three weeks before I heard whether my thesis was accepted almost unbearable. One evening as we had dinner the phone rang. It was the head of the department with the wonderful news that it was accepted. I almost collapsed with happiness. In June 1968 I was awarded my master of library science degree (MLS). At that time, the shortage of librarians all over the country meant that for every graduate there were five openings, and libraries competed fiercely for us.

This professional degree meant so much more to me than straightforward academic accomplishment. To me, my degree represented freedom: freedom to support myself, freedom to enter the world of professional women, freedom to earn my own money and decide my own future. And it meant liberation from the yoke of dependency under which I had so chafed. No longer would I be demeaned by having to beg my husband for money or ask his permission to do something.

I had never accepted the traditional role of women in my own culture, but my financial dependence had thrown me into that role here in the United States. Now I was ready to be my own person. Almost forty, I felt for the first time that I was a grown woman. I was still a wife and mother, but now I could have my very own checking account, my very own credit card, and my very own car.

These gains had come at a great cost. Our household had come to resemble a war zone, with two cultures living uneasily side by side. On one side was an Iranian man, remote from the daily business of his family and unchanged by American culture; on the other side, an educated, westernized woman with American children. Everything domestic—be it raising and educating the children, cooking, cleaning, entertaining, or shopping—was my responsibility. As the sultan, the king, Khosropur ordered us around, gave us money as he saw fit, and never consulted me, even on major issues such as buying a house. When he bought our house, he was stunned when the bank informed him that we both must sign the mortgage. He insisted, "Why does she have to sign? What does it have to do with her?"

I don't believe he saw me as a partner or even an adult. I was a doll, or just one of the children in his little kingdom. In our life together, Khosropur bought two houses, the first on Military Road, then when Sudi was thirteen, a house in Chevy Chase. He involved me in neither of these purchases, presenting them as a *fait accompli* when he took me to sign the contracts.

Even the furnishing of the homes was under his control. I noticed that the sofa in our living room looked shabby and chose a new one. When the sofa was delivered, Khosropur went at once to the store to arrange for it to be returned, saying, "I am the one who decides whether we need a sofa. This is my home, these are my children. If you don't like it you can go back to your mother." Not only did I not go back to my mother, I went back to the store and arranged for the sofa to be delivered all over again. My husband was too embarrassed to rescind my order.

We barely talked, and if I walked in on a conversation, he would stop talking immediately as though I couldn't possibly understand or contribute. He was not affectionate and was often away, either on business or on holidays that he took alone.

About to travel home to see my mother, I asked Khosropur to get me some Iranian money from the bank; but he said no, it would be better to ask his brother in Tehran to advance some from their business account. I had no access to financial records, so I was very surprised to find out, by accident, that my husband and his brother had been investing in business interests in Iran. Soon after arriving penniless in Tehran, I went to visit my brother-in-law and his family, accompanied by a few of my family members; when I mentioned my husband's instructions, my brother-in-law laughed, said that Khosropur must have been joking, and gave me nothing. It was humiliating being disgraced in front of both families. My sister Cherry felt so ashamed for me that she wrote me a blank check immediately.

There were many other times during the marriage that I felt humiliated and betrayed. Even before we left Iran, I suspected Khosropur of dalliances with other women, including our maid. It did not take long before I saw evidence of similar behavior in Washington.

Soon after we arrived, Maman sent me a pair of beautiful gold earrings. It was just before Christmas and Khosropur told me to wrap them up as a thank-you present for a woman in the staff relations department at his office who had been particularly kind and helpful to us when we first arrived. I was surprised at this generosity, but not as surprised as I was a week later, when we attended the staff Christmas party and I watched my husband dance all evening with his secretary—who was wearing my earrings.

I recall one embarrassing occasion when I was at home with the children. The manager of the apartment called to ask if she could come up for a few minutes. She arrived with a big box in her hands, and opened it to show me the black negligee inside. "Your husband bought it for my birthday," she said. Her eyes narrowed at my discomfort as she told me about their affair.

One of my worst experiences came after a party. Khosropur had paid a lot of attention to a very voluptuous woman, whom he offered to drive home. Blanche was baby-sitting, so I suggested we stop by the house so that she could be driven home too. Blanche was ironing when I ran in, and said that she preferred to finish the job and then find her own way home. When I ran back to the car to say that they need not wait, I found them passionately embracing in the car—right in front of our apartment. I was angry and hurt, but my husband was humiliating this woman as much as he was his wife. He simply did not regard women as full human beings, worthy of respect and consideration: If he wanted another woman, well, in his opinion it was his right and I had no business criticizing him. Interestingly, the only woman for whom Khosropur did not feel disdain was Sudi. She was his daughter and perhaps this qualification alone allowed her full personhood.

My husband may have been a philanderer without a conscience, but he was also suspicious and jealous, expecting his wife to behave with the utmost decorum. Not long after we arrived in Washington, I became aware of the number of churches that Babak and I passed on our daily walks along 16th Street near our apartment. I wondered how there could be so many varieties of Christianity? I was familiar with Jesus—he is recognized in Islam as a prophet—but there was only one of him, so why the need for so many ways to worship? When I was growing up in Tehran, there were several mosques, some Armenian churches and perhaps a Catholic church. In Switzerland, I had not noticed much variety. I decided to explore. Every Sunday, I attended a different church. I could see they all read the Bible, said prayers, believed in Jesus. One day, I felt a familiar presence behind me. I turned around, and there was Khosropur. He had become suspicious of my weekly outings and followed me. He thought I was conducting an amorous affair every Sunday morning. I am still puzzled by the churches. I don't believe religion is how you pray, where you go, but how you stand up in the service of mankind. I have always liked what the great thirteenth-century Sufi poet Rumi wrote about places of worship:

I tried to find God. I went to the mosque, but I could not find Him there. I went to the synagogue, but He was not there. I went to the church, but did not find Him. I went to the Buddhist temple, but did not find God. I went to the top of the mountain, but He was not there. I went to the bottom of the valley, but still did not find Him. Exhausted, I went home. I sat in my room and looked quietly into myself. I found God in my heart.

I gave up my peripatetic churchgoing and went back to the church of my own heart, reading Saadi and Rumi and meditating on the wisdom of their words.

In the midst of all my domestic and educational activities, I was also engaged in getting to know the ropes of Washington social life. Khosropur was part of the diplomatic circle, and I was expected to attend four or five cocktail parties and several dinners a week. Washington was quite a small provincial town in the 1950s and '60s, and most people in this circle knew each other. There were only two newspapers then, the *Washington Post* and the *Washington Star*, and society dinners and parties were covered by both of them.

After we had established ourselves, Khosropur told me that it was time to start returning the invitations we had received, and that I should prepare to be hostess to delegations from the fourteen countries he represented at the World Bank. I had experience with party giving in Iran, but there it was so easy—I had a cook, two servants, and a driver to carry out my instructions. All I needed to do was play the hostess. Now it was completely different.

I immediately set out for a bookshop in Georgetown that carried foreign language books and purchased the French edition of Emily Post's *Etiquette* and several cookbooks in French. From then on, I kept a journal in which I jotted down the details of each party we attended—invitations, table settings, flowers, food presentation and seating plans. I became a party sleuth and my journal soon overflowed with ideas. Unlike Persian parties, where food is served buffet style at a big central table and guests serve themselves and either sit around this table or on chairs and sofas around the room, I noted that it was fashionable in Washington to seat guests at a number of small tables, each decorated in a different color. Tiny ashtrays and salt and pepper shakers, elegant cigarette boxes and lighters (everybody smoked back then), porcelain place cards, silver candle-holders, and napkin rings were a must on each table. No detail escaped my watchful eye as I studied the art of the Washington hostess.

In 1950s Washington, a small number of celebrated hostesses set the standard for excellence in entertaining. One of these, Perle Mesta, a wealthy widow who entertained lavishly in her huge Kalorama apartment in The Rochester, for some reason took me under her wing. Perle's cocktail parties and dinners were renowned for bringing together powerful, rich, and famous people, and were regularly described in the newspapers. I had met her several times when one day, she invited me to her home for lunch. I prepared myself carefully in a beautiful dress—short, in the pre-Kennedy days—and hat and gloves, anticipating the usual luncheon crowd of elegantly dressed women. Arriving at the apartment, I soon realized I was the only guest. I was astonished. Why had she singled me out? She took my hand just like a mother might, looked me in the eye and said, "I am going to teach you everything I know." I have been fortunate in life; whenever I have need of a teacher, one seems to arrive.

I don't know why Perle took a liking to me. Perhaps it was my curiosity and determination to learn the culture. Perhaps she had noticed my concentration on details at parties. Whatever the reason, she was a godsend and we became close friends.

When I told Perle that in a couple of months, the annual meetings of the IMF and World Bank would bring all the central bankers and finance ministers and their entourages to Washington, and that I would be expected to host a big party in honor of the delegates from Khosropur's countries, she went into high gear. Together we swept through The Hecht Company's housewares department, choosing lovely embroidered table linens in white, pale blue, pistachio, and light pink, and candleholders, small silver vases, ashtrays, and cigarette boxes. Next, Perle introduced me to Ridgewells catering company, and helped me place an order for some European food. I wanted to serve Persian food as well, but having never cooked before, I was filled with trepidation. An Iranian friend who had learned to cook—a rarity, since Persians of the class who traveled abroad tended to have cooks to prepare their meals in Iran—taught me how to make one dish and I practiced it several times.

The party was in late September. As the date approached, I became very anxious. The night before the party, I was so scared I could barely sleep. However was I to entertain all these distinguished people? I had invited Perle—she actually turned down another invitation to come to my party—and she arrived early. When Blanche opened the door and I saw Perle, I almost screamed with happiness and relief. She hugged and kissed me and said I looked beautiful, then inspected all the table arrangements before moving on to the kitchen to check on the food. When she came back to give me an "A" rating, she took one look at me, shivering with apprehension, and asked the butler to pour me a sherry. I was to calm down, she told me, or the guests would see that I was a novice. At that moment, Khosropur appeared, having contributed nothing but the guest list.

The dinner was wonderful. Even my Persian food was a success and everyone remarked on how exotic and delicious it was. After dinner, the men went to one side of the living room for a while to smoke and talk while the women touched up their makeup and chatted on the other side. Then all the guests mingled until about eleven o'clock. Their talk and laughter was heavenly music to my anxious ears. When the last guest had departed, I collapsed on my bed like a dead person. It was over. I had done it. And I had lost my fear of entertaining.

I began to give parties at least once a month, enjoying my social life more as my English improved and adding in a little Persian touch here and there to distinguish my parties from those of others. I even appeared in the society columns as "the charming Mrs. Khosropur." For one who had been raised in intellectual circles, it was fascinating to watch the world of power and politics play out in Washington parlors. Khosropur left me to fend for myself at parties, so I made my own friends among people I met.

Eisenhower and Nixon were in the White House when we came to the United States. One afternoon in October of 1959, I was invited to a tea with Mamie Eisenhower at the White House. The guests were the wives of economic directors at the IMF and World Bank, and the wives of governors of the central banks of member countries who were in Washington for the annual meetings of the IMF and World Bank. The First Lady was impressively informal, interacting with her guests with ease and charm. After the stiff pomp and ceremony of the Shah's public appearances and the gilt and mirrored splendor of his palaces, the simplicity and hominess of the White House was quite an eye-opener.

To the accompaniment of the Navy Band, we were provided with name tags that indicated our country of origin and then led towards the reception room. To my great surprise, I spotted my next door neighbor conducting the band; until that point, I had no idea that he was even involved in music. By the look on his face, he was equally surprised to see me on my way to tea with the First Lady.

Mrs. Eisenhower was standing at the door to greet us individually, a welcoming smile on her face. She looked pretty in a short, full-skirted blue dress that matched her eyes. Her rosy cheeks were framed by her trademark hairstyle and she wore a simple pearl necklace. When she got to me, she put her arms around my shoulders and peered in through the veiling on my red hat. "My dear," she said, "you are very young!" It was true; I was by far the youngest woman there.

Once we were all assembled, we were directed to the tea room. One table was presided over by two ladies, each manning a large silver tea service. The other was laid with an array of cakes and sandwiches, chocolates, and sweets that, for me at least, seemed like a feast in a fairytale. In Iran we had fruits rather than desserts and, at least in my family, cakes and sweets were few and far between. I was quite dazzled and only a sense of propriety kept me from racing over and grabbing handfuls of goodies. That, and the memory of my visit to the doctor.

When we moved into our apartment at the Woodner Hotel on 16th Street, I discovered a treasure trove one day. I had run out of milk and asked the doorman where I could buy some. Actually I pointed to my purse and said, "Milk? Milk?" He took me to a room off the lobby where there were some vending machines, including one that dispensed small cartons of milk. I also noted one that sold chocolate bars, an almost unheard of luxury in Iran. I made many journeys to that little room. I also consumed enormous quantities of ice cream, amazed that such a glorious treat was so easily and cheaply available. I had it for breakfast, lunch, and dinner. Every time I went grocery shopping with my husband, I loaded up the cart with gallons of ice cream in heavenly flavors. When I went for my checkup, the doctor could hardly believe how much weight I had gained. He was stunned when I cheerfully described my diet. People weren't nearly so conscious of what they ate in those days and sweets were a part of every meal. Still, I had rather overdone it.

The First Lady did not give a speech; instead she circulated among her guests. Her relaxed manner and hospitality made everyone feel comfortable in what could have been an intimidating setting. Many years later, when I was the president of the Iranian Women's Association of the United States, my vice president and I were invited to the Shah's palace for an audience with Queen Farah. What a contrast. We were escorted through the palace by a succession of silent and elegant men in expensive suits, finally finding ourselves in a large formal room filled with Persian rugs, antique gilt furniture, and glittering chandeliers all reflected a thousand times over in the many mirrors. Already intimidated by the cold formality of our reception, we were further diminished by the many instructions showered upon us by a supercilious official who had glided in behind us. At the end, he looked at us sternly and said, "If the Queen asks you if you would like to take tea, you will say 'NO!'"

As we sat there mulling over this advice so at odds with traditional Persian hospitality, the Queen entered the room looking very elegant in her chic summer silk dress set off by magnificent jewels. She shook our hands very pleasantly and invited us to sit down. She was gracious and kind and interested in our work with the Women's Association, promising us help if we needed it, a promise she later honored. Then came the fatal question: "Would you like to take some tea?" Rebellious thoughts flashed through my head, but with a quick glance at each other, my colleague and I sat up like little lap dogs and whined, "No, thank you." The whole environment conspired to produce subservience. I wonder if Farah was aware of the protocol. A cup of tea would have been most welcome right then—perhaps for her, too.

Farah Diba had been in the same class as my youngest sister Cherry at Jeanne d'Arc, the French school in Tehran. She had then gone to Paris to study architecture at Ecole Speciale d'Architecture. Before she finished her studies, she was tapped to be the next queen, reportedly at the suggestion of Princess Shahnaz, the Shah's daughter from his first marriage to Princess Fawzia of Egypt. With no possibility of a male heir to the throne, the Shah divorced his second wife, the beautiful and popular Soraya. An introduction was arranged by Shahnaz's husband, Ardeshir Zahedi, son of the prime minister who had replaced Mossadeq. Zahedi was Iran's ambassador to the United States from 1959 to 1962, and again from 1973 to 1979 and was famous for his lavish parties at the embassy.

The marriage took place at the end of 1959, with Farah resplendent in a Dior wedding gown trimmed with mink and encrusted with about thirty pounds of jewels. It was a far cry from her life as an ordinary student from an upper middle class family.

Even more fabulous was Farah's elevation to crowned Empress in 1971 during the festivities at Persepolis, the ancient capital of the Persian empire. Tens of millions of dollars were spent to entertain, in epic movie style, a vast crowd of royalty, heads of state, and other notaries in the desert to celebrate 2,500 years of the Persian empire, to hold the coronation, and to commemorate "Reza Shah the Great," the current Shah's father. Never mind that the Pahlavi "dynasty" was less than fifty years old, having started when this former Cossack was put in power by the British to crush the democratic movement of the early twentieth century and took the name Reza Pahlavi. And never mind that his son's place on the throne had been saved by a combined CIA/British Intelligence-sponsored coup in 1953 after the pro-democracy, nationalist prime minister, Mossadeq, tried to nationalize oil and limit the power of the monarch. It was during the purges that followed the return of the Shah that my brother Mehrdad was imprisoned, and sentenced to death, for his part in that uprising.

Twice in the twentieth century, democratic movements were crushed in Iran. Each time they were replaced by dictatorships that relied heavily on outside support. It is no wonder that Iranians remain suspicious of, even hostile to, the U.S. and Britain, and that when finally the Shah was overthrown in 1979, he was replaced by an inward-looking, hard-line theocracy. But all this history of repression and foreign influence was brushed aside in the silken opulence, the dazzling pageantry, of Persepolis. The spectacle of the Shah's coronation and Farah's elevation to Empress was one of the greatest PR stunts of all time. The Shah was able to harvest and appropriate the glory of the Persian empire in the presence of the world.

I was glad my father did not live to see the return of his country to an even more repressive dictatorship. And I am grateful he did not live to see his son jailed for political activities. Mehrdad was so encouraged by the nationalist movement and the appointment of Dr. Mossadeq as prime minister, and by the referendum on nationalizing oil to end the bleeding of Iran through foreign ownership and domination. The demands of the people and the parliament had elevated Mossadeq. The Shah had fled. Who would have guessed that this tide of freedom and democracy could so easily (and so cheaply) be turned by American and British intervention, using the army and paid mobs to do their dirty work? When I heard on the radio that Dr. Mossadeq had been arrested, I cried bitterly, for Iran, and for my father's dreams of democracy.

The palace, a fortress to protect the Shah, was a very different environment from the homey atmosphere of Mamie Eisenhower's White House, where we were treated warmly, almost like friends. It was clear that Queen Farah was on an entirely different level, polite but untouchable. The aura of power of the monarchy in Iran separated the royal family from the discontented populace. The presidency in America, arising as it does from the will of the people, created an atmosphere of equality and welcome at "the people's house".

I was invited for tea at the White House a second time, during the Kennedy administration. By then, Jackie Kennedy had transformed the White House into a more formal and elegant place. There were more guards and more protocol. The Navy Band was there again, and my neighbor conducted the musicians.

This time, the vice president's wife, Lady Bird Johnson, joined Mrs. Kennedy in welcoming the guests, again the wives of IMF and World Bank executive directors and Central Bank governors. Once the guests had all been greeted, the slim and stylish First Lady left. (We later heard she left for a ski trip.) Mrs. Johnson took over the duties of hostess. Mrs. Johnson was down-to-earth and warm. She mingled among the guests, engaging in conversation and urging us to enjoy the tea and the spread of cakes and sandwiches. I had already met both ladies earlier in 1962 at a gala reception at the Iranian embassy.

During the Kennedy presidency, the Shah of Iran made a state visit to the United States. The Iranian embassy held a reception, inviting the president, the vice president, most of the cabinet and their wives, various VIPs, and a number of Iranians to meet the Shah. I was a student at American University by then.

The annual meetings of the World Bank and IMF were in New Delhi that year. I had accompanied my husband, and we visited Japan, Hong Kong, Hawaii, and California as we made our way home. We were in San Francisco when Khosropur was called back urgently to Washington. I planned to spend a few days there before traveling to Florida to pick up Babak from my brother Hushang's house, where he had stayed while we were away. No sooner had Khosropur arrived back than he called me in great agitation to tell me of the Shah's impending visit, insisting I return as soon as possible to purchase a long gown for the reception.

It was raining when I got home. Leaving Babak with Blanche, I set off to American University to register for the next semester. Then I hopped straight on a bus to the downtown shopping district to find my dress. After a frustrating and fruitless search through the offerings at Garfinkel's, Woodward & Lothrop, and Hecht's, I finally staggered into Erlebacher's on Connecticut Avenue, close to the White House. Under normal circumstances, I would never have dared shop in this, the most fashionable and expensive boutique in town—Khosropur would have killed me! But these were not normal circumstances and this was my last resort.

As I entered the shop, I must have looked like a homeless student in my raincoat and flat shoes. My hair was wet and lank and stuck to my head, my clothes were wringing wet, and I probably had a frantic air about me. A shop girl tried to bar my entry. These were times when women really dressed up to shop, especially in an exclusive place like Erlebacher's. Desperate and exhausted, I insisted that I be shown the evening gowns right away. The shop girl just as insistently tried to steer me out the door.

As our voices rose, the manager came out to see what this most unseemly commotion was about. He, too, looked me up and down, his practiced eye appraising me none too favorably. "What do you want?" he demanded curtly. I told him I needed a long dress to wear to a reception in honor of the Shah of Iran. He looked at me suspiciously. I told him that President and Mrs. Kennedy would be among the guests. Disbelief played across his smooth features. "What is your name?" "I have the money to pay and I insist on seeing your dresses. What does it matter what my name is?" I said archly, trying to muster as much dignity as my drowned gypsy appearance allowed. Still he persisted, until I finally told him my name. Not satisfied, he asked, "Who is your husband?" (Can you imagine this happening today?) Rising to the top of my five feet two inches, I replied, "I am the wife of Dr. Ali Akhbar Khosropur, executive director at the World Bank." I sounded just like my mother saying "I am the wife of Malek o'Shoara Bahar."

The manager slid away with the information. When he returned, what a transformation! Ushering me into a chair, he clapped his hands and ordered that

I be shown all the suitable evening dresses immediately. A parade of models soon materialized, wearing exquisite creations. Sitting in an ever-expanding damp spot on the velvet chaise, with water dripping down my face in little rivulets, I chose a strapless white Italian lace gown. Then, for good measure, I asked that a suit that had caught my eye be brought to the fitting room too.

Both garments fit like a dream. With an imperial wave of my arm, I said nonchalantly, "Have them delivered in the morning." As I left the boutique in triumph, I told the girl who had so rudely tried to bar my entry, "Don't ever judge a person by her appearance."

The reception, held in April 1962, was quite an experience. It was small—about sixty people—and very formal. The blue-domed Iranian embassy was filled with flowers and made a beautiful backdrop for all the women in their lovely gowns. Guests went through a receiving line, made up of the Shah and "Shahbanou" (a title created for the Shah's wife), President and Mrs. Kennedy, and Vice President and Mrs. Johnson. The Iranian ambassador made the introductions.

President Kennedy was a tall and commanding presence and much more handsome than I had imagined from photographs in the papers. As I shook his hand, I fell instantly in love. Mesmerized by this god-like person, I dreamily made my greetings then moved to greet Mrs. Kennedy. At least, I tried to. I was rooted to the spot and it was not only the magnetic power of the president; one of my gold high heels had become entangled in the carpet fringe. I had no choice but to step out of my shoe. Worse, I had to bend down and retrieve it.

To the amusement of all—my husband later told me the Shah was hysterical— I completed the receiving line with shoe in hand, bobbing up and down with each step. It was some consolation to see that my white gown was among the most beautiful worn that evening. I wish I had kept it. Somehow, when one is young, these things do not seem so important.

Queen Farah wore a long chiffon gown. Her thick hair was worn up, encircled by an incredible tiara of pearls and diamonds. The main reason for the visit was to seek financial aid from the United States. When you come to beg, it may not be wise to cover yourself with jewelry.

Mrs. Kennedy had a new hairdo that instantly became a fashion sensation. Most of her dark hair was swept up into petal-like pieces that created the effect of a flower, with the hair at the back hanging loose. She wore a plain black dress, sleeveless, with a square neck that showed off her pearls. I was surprised to discover many years later that the famous pearls she wore that evening, auctioned after her death for quite a sum, were faux.

There were speeches and toasts and a sit-down dinner. The tables were arranged in a large, open square with the Shah and Farah seated in the center of the head table, flanked by the Kennedys and the Johnsons. The Shah welcomed the president and vice president to the Iranian embassy, and Vice President Johnson welcomed the Shah and Farah to Washington. Then President Kennedy made a long speech about the value he placed on good relations between the two countries, emphasizing the importance of Iran in the Middle East. He ended by announcing that the U.S. would provide financial aid to Iran.

The Shah was a very good client for U.S. weapons, planes, and other military equipment, and welcomed tens of thousands of American advisors during his reign. Many Iranian military personnel were sent to the U.S. for training. It was a cozy relationship: the U.S. had a strong ally, a reliable supply of cheap oil, and a customer hungry for military equipment, while the Shah had the might of the U.S. behind him.

Or so he thought until the Revolution of 1979. Then the man who had often been portrayed as a puppet of America found himself an unwelcome guest in the country that had hitherto done so much to keep him on the throne. As my father had said, "The palace of the king is no more secure than the little shack of the poor."

The bitterness that has characterized the U.S.–Iran relationship for the past thirty years had its origins in the rage that poured from the students who took over the U.S. embassy in Tehran in 1979. The students called that embassy (not without cause, as a painstaking reconstruction of mountains of shredded documents showed) a "nest of spies." They seized the personnel there as hostages. These hapless victims of long imprisonment, humiliation, and torture were the only representatives within reach on whom to vent the enormous pent-up anger. The demonstrators unleashed justifiable rage at the long history of economic exploitation and shameless meddling in Iranian politics, practiced by first the British and Russians, and later by the United States.

Every time I pass the Iranian embassy in Washington, D.C., so forlorn and uncared for today, I feel pain in my heart. So many of its blue tiles are now missing after the paint applied in the anger of the hostage crisis was removed. The two countries that I love remain divided and hostile, and increasingly ignorant of one another. I hope that I live to see the flags flying once more on both the Iranian embassy here in Washington and the U.S. embassy in Tehran.

When I look back on those high society days, I am stunned by my naïveté. I was in my early twenties when I entered the rarified world of Washington parties. My English was a work in progress, which meant I understood very little of what I saw on television or in the newspapers. My husband made no effort to educate me about the people with whom we socialized. He liked to enter with me on his arm, young and pretty and eager, but soon left me to my own devices. Because I did not really know who anybody was or appreciate the exalted positions many of them held, I saw them all as interesting people and was spared the anxiety of trying to be deferential. Perhaps the friendly confidence I exuded through ignorance and guilelessness was refreshing and charming to many of the people whom I met. Whatever the reason, people were always attentive and kind to me, interested in Iran, and patient with my efforts to speak English.

One evening at dinner, I sat next to Vice President Nixon and thought he was just a nice man who seemed vaguely familiar. Trying to make conversation with me, he commented that he really admired Persian carpets and that the Shah had given him a beautiful one. "Oh!' I replied. "You must be important if the Shah gives you a carpet!" It was only when I got home that I discovered why everyone at the table had found my comment so hilarious. I often sat and talked to Supreme Court Justice William Douglas at parties. He was so interesting, so knowledgeable, so liberal, and loved to discuss his experiences in Iran—he had learned impeccable Persian while traveling with the nomadic Qashqai tribe—and the culture and history of the Middle East.

Richard Ettinghausen was another man I was always delighted to see. He was assistant director at the Freer Gallery when I met him, and we became friends after I asked him to show me the collection of Persian art there. At the time, he was teaching at the University of Maryland in the department of Middle Eastern art and philosophy. We did some research together and I even did a little teaching with him. It was through the association with Dr. Ettinghausen that I first became interested in Sufism. Both he and Eugene Black, then head of the World Bank, with whom I also became friendly, served on the cultural committee of the Iran-American Society. While an undergraduate at American University, I was president of the Iranian Women's Organization, so we had various threads to our relationship.

With Robert St. John, the veteran war correspondent and prolific author, and his delightful wife Ruth, I developed a friendship that lasted almost half a century. Robert died in 2003 at the grand age of 101, an astonishing repository of knowledge.

I interacted with so many famous people and, in most cases, never knew it at the time. Even my mentor, Perle Mesta—it was years before I discovered how famous she was, how accomplished and how rich. Little did I realize at the time that she was *the original* "hostess with the mostest," a former ambassador to Luxembourg, the inspiration for Irving Berlin's *Call Me Madam*, and a powerful Democratic Party fundraiser. To me, she was just kind Perle, who initiated me into the world of the Washington hostesses.

I blush now to think of the casual attitude I had towards these people, powerful players in a city in which so much was decided in parlors and behind closed doors. I was full of curiosity, sociable, vivacious, and found this new glittering life exciting. I loved the clothes, the fairy tale transformation—and was close enough in age to the tree-climbing tomboy I had been to approach my social life as a thrilling game, not realizing that the people I associated with were among the most powerful in the world, that this was not "normal," but rather amazingly privileged.

By day, I was a co-ed trudging around campus and taking the bus; by night, a glamorous partygoer arriving in a limousine. It was hard to find time for study; many were the nights that I came home late or waved off the last guest, then sat at the kitchen table with my books until morning. And in between college and partying, I was a mother, raising children, attending PTA meetings, and scheduling parent-teacher conferences with an energy that only youth can provide.

Khosropur was remarkably absent from much of my life, including anything to do with the children's schooling. I recall meeting with the principal of Babak's school to discuss a disciplinary issue. The principal asked me, "Doesn't this boy have a father?" When I said yes, he did, he asked me, "Why does he never come into the school?" I said, "My husband is a very busy man." The principal shot back, "Robert Kennedy is the attorney general of the United States. He has time for his son."

I think of those first fourteen years in the United States as an extended metamorphosis. Like the butterfly for which I was named, I spent these caterpillar years eating voraciously at the fruits of knowledge and experience, determined to emerge with bright, strong wings. I hid many of the transformations from my husband—easy enough to do since he paid so little attention—rather as the chrysalis shields its reformation behind a hard little shell. And when I finally emerged, I was indeed completely transformed from the young bride who had arrived in Washington. I had learned English; I was raising three children; I had a graduate degree; I had achieved success as a hostess, throwing several parties a month and attending many more; I had a wide circle of interesting friends. And soon I would have a professional job, the first paid work of my life, and be financially independent.

My first choice for a workplace was the Library of Congress, which had been the initial inspiration for my graduate degree in Library Science. I applied there and was one of three students from our class offered positions at Grade 9. The other two students, both men, began immediately; but I asked for a month's delay so that I could visit my family in Iran. I was told that I could sign the contract on my return.

In September, imagine my shock when the contract with which I was presented was for Grade 7. I questioned it, saying that my classmates were already at Grade 9, and that this was what I also was promised. I assumed it was a mistake. The head of administration gave me many reasons, but I rejected them all. I told him that I knew three languages whereas the other two were not only not fluent in other languages, neither of them had a Middle Eastern language. I told him that my inferior offer was solely because I was a woman, and tore up the contract in front of him. Despite the fact that the money—even at Grade 7—was excellent,

I knew I would rather work for less in an institution that did not discriminate against me. I was humiliated by my second-class treatment. This was not why I had liberated myself through education.

My first job was at American University. It was wonderful to go back there as a professional. I was a catalog librarian in 1968–69, earning $7,000 a year. That was much less than the $14,000 I might have made at Grade 9 at the Library of Congress, or even the $11,000 at Grade 7 there. But I felt respected as an equal, and that was more important to me.

From 1969 to 1970, I was hired by the University of Maryland to catalog a recently acquired collection of Arabic and Persian literature. My salary went up to $8,000.

In 1970, I moved to the Fairfax County Public Library system in Virginia. I worked there for four years in various libraries as a reference librarian and a reader's advisor. One of my duties was to read stories to groups of children. It makes me laugh when I think back to my performances. I would read very animatedly and the children would gaze at me with rewardingly rapt fascination. My strong accent probably rendered the story quite unintelligible to them and they were mesmerized instead by this strange, lively woman with the weird way of talking.

My husband had thought I was not intelligent enough to drive, and for a long time would not permit me to get a driver's license. Just before I was accepted at Catholic University, he was away for a week at the United Nations in New York and I asked a friend to teach me to drive. When Khosropur returned, I showed him my new driver's license and asked for a car. He bought a new car every two or three years for himself, but for me the first model he had bought in the United States—an old Chevrolet with no air conditioning—was good enough.

The very first thing I did with my first paycheck was to put a down payment on a brand-new car, one that I chose myself. It was a pistachio-green Corvette. How I loved that car! I also bought a pair of totally impractical navy blue shoes with the highest heels imaginable. They were beautiful, hand-made with white working on the leather and very expensive. I reveled in the luxury and the self-indulgence of the purchase. Sitting in my sports car, zooming around in my high-heeled shoes, with my checkbook sitting snugly in my alligator handbag, I thought I was the queen of the world.

While my salary was decent, I wanted to improve my position. I applied twice, without success, to the IMF–World Bank Joint Library. After some research into what kind of people they were hiring, I discovered that Arabic was in high demand. OPEC, formed in 1960, had recently begun to flex its muscles and the IMF and World Bank increasingly focused on oil prices, which had risen dramatically. A number of member countries in the Middle East and Africa spoke Arabic and the Library was increasing its Arabic language holdings.

Georgetown University had a department of Arabic studies and I enrolled immediately. I studied for two years with a wonderful professor, a very scholarly woman who had studied Arabic in her native Germany. Then I reapplied for the IMF–World Bank position.

This time, I received a call for an interview and bingo! I was offered a job as a catalog librarian in Arabic, Persian, Turkish, and Urdu. My salary was $21,000 a year—tax-free. I was in heaven. I worked at the Joint Library from 1974 to 1992. Towards the end, I was earning far more money than my husband had ever earned in this country. I—who was too stupid to drive a car, too intellectually limited to finish high school, too foolish to manage my own finances, good only for having children and acting the hostess—was independent.

Total independence came suddenly. I had long planned to leave my husband—dreamed about it, studied for it, worked towards it—but first I had to get my children established. Babi had graduated from college, Mehri had recently married a lovely man and had a good job, and Sudi was just a few weeks from finishing high school. I was almost there. But just before I could walk out with my head held high, Khosropur made a devastating mistake that precipitated my departure.

I had made use of one of the benefits of working for the IMF at the time by bringing a young Philippina housekeeper from abroad on my visa. I was away in Chicago when Sudi called, begging me to come home immediately. Apparently the housekeeper's sister had telephoned Khosropur, angrily demanding that he keep his hands off the young woman. He took the call in the kitchen, moving into the study so that Sudi could not hear the conversation. But he left the phone off the hook, and when Sudi came into the kitchen, she overheard the heated exchange.

I was disgusted that my husband should care so little for propriety that he not protect his daughter from his sordid secrets. I flew straight home and confronted him. Of course, he denied everything. I was devastated and even considered suicide. But I decided that, after all my preparations for independence, this was not the time. There was no timetable for killing myself, I thought. If I couldn't make things work, there was always next year.

Sudi urged me to leave. I had a good job. I could do it now. After packing a few things, I walked away from my husband, my home, and my oppression. Twenty-five years. It was surprisingly easy to leave it behind. But walking into the apartment I rented, empty save for a bed, was more bitter than sweet. Twenty-five years of hard work had come to this: an empty apartment. I had chosen an apartment building close to the house, and Sudi divided the summer before college between the two places.

Khosropur had one last insult in store for me. Prior to walking out, I had arranged for a big party to be held during the annual meetings of the World Bank. The invitations had gone out and I had placed the order with the caterer. As the date approached, Khosropur came into my office. It was the first contact we had had since I left. He suggested that I come back and host the party. "Then," he said, with absolutely no trace of irony, "then you can leave again."

In 1980, I bought an apartment in Dupont Circle, another milestone in my quest for independence. I loved it. I could walk to work, walk to dozens of restaurants. After so many years in the suburbs, being in the city was energizing and I felt almost unreasonably pleased with myself. I was dating. I had a lot of friends and had found an inspiring Sufi teacher in the managing director of the IMF, Dr. Wittaween, who organized a small group of interested people that met weekly. Once more, a teacher appeared when I most needed one.

Sufism is not a religion, although followers respect all religions, but a beautiful philosophy that seeks harmony, love, and beauty in a world in which human beings and nature are seen as one. I was struck by the similarities with my father's ideas; perhaps this was what attracted me. After Dr. Wittaween left, I continued teaching the class, as I still do today.

In 1985, Khosropur died. Overnight, I became the mother of a teenage boy, Farhad, Khosropur's nephew. After the revolution in Iran, both of Farhad's parents were jailed for six years and he was sent to boarding school in England. Khosropur tried to bring him to the United States, but the hostage crisis effectively cut off visas for Iranians. I could not bear to think of this poor boy all alone in England, so I arranged to adopt him. Because of the semi-diplomatic status accorded to employees at the IMF, I was able to get a G4 visa and bring him to the United States. He was fourteen and a complete stranger to me. He lived with Khosropur for a year or so, and after Khosropur's death I took him in. My sophisticated city life ended abruptly when I sold my apartment and moved back into the family home. It was an odd sensation going back for the first time, but so much had changed in my life that it soon seemed a friendly place again.

It was hard to have a teenager in the house. After quite a tumultuous time with Babak, Sudi had been easy, a good student, and we enjoyed a loving mother-daughter relationship. Not that she was perfect: Her father had bought an elderly convertible in which Sudi drove herself and a group of friends to school. One day I happened to look into that car and to my horror, I saw that she had removed all the seats but the driver's seat, and that had no back. But I had almost forgotten—or possibly repressed—how difficult raising an adolescent boy could be. Suddenly I had to learn about discipline and football, cook mounds of food, wash endless pairs of socks, and watch my basement be transformed into a gymnasium. I read the riot act to Farhad, telling him that while he was with me he had to study, because I did not accept mediocrity and that if something happened to me, he would have no one. And no girls until college.

Farhad kept me on my toes in every way. One day when I went to look for him in his "gym" downstairs, I found him putting up a huge poster of Joan Collins—then starring in the TV series "Dynasty—on which he had written: "Shame on you! She is your age!" I was a bit chubby then, and he shamed me into doing so much exercise with so many weights that I could hardly move the next day. Another time, when I was upset with him over some transgression, I told him that he would receive no more allowance. Later I found a message taped to the refrigerator: "You can punish me any way you want, but not monetarily." He had such a sense of fun and was so charming that I could never stay upset with him. Even if he didn't always do what I wanted, he did what he did with a smile.

Farhad lived with me while studying electronic engineering at George Mason University. His parents were eventually released from prison but one day his mother, who had to report to the police every week, was assassinated. Telling Farhad that his mother, whom he had not seen for so many years, had been brutally killed was one of the most painful things I have ever done. He was finishing his final exams when it happened, and after a lot of thought, I decided to wait until after the last exam to break the sad news. Fortunately Sudi, who had meanwhile earned a master's degree in drama therapy at NYU, was back at home while training at St. Elizabeth's Hospital in D.C.; so between us, we surrounded Farhad with love and support.

These two young people were very close—I might say "partners in crime," because in one week they totaled three cars between them. There were no injuries, although Sudi was thrown into the street in one accident; but my car insurance skyrocketed and I was furious.

When Sudi left again, this time for California where she has lived ever since, I was grateful that I still had Farhad. I missed my daughter terribly, but the nest was very definitely not empty. I had not asked for Farhad or Mehri or, for that matter, various nieces and nephews of my own whose education I sponsored. They dropped into my life. And how grateful I am for these young people. There is nothing more worthwhile than seeing children—it doesn't matter whose—on the path to success.

Suddenly, I was alone again. Farhad left to build a successful career in engineering. His father came from Iran to spend his last five years with his son, and Farhad mischievously told me that everything he did well, his father claimed as good genes; everything wrong was attributed to my bad upbringing. I missed his presence. It had not been easy, but oh, it was worth it. I came to adore this lovable cuckoo that had appeared in my nest. He was, and is, irrepressibly funny and loving; and he and his adorable wife Maryam have repaid me a thousand times over by simply being in my life. And my wonderful Sudi, making her documentaries and living happily with her lovely husband, Rod; I cannot imagine an existence without them. How I wish my father had lived to know them. How I wish they had known him.

Like many women in oppressive marriages, especially foreigners who lose their network of support from family and friends when they come to this country, I had been isolated and undermined by my husband. At first, he controlled almost every aspect of my life—the house in which we lived, our finances, the people with whom we socialized, even my education. But as I persisted at university and first Babi, then Sudi started school and became at home in our adoptive culture, I gained my independence. Little by little I remembered who I was. I was the daughter of a stubborn, capable and determined woman. I was the daughter of a poet who wrote of women:

You are at once both delicate and strong.
Both the oyster's pearl and its nurturing sea.
You are blessed with a keen intelligence
And know full well the power of your mind.
You are both architect and mason,
Building happiness in the world.
When men are blind to women's strengths,
Blind to their worth, society is crippled. How sad.
For where women are paralyzed, so too is the culture.

—from *Aye Zan* (A Woman)

THE WOMEN'S MOVEMENT

I N 1961, confronted by the fact I was not accepted into law school because I was a woman, I began to wonder how I could change this situation.

While still an undergraduate at American University, I had met a very lovely Lebanese-American woman, Patty Mason; tall and slender and elegant, always with a smile on her lips. I was in the cafeteria one day when Patty asked if she could sit with me. We introduced ourselves and started to talk. I was Iranian. She was born in Lebanon. We both spoke French. We looked somewhat alike with our dark hair and eyes. The discussion that started with lunch continues to this day. Patty was in her last year of law school when we met and she encouraged me to apply. Law interested me and I imagined us working together. It didn't work out that way, but we continued to meet and talk.

It was to Patty's law office on K Street NW that I went to share my bitter disappointment at the discriminatory treatment I had received at the Library of Congress. When I told her what had happened, Patty said, "You are not alone." That was when I realized the sad truth—there was no law to protect women. Women in the United States were subject to discrimination at every turn. Patty said men were seen as the head of the family and deserving of more, whereas women—many of whom actually were heads of their families—were seen as having support from family and husbands.

The decade of the 1960s was a very interesting time to be a university student. All around me, students pushed for change. Terrible images from the war in Vietnam and scenes from the growing civil rights movement in the South filled the television screen every night, spilling over into classroom discussions and campus life. Many of us were filled with a desire to do something about it. At the same time the Women's Liberation Movement was gathering strength.

It all seemed to me to have the same root cause: inequality. One group—be it men, whites, or Americans—sanctions, even codifies into law, the use of power over another grouped deemed "inferior." My father had championed the cause of humanism, fighting all his life to expose attacks on personal, social, and political freedom. I saw that these inequalities were not restricted to backward countries like Iran, but also rampant in the United States, the self-styled beacon of freedom for the world. The old bastions of power came under increasing attack, and students on campuses across the nation played active roles in what amounted to a revolt against "business as usual."

With the sting of my law school rejection fresh in my mind, and the daily humiliation of living with a male chauvinist, I began to research why and how, in a country that talks of democracy and freedom, more than half of the population was treated poorly. I saw that indeed I was not alone. Women all over the country began to wake up to their position, just as blacks were doing. Every year, millions of girls and women graduates confronted the same truth: America accorded men and women different social status, with women definitely on the lower rung. Most people saw women as mothers, teachers, librarians, and nurses. Although 90 percent of librarians were women, men occupied 90 percent of the library administration positions.

Women were waking up. President John F. Kennedy ordered a commission on the status of women in 1961. Its conclusion: A big difference exists in compensation to women relative to men in the workforce. The 1963 Congress mandated equal pay, but inequities persisted.

Like many of my contemporaries, I read Simone de Beauvoir's *The Second Sex* and I found it illuminating. After Betty Friedan burst on the scene with *The Feminine Mystique*, more and more women started forming discussion groups to air their grievances and problems. Then in October 1966 the National Organization for Women came into being when three hundred women and men got together to look into women's rights and organize day care centers for working women. Patty Mason called me and suggested we join. We did. The Statement of Purpose of

NOW, as it became known, was to create the conditions for women to fully and equally participate in all aspects of society. Betty Friedan, one of the co-founders of NOW, spoke in terms that resonated strongly with me, particularly when she talked of humanism as a guiding principle.

In 1971 I worked at the Dolley Madison Library in McLean, Virginia, when a new group came together in Washington: the National Women's Political Caucus. I knew that only through political participation could women's rights be heard and represented. This group, which sought to identify and support women seeking public office, represented our best hope. I took a month off work, without pay, to help organize the first national caucus.

Patty Mason and I and ten other women in Washington, D.C., including my neighbor Alice, worked very hard over several weeks to facilitate the meetings that were to be held on July 10 and 11. We organized speakers, selected venues, planned accommodations, arranged the breakfasts, lunches, and dinners, and managed publicity. Actually, publicity all but took care of itself, because the major television networks and newspapers pursued us for information. The event became a national sensation. The more I worked on that conference, the more I loved the participants and identified with the struggle of women for dignity and equality.

Finally, the great day arrived and dozens of women, black and white, representing every walk of life and from all over the country, gathered at the Statler Hotel. This was the same hotel that had been my first home when I arrived in the United States eighteen years earlier; now it hosted the first convention of the National Women's Political Caucus. There was only one foreign woman participant, and that was me.

Our goal was a grand one—to help women get into politics, to change politics from a stage for white men only, so that sexism and racism could be opposed from within the political system and women's issues could get the attention they deserved. It was a non-partisan agenda, concerned only with equality.

During the convention, I was in heaven. I saw finally that my frustrations had a productive outlet and that my daughter might see better days. I listened to the powerful words of Bella Abzug, Shirley Chisholm, Gloria Steinem, Betty Friedan, and others, and I exulted. I remember especially one woman, a black farmer from the South, who stood up and told us, "I plow and seed the fields, I cut trees, and do everything myself with no help. And I am a woman!" A couple of men were also present, including Dr. Benjamin Spock, the pediatrician whose book *Baby and Child Care* was a staple for families raising children. Dr. Spock apologized to the audience for his sexist approach to child-rearing that encouraged parents to view their boys and girls quite differently—the next edition of the book incorporated his more enlightened view. A few months later, when I heard Helen Reddy sing "I am Woman, hear me roar," I threw my arms in the air and roared.

When the case of Roe v. Wade gained national attention, I followed it closely. I felt strongly that a woman's right to control whether and when to have children was fundamental to her true emancipation. I had been lucky; I had enough resources to pay Blanche to help with my children so that I could pursue my education and work. Even though I had at first been horrified to find that I was pregnant with Sudi, her birth meant only a delay of three years in my plans. But when I thought of my mother and how she had suffered to support all those children, of the countless women trapped by unwanted pregnancies, I knew this was a pivotal moment in the nation's history. With a number of other supporters, I joined the vigil outside the Supreme Court as they debated Roe v. Wade in the late fall of 1972. Some opposed to legal abortion showed their contempt by pelting us with eggs and tomatoes. I was not so stalwart as those who braved the cold and stayed overnight. Instead I went home to my children, but I stayed with the vigil keepers in spirit.

It is a magnificent strength of this country that people are free to express their opinions. Let us hope it remains that way. The avenues for expression have now become so varied, the speed of communication so rapid, and the opportunities to disrupt or distort the free flow of information so tempting to those who fear the power of public opinion, that it is hard to discern the fleeting fact from the enduring truth. I wonder how my father, whose pen and voice were his only tools to fight for freedom and reveal corruption, would react to the Internet, to Twitter and Facebook and Wikileaks. I imagine he would rejoice that multitudes of protesters can be mobilized and that government propaganda can instantly be debunked using tiny cell phones—as we see happening today throughout the Middle East, including Iran. Given this democratization of information and the instant communication made possible through today's technology, it is increasingly difficult for oppressive governments to smother their people's cry for freedom and democracy.

On the other hand, with the labor of penning one's words comes the space to reflect and examine one's thoughts, even to discard one line of reasoning and start again. There is so much noise in today's world, so little silent reflection. I think of my father, sitting in his tiny, dark cell, conjuring up the silvery clarity of the nightingale's voice crying "Truth! Truth! Truth!"

My work on the status of American women led to research into the status of women in developing countries. By then I had taken a position as research librarian at the Joint World Bank–International Monetary Fund Library. I spent two years collecting documents from all over the world and discovered some appalling facts. In India, for example, despite a law prohibiting women from being burnt on the pyres of their dead husbands, families still practiced this awful custom. In China, baby girls were being suffocated in the hope that a subsequent child would be a boy. In African countries, women were suffering genital mutilation that destroyed their bodies and any hope of sexual pleasure. Although the life span of women is generally longer than that of men, in Africa women were dying younger from overwork and the custom of receiving the smallest portion of the food they prepared for their families.

I compiled all my research into an annotated bibliography of the status of women around the world.[6] The International Monetary Fund printed my work in 1985, without acknowledging my authorship, and sent a number of copies to the United Nations Women's Day in Nairobi. When they went like hot cakes at the convention, a publisher approached the IMF for publishing rights. The book was published commercially in 1987 by G.K. Hall & Company of Boston, Massachusetts, again without my name on it to my great chagrin. It won an award from the Government Documents Round Table (GODORT) Notable Documents Panel of the American Library Association as one of the Notable Documents of 1987. That book was always dear to my heart. Now that my book of short stories, Abe Porteghal, has been published (Darkou Publications, 2010), I am revisiting that earlier work and bringing it up to date, because I see it as one of the really important areas of research.

In 2010, I bought a computer despite the misgivings of several acquaintances who pronounced me "too old at eighty-two to learn the computer." Since I felt that I did not have time to bumble along and learn the hard way, I took lessons three times a week and practiced for hours a day. From not even knowing how to turn on the computer, I am now able to navigate the Internet and use a word processor, and I am doing what I love—researching the position of women around the globe, albeit this time from the comfort of my own apartment. And this time, I will get the credit!

It is odd, I suppose, that I was involved in freedom movements while I endured such a struggle to free myself. And I couldn't even vote. One would suppose my upbringing, where freedom was espoused as a right even as this right was thrown into question by my family's experiences, might have predisposed me to fight more vigorously for my own place in the world. I think I was so shocked to find myself at such a disadvantage in a foreign country, totally at the mercy of a husband who all but ignored me, and responsible for various children, that I put myself in a special box labeled "later." Certainly I developed a plan to educate myself until I could be self-sufficient. Intellectually, I identified with others who were struggling to realize their self-worth and independence. But I don't believe I saw myself as a mature woman with rights and legitimate needs until I walked away from my second marriage.

Even that is perhaps an exaggeration. I always hoped that a man would come into my life, one with even a fraction of the intellect and humanity with which my father and my brother Mehrdad were endowed. In 1990, I thought I had found such a man, but it was just a chimera. I married again, and for my mistake I suffocated in that marriage for four years until I saw that my choice was to leave or die. Almost overnight I chose life. I moved out and within a week, I had sold my house and moved into an apartment. It was in the same building into which I had moved when I left Khosropur.

I threw a big dinner party in the new apartment for all my friends, many of whom I had not seen for a long time because my husband had sought to isolate me from the friends and activities that had always been my sustenance. At the party, which had been planned some time before, albeit at a different address, I was almost giddy with relief, and so were the friends who had watched me slide downhill, both physically and spiritually, in that awful marriage. One guest sent a huge floral arrangement with a one-word message: LIBERTY! Others brought champagne.

Some friends who were heading off to Maine that week invited me along. In an instant, I accepted. This was the new free me. I had almost forgotten who I am; the person I worked so hard to become. But I have found that if you respect yourself enough, you will grab at life. The week of swimming, laughing, and talking freely among dear friends by a lake in Maine repaired my broken mental and physical health. Even a near calamity when our canoe sank and we all became entangled in submerged fishing lines as we tried to swim to shore was not enough to dampen my newfound enthusiasm for life. I felt like the Phoenix, purified by yet another fire and ready to rise again, albeit a little damp around the edges.

In 1990, the same year that I foolishly married for the third time, I became an American citizen. Even though I had lived most of my life in the United States and my children are American citizens, I had a United Nations GIV visa, first through Khosropur, then through my employment at the IMF. In 1992 I voted in my first-ever presidential election. Actually, it was the first time in my life that I had voted at all! I was so excited that I almost charged into the booth before the person ahead of me had left—sixty-four and giddy as a girl. It was exhilarating and I was sure that on my vote hung the future of the U.S.A.

Lately, I find myself disenchanted with politics and wonder if the time for individual effort has passed as an effective political force. I see more in common than I care to between our current political environment and that of my native Iran, where the preordination of candidates for office and the ideological, arrogant abuse of power at least has an open face. Like my father, I abhor war and human oppression; but I see it all around and it grieves me deeply that so little has changed since he cried, "I curse you, shrieking owl of war!"

Indeed, the owl of war, "dripping blood from its insatiable maw," seems to have grown ever more greedy and arrogant in the half century since my father's death, and "the gains of war" that he threw back in the owl's hateful face seem to have proven irresistible to those who wage it. The cause of peace he so cherished has faded into ineffectual mumbling, and "war" and "peace" can be uttered in the same unblushing breath as justifications for unholy acts of terror. Oh my father, how disillusioned you would be! But then you would take up your pen and compose an impassioned argument for reason and human dignity. Would that your pen were here now to show us a better path.

Father's revolutionary poem *Bird of the Dawn* was set to music and has become an anthem in Iran. Although the government in Iran banned it, this poignant and inspiring song found a groundswell of popularity. It was sung at a fundraiser for the victims of the Bam earthquake in December of 2003. The earthquake killed more than 43,000 people and injured 20,000 more. Bam is an ancient city—over two thousand years old—and the earthquake destroyed most of the mud brick buildings. A father and son sang the anthem at the end of the fundraiser. The popular song is now unstoppable.

So my father's pen is still showing us a better path. My wings have been clipped many times. Each time I escape my cage, just as Father enjoins the bird to do. Like that bird, I "start singing . . . the universal song of human freedom" and I do not stop.

THE U.S. CIVIL RIGHTS MOVEMENT

When you pound a nail into a rock,

The resistance is like that of a person oppressed;

The greater the challenge faced, the greater the strength to resist.

—from *Pafeshari Mikh* (Resistance of the Nail)

W E MOVE back in time. It was 1955. Khosropur and I had arrived in Washington, D.C., with our little son Babak the previous year. I was young and naïve and spoke little English, although I was trying to learn. One night we decided to go to a movie and I looked in the *Washington Post* to choose a show. I found one that started at eight thirty at a theater on U Street NW, and we set off. We knew where to go because we had previously gone to nightclubs along U Street to listen to wonderful music. A parking spot materialized close to the theater's entrance and we purchased our tickets from a young black woman. The film had not started but the lights were off and coming attractions were being advertised on the screen. With some difficulty we found a couple of empty seats in the back of the theater. Once my eyes had adjusted to the dark I realized that all of the other people in the audience were black. This did not surprise me; my only thought was that black people liked the same movies as I did. The film ended at around eleven. We walked back to our car and drove home.

The next morning I was talking to a friend about the film we had seen. She asked me where it was showing. When I told her it was on U Street, she gave me a look of amazement and fear. "You went to U Street?" she gasped. "You went to a *colored* movie theater?"

I was stunned by her reaction. "Why shouldn't I go to any movie I choose? What do you mean, colored theater?" She told me that what we had done was extremely dangerous and that Negroes might kill white people who go to their movies. She lectured me further on the fact that whites in the United States felt that they were a superior race, that colored people lived under different laws and had a separate social life.

I could hardly believe what I was hearing. I stopped her, saying that I understood slavery had been abolished in President Lincoln's time. She did not address that point. She warned me, "Don't do that again. Don't go to that section of the city."

After my friend left, I thought about what she had said, but I didn't believe her. I could not accept that the United States, a symbol of freedom for so many in the world, could have two sets of laws, one for white and one for black citizens.

A few days later the TV, radio, and newspapers carried stories about the ambassador of India, who had been traveling in the southern part of the United States. He stopped at a restaurant to have lunch and had been thrown out by the manager, who told him he had to go to the black section of town. The incident caused great embarrassment to the American government and an apology was issued to the Indian government.

As I thought about this incident, I wondered how people were meant to recognize if a person was Indian, or African, or any other nationality. Why should it matter if a person's skin were dark or light? What did this have to do with eating lunch? Was the only reason the incident caused embarrassment that the man had status as a foreign ambassador? What about all the others who were routinely excluded? There were no articles about that.

In the mid-1950s, my brother Hushang, his American wife Marilyn, and their eight-year-old daughter Roxana were living in a small town in Florida. One morning when Marilyn was driving Roxana to school, her car overheated and broke down. It was hot and they were on a country road. Marilyn hoped someone would come by and help them with a ride. Eventually a school bus appeared, slowing down when the driver saw the car and the two figures stranded by the side of the road. He stopped and asked if he could help. Marilyn was grateful when he obligingly agreed to give them a ride to Roxana's school. The other children on the bus were quiet, and all was well until the bus pulled up in front of her school. The bus driver and all but the two new passengers were black. It transpired that it was against the rules for a "Negro" bus to come into a white school area and even worse that the driver had carried white people on his bus.

The administrators and others at the school were extremely upset and angry. Hushang was called from work. The bus driver lost his job and Hushang nearly lost his job, too, in another school district. All because a compassionate bus driver had helped a woman and her child get to school safely. My brother's family soon left the South, unwilling to raise a child in a place that embraced such oppressive laws. Roxana was strongly affected by her experience, learning at a very young age that good people can suffer terrible consequences from kind acts simply because someone has the power to make it happen.

Earlier that year we had our own experience of Southern discrimination. We decided to vacation in Florida and, to see a bit of the country, included a three-day road trip from Washington through Virginia, North and South Carolina, and Georgia. It became clear as we traveled that blacks and whites were leading very different lives. Everywhere we stopped, we saw water fountains, often side by side, marked "For Whites Only" and "For Coloreds Only." In streets and parks, black people were denied benches to sit on; they too were labeled "For Whites Only." Public toilets were the same. The movie theaters and restaurants were separate as well. I was used to people facing discrimination for their political beliefs or their gender in Iran—but this was America! I was discovering the truth of what my friend had told me: there really were two separate races of people living in the same country with different laws. And I saw that white people did believe that they were superior to black people. What I didn't know was how this reality would soon affect my family directly.

In Miami, we were staying at a hotel, enjoying the sunshine. Babak was playing in the pool while I lounged in a chair nearby. Suddenly the manager of the hotel blew a loud whistle and started shouting, "Hey! Nigger! Get out! Hey! Get that nigger out of the water!" I had heard the word "nigger" used to refer to black people although I didn't yet know what it meant. I looked around the pool and I couldn't see a black person anywhere. Then it dawned on me: He was pointing to my son, to my little Babak, whose olive skin quickly becomes dark when exposed to the sun, and was yelling in a loud voice, "Nigger! Hey nigger! Who gave you permission to swim in a white pool?"

I jumped from my seat and shouted at the manager, "This is my son! We are guests at your hotel." The manager saw me as a young white woman, and looked confused. "Oh, I didn't know he was your son; he's colored." One of the hotel staff was now trying to drag Babak out of the pool. When I shouted, "Who do you think you are, taking my child out of the pool?" the manager looked at me and asked, "Well, is he white or colored?"

"What difference does it make?" I protested. "I am your guest, and you have no right to throw him out of the pool!" In my rage, I told him that he would regret attacking my son. I would ask my husband to complain about him to the government. I had no idea how naïve my words were. The manager looked at me, a great sarcastic smirk on his face, and turned away without a word, leaving us standing there. I was shivering despite the heat and muttering to myself, "Is this America? America where everyone in the world wants to come and live? Is this Lincoln's and Washington's America?" I took Babi by the hand and we returned to our room.

Khosropur was lying on the bed, taking a nap. He was alarmed to see me shaking with anger and asked what had happened. When I told him that the hotel manager had tried to throw Babak out of the pool because his skin turned dark in the sun, that they thought he had no right to use the pool, he tried to soothe me, saying, "That is not important. In America, black people don't have the same rights as white people. Didn't you know that?" I shot back, "Are you serious? Different rules for black and white? I don't—won't—understand that. How could the color of your skin make your destiny?" He tried to calm me. "Don't take it so seriously. This is not our country. It doesn't matter to us how blacks are treated. Why should you care?" I was speechless. Then I said, "It *does* matter, even if it's not my country. All human beings are the same for me and the color of a person is not important. How can you accept these stupid laws?" He turned his back and did not answer.

That afternoon we planned to take a tour bus around Miami Beach. The bus had signs that indicated that one part was designated "Whites Only" and the other part was for "Coloreds." The line was clear—even if there were no seat available at the back of the bus and the front section was empty, a black person could not move past that powerful boundary. As I understood the meaning of this awful and arbitrary line, I felt sick. In Washington, D.C., buses and trains did not attempt to separate people. I told Khosropur we should get off the bus and use our car to see Miami Beach. When he saw my distress, he agreed. But between the bus and our car he told me, "You should not care about Americans. We are Iranians and we should take advantage of the good things that America offers and ignore the others." But it was impossible for me not to care, although I did not know what, if anything, I could do about it.

After we returned from Florida I was talking one day to our housekeeper, Blanche, about our trip and about the injustices I had seen. Blanche looked at me levelly and said, "Mrs. K, this is the beginning. You have just opened your eyes and seen how we have lived all these years."

I thought about what she said. I decided to talk to my English teacher, Ella Harllee, whom I respected and trusted. I asked her how such injustices could persist in the country that I believed to be the home of freedom and equality. As a young Persian woman coming to America, one who had witnessed injustice—indeed, experienced it first-hand—I idealized America's promise of liberty and justice for all. My expectations were so very different from the shocking reality I met.

Ella shared my views about discrimination. She told me to go to the National Archives and read the Constitution and the Bill of Rights—the actual documents—for myself, so that I might gain an appreciation for their intent and majesty. The harsh realities of life for black Americans began to consume me. It was all so wrong, so against everything in which I believed. The more information I gathered, the more sadness, hurt, and indignation I experienced on behalf of my fellow human beings. I could not bear to see the United States, my adoptive country, divided by color. I became intensely attentive—obsessively attentive—to the news and felt I had to know every minute what was happening all over the country in issues relating to race. I had never so eagerly awaited my husband's return from the office, bombarding him with questions and demanding he watch the news and tell me what was happening.

On December 1st of the same year as our troubling trip to Florida, the story of what Rosa Parks did in Montgomery, Alabama, was all over the news. Then came the bus boycott, the fines, police harassment, trickery, deception, and finally violence. Dr. Martin Luther King's house was bombed. Every day the news got worse and worse, but I couldn't stop watching and reading. I was still angry about our small indignity in Florida and it was nothing, nothing compared with what was happening in Alabama. I remembered my father's words: "In life, always take the road of truth even though you may lose. Always take the side of the oppressed. This is the purpose of life." He had said to me that the only people he despised were the oppressors. It helped me to ask myself: If Father were alive and could see what the government was doing to these oppressed people, what would he do about it?

The boycott went on, and the black community became ever more united. I was elated about the triumph of reason and decency when the Supreme Court ruled on bus segregation in 1956. Now things would improve and whites would see that integration was not only possible, but also the right thing. But no—a wave of terror broke out. White snipers shot at the buses, churches were bombed, the homes of black leaders were bombed, cab companies were bombed. The images in the media were appalling. Little *children* were killed! I thought about the times my father fought for freedom in Iran, of his imprisonment, his exile, the assassination attempt he escaped. He had faced terror again and again, but he never stopped fighting. I heard his voice from prison, talking to me. I remembered part of his great epic poem *Morghe Shabahang*, written while he was in prison:

Listen, my daughter. Listen very carefully.
Oppression strangles life.

But after every dark night, there is always a dawn.
While I may not live to see justice, I want you to remember:
You must stand up and fight for what you believe.
When you fight for freedom, you stay the oppressor's hand.
I want you to remember. Fight for your own liberation
But fight also for all who have been enslaved.

Increasingly agitated, helpless, and anxious, I watched as peaceful sit-ins turned violent, as white teenagers attacked black students. Police dragged people into the street, beat them, hosed them, jailed them, trampled them beneath the hooves of horses, killed them. Thousands were arrested. But when I heard the voice of Dr. Martin Luther King, I heard the voice of Gandhi and the call to work through peaceful means.

Then came the news of the Freedom Riders, and of martial law. I could hardly believe it. The army called in because people exercised their guaranteed rights! I had come from a country where people were afraid to speak their minds, where the army could step in, where you could be thrown into jail on a whim—but again, this was America! I watched terrible things on television. I saw the police use dogs, cattle prods, fire hoses, and bull whips against American citizens who were only asking that their constitutional rights be respected. In Iran, repression was carried out secretly. Here it was out in the open, shamelessly, on television for all to witness.

In the spring of 1963, the children's march in Birmingham ended in a show-down. We all watched on television and read in the newspapers. Children were hosed with powerful water pressure and attacked by dogs. I thought, "These could have been my children." It was amazing and terrible. It was not the same form of oppression we suffered as children at the hands of the Shah. Here were free adults doing violence to children who were innocent, who should have been protected by the very people who inflicted the harm. It was shameful and cor-rupting of all who participated.

But as my father said, "After every dark night, there is always a dawn." Bit by bit, even though every step of the way they met fierce resistance, black activists achieved their goals through peaceful means. For a different struggle in a different era Father wrote a poem, *Koushesh va Omid*, "Perseverance and Hope," that was taught to schoolchildren to inspire them never to give up on their dreams:

A little spring bubbled up from the earth.
It trickled happily down the mountain
Until suddenly, a large boulder blocked its path.
Humbly it said to the stubborn stone
"Be kind to me, blessed one, and let me pass."
The proud and selfish boulder, jealous of its situation,
Slapped his face and growled, "Go away, sonny!
I won't move for the likes of you!"
Undaunted by the stony response,
The spring gathered its strength and began to press.
It dug and delved and strove until
A little path was carved around the boulder.
With perseverance, you can achieve anything in life.
No goal is beyond your reach.
Go on, work with hope in your heart
Because despair begets nothing but death.
If you persevere in all your endeavors,
Any obstacles on your road will dissolve.

I saw that this was happening in the South. What started as a trickle rapidly turned into a flood. Like many others I felt elated, but also angry and helpless, knowing I wanted to do something but not knowing how I could join my voice with the great river of those crying for freedom. By merely witnessing these events, I felt responsible. Then came an announcement that a march was planned in Alabama for Sunday, March 21, 1965. It was to be a fifty-mile march starting in Selma and ending in Montgomery, led by Dr. King. Immediately I knew what I could do.

My husband was away on a trip to Africa. I asked Blanche if she would stay with Babak and Sudi for the weekend while I went to Alabama. She was willing to stay but she told me it would be dangerous. When she saw how firmly committed I was, she offered to help. "You can stay with my cousin in Montgomery. She will pick you up from the airport and you can march with her behind Martin Luther King. At least you won't be alone," she said.

I left at ten o'clock on Saturday, March 20, arriving in Montgomery at four in the afternoon. Blanche's cousin, Mrs. Andrea Black, waited for me with a big sign with my name on it. When I approached her and told her my name, she hugged and kissed me and thanked me warmly for coming.

We took a bus to her home, both sitting in the back. She lived with her husband and two young sons in what the whites called the "colored section" of town, in a small wooden house with peeling paint, much in need of repair. We went up a few steps to a covered porch, furnished with two small wicker chairs, then through a screen door. A kitchen with a modest table and a few chairs occupied the right side of the house; there were two bedrooms on the left. Behind the kitchen was a small room with a little wooden bed that Andrea had prepared for me. Poverty was very much in evidence; they had so little, but everything was neat and clean.

After a while, Andrea's husband returned home from his job as a truck driver. Like Blanche, Andrea was Jamaican, but Mr. Black was American. They had met in Washington, D.C., when Andrea was working for a diplomat, and then moved south to be near his parents when they were expecting their first baby. While the children, who were about the same ages as mine, were at school, Andrea worked in white people's houses, doing their ironing.

I brought my bag, containing little more than trousers and walking shoes, into my room. The room had a window with a white shade that opened onto the street. There was a small table with a lamp on it, and on the wall behind the bed, a cross. Tired, I lay down on the bed, enjoying the wonderful aroma of coffee percolating and what smelled like a lovely stew simmering in the kitchen. I listened to the sounds drifting in from the street—children playing and talking to each other, but I couldn't understand what they said. I closed my eyes and let my mind wander back to Iran and my father's house, to my mother, my brothers, my sisters, and my nanny. Here I was, in the home of a complete stranger, feeling safe and welcomed.

I was lost in my thoughts—or maybe I was asleep—when Andrea called me to dinner. I jumped up, embarrassed that I hadn't helped her. The kitchen was also living room, dining room, and workroom. Andrea's husband was setting the table and seated me between himself and their elder son. We sat together and held hands while Andrea's husband said grace in his deep voice: "Dear Lord, we thank you for our food tonight. Lord, we thank you for our dear guest who is here with us tonight. Dear Lord, we ask that tomorrow's march will be peaceful. Lord, please help us."

My guess was correct—dinner was a stew, and it was delicious. After the children went to bed we sat in the kitchen and talked. I told them about Iran and our life there, and translated one of my father's poems, "The Beggar Girl," for them. They loved the poem and asked many questions about Iran.

The atmosphere between me and this kind and hospitable family relaxed over the course of the evening. I think they had been wary, even a little suspicious of my motives in coming to Selma. They probably wondered if I were one of those whites who want to show off how liberal and progressive they are by getting involved in black causes. Once they learned how my family had been subjected to the cruelty and oppression of arrogant and powerful people, that my father had fought against that power and made a common cause of all oppression, they embraced my participation.

Andrea and her husband were religious people whose faith informed every aspect of their lives. They talked about the other marches and demonstrations in which they participated. Mr. Black said a prayer, thanking God nothing happened to him before to prevent him from carrying out his duties as a husband and father. He asked for protection for us all the next day. These courageous people seemed more concerned for my safety than their own. I was grateful I would march beside them.

We were in bed by nine o'clock, as we had to get up very early to catch the bus to Selma. I slept very deeply that night.

In the morning, Andrea said softly, "Mrs. K, please get up; coffee and breakfast is ready in the kitchen." Breakfast was bread and butter and jam. I asked who would stay with the children. Andrea's husband was just saying that his mother was coming when she walked in. I rose and she came over and hugged me, saying, "Thank you for your support. I will be here until you come back." The warmth and hospitality of black Americans I have known always reminds me of Iran, where a guest is seen as a gift and hospitality is a point of honor.

We joined many neighbors who were heading down the street to the church where three special buses waited to take us to Selma. I sat next to Andrea and her husband sat behind us. When the bus started to move, everyone sang "We shall overcome" and various religious songs. As one person began a song, everybody else would pick it up. It was joyful, full of energy and hope. I had never experienced anything like it.

It took us about two hours to get to Selma, where several thousand people stood around the church, waiting for Dr. King. When he arrived, he went to the microphone and spoke to us in his powerful voice, inspiring us to march on Washington itself if we had to. It was hard to hear, because helicopters were flying overhead. The media filmed us on either side of the street, and the National Guard stood there.

Then the march began. We took each other's hands and began singing "We shall overcome" over and over again. Behind the National Guard, white people held big insulting signs and cursed and shouted at us, but we remained completely calm. I wondered how many of the marchers had been beaten back in other peaceful demonstrations. How brave they were.

I was absolutely stunned by the organization, the humanity, the dignity, and the politeness of the marchers. We walked slowly through the city without incident. When we crossed the Pettus Bridge, where Dr. King and other protesters had been turned back in an earlier march by state troopers armed with clubs, tear gas, and electric cattle prods while whites cheered them on, our steps quickened and our voices grew louder. This time, the march was allowed to pass because federal troops protected us.

As my own voice merged with those of all the courageous people around me, I was reminded of my father's words in his poem *Naleh Melat* (The Cry of the People):

There is a sound

More powerful and fearsome than the boom of a cannon

Or the howl of a warrior in battle,

More than the crash of lightning in the darkness,

The typhoon pounding the shore with killer waves

Or even the roar of an erupting volcano.

More powerful than all these sounds is the cry of injustice

From those without hope,

From those who have been oppressed.

This is the loudest sound of all.

Night approached. It was the first day of spring and the air was cool. The marchers took Route 80 from Selma, covering over seven miles by the time we reached the first campsite at the property of a black farmer named David Hall. A few buses were parked in front of the farm and the women and older men were asked if they wished to return to Selma. The march would resume the next morning and the organizers hoped to cover more ground on the second day.

Andrea's husband, along with most of the men, remained. Andrea and I took the bus back to Selma and then to Montgomery. It was close to midnight when we got back to her house. Her mother-in-law was waiting for us but the boys were asleep. I spent the night in the same little room behind the kitchen and returned to Washington the next day.

My children loved Blanche so much that they had hardly missed me. When I arrived home, I told her everything. I followed the rest of the march on television. On the second day, the marchers reached the outskirts of Montgomery. Thousands more people joined the march and they arrived at the State Capitol building. Dr. King took the microphone and spoke to the crowd. "What do we want?" he asked. "Freedom!" they roared with tremendous power. Indeed it was "the loudest sound of all."

When Dr. King was assassinated on April 4, 1968, I cried more than I ever remember crying before. Khosropur commented, "If I had been assassinated, I don't think you would have cried like that." He was right. My only comfort was the knowledge that Dr. King's words of truth and inspiration remained with us, and that his leadership did not die with him.

Today, at least in law, we have equality, and many improvements came from the Civil Rights movement. But no law can change divisions in the heart and mind; that takes generations and education. It is up to each of us to refuse to countenance the oppression of any person, for any reason, to strive and strive until we carve a way around the many boulders that stand in our way and in the way of our fellow human beings, to fight for our own liberation, but fight also for all who have been enslaved.

EPILOGUE

WITH SURPRISING speed, the Revolution of 1978–79 in Iran brought down the Pahlavi monarchy and replaced it with an Islamic theocracy under the supreme leadership of Ayatollah Khomeini. What happened in Iran was a true revolution. The wheel turned and the top went to the bottom and the bottom came to the top. Those who had been powerless and oppressed were suddenly in charge. The privileged, the powerful, the well-connected had the rug pulled out from under them. Those who did not escape the country in the tumultuous months of demonstrations and strikes faced the loss of position and property, imprisonment and in many cases, execution.

Opposition to Khomeini's appointed government was declared "warring against God." His followers systematically crushed royalist opposition and competition from other groups that had worked for the revolution. They took control of the military, police, government offices, and means of communications. After a brief, hopeful period, the provisional secular government was disbanded. Khomeini's vision of an Islamic Republic of Iran began to materialize. The Revolution had been hijacked. Very early on, Khomeini established the *Pasdaran*, or Revolutionary Guard, as his enforcement arm. The Revolutionary Guard has evolved into the strongest player in the economy and politics of Iran today.

Overnight, everything changed profoundly. Women who had been used to wearing what they liked had to don *chadors* in public and morality police roamed the streets, beating and arresting those who did not comply. Men abandoned neckties as too Western, and sported beards as a sign of piety. Women were not allowed to be in the company of any man who was not a relative. If the police found a man and woman walking together in the street, they would stop them. If they had no document showing the woman was the sister, mother, daughter, or wife of the man, the couple would be taken to the police station.

The marriage age was dropped, and girls were considered legally mature enough at age nine to consent to marriage. Boys and girls were separated in schools and universities; in many other areas of life, gender segregation became the norm. While the position of women had crept forward only slowly under the Shah, and *sharia* law was the basis of "family law," the post-revolutionary climate for women was particularly shocking for the westernized middle class and elite sectors in Iran.

I did not go to Iran for many years after 1979. For one thing, I was not confident I would be able to leave again. I did not have an Iranian passport. And even after I had a U.S. passport I could not use it to visit Iran. If you were born in Iran, you must travel on a Persian passport when you are there. Following the hostage crisis of 1979, diplomatic relations between the U.S. and Iran ended, and with the Iranian embassy in Washington closed, I could not renew my Iranian passport. The long years of separation from my family and friends were extremely painful for me, but finally I was able to get a new Iranian passport through the Iranian Interest Section at the Pakistan embassy. I could go to Iran. But would I go? It seemed Iran was always on the front pages and none of it was good.

The Cultural Revolution, so like China's with its purges and thousands of executions, the eight-year war with Iraq during which half a million died and Iran's cities were battered nightly by air attacks, the hostage crisis, Iran's increasing isolation—I watched the news like a person possessed. I was afraid of what might happen in a country that had become totally foreign to me, where public executions were common, where women could be beaten or arrested at the whim of the morality police, where even getting in a taxi alone was impossible, and where staying in a hotel was forbidden to me.

In 1982 I decided to enlist the help of my sister Cherry, who was visiting her daughter in Paris. After spending two wonderful weeks together in Paris, the three of us flew to Iran on Iran Air. As we approached Tehran, the pilot announced in a loud voice that all the women on board, Iranian or foreign, had to enter the country wearing *hejab* or Islamic clothing. This meant a very long robe or ankle-length coat over the clothing. Hair must be covered by a scarf or *chador*; only the face and hands could show.

Reza Shah had banned the *chador* in 1936, but after his forced abdication many women from conservative families took to wearing it again. It was considered backward and lower class by most middle and upper class people during the era of the Shah's reign, and women who wore it were discriminated against in many workplaces and elite social settings. It would have been amusing to watch a plane full of fashionably dressed women quickly disappearing behind shapeless, dark coats, and covering their elegant hairstyles with *chadors* or scarves, if I had not been so nervous. During the whole flight from Paris, I had been increasingly anxious. By the time Tehran appeared below us, I felt sick and shaky.

As a precaution against having my U.S. passport taken from me, which I heard had happened to other Iranian Americans, I took a handbag made with a false bottom so that I could hide it. As we touched down, I cursed the day I had thought up such a foolish scheme. The passport seemed to be burning through my bag and into my legs. The authorities would be sure to find it and then what would happen to me?

Once the plane landed, a bus drove up to meet us on the tarmac. On the bus was written *Marg bar Emricah*, "Death to America." We were directed to the women's line for immigration. My sister and niece went through very fast, but my Iranian passport was confiscated and I was taken for interrogation. It was very, very frightening. Police surrounded me and pointed their guns at me. I could feel their revolutionary zeal even though thirteen years had passed since the Revolution. It seemed all these men despised me for arriving on a plane from elsewhere and for being a woman.

The authorities questioned me for seven hours. Why had I not returned to Iran? I explained I had no passport. There was no diplomatic relationship between Iran and the U.S., so there was no embassy. Many other questions were fired at me, such as Do you believe in the Revolution? Do you support Ayatollah Khomeini? Are you a communist? I was expecting to be sent home on the next plane or, worse, arrested and thrown into prison.

As morning came and the sun rose, the night shift ended and the day shift took their place. Instead of the very aggressive and misanthropic official with whom I had been dealing, a nice young man appeared. He took my passport and started to read it. My last name, where I was born . . . all of a sudden he saw the name of my father, Mohammad Taghi Bahar. He looked at me with great amazement. "Are you really the daughter of Malek o'Shoara Bahar?"

"Yes, I am."

Then slowly he said, "Your father was the father of our education system. He was a great poet who gave great service to this country."

At this point I started crying. I was exhausted from the trip, from the seven hours of interrogation and the fear. The tears rolled down my face as I said in a loud voice, "Because of the services of my father, and because my family has done so much for Iran, is this the reason you won't allow me to enter the country of my birth?" The young man right away picked up all my belongings, which were scattered on the floor, and put them into my suitcases. He called for someone to take the suitcases and told me I was free to join my family. He added, "I am sorry you endured so much pain on your first visit back to Iran." And I believed him.

I felt my father had come to my rescue, and remembered how my mother, arriving at London Heathrow, had loudly proclaimed in Persian that she was the wife of Malek o'Shoara Bahar as though that was the magic that opened any door. I cleaned up my face but I knew I looked like a tired old woman, especially without makeup and with my hair covered up. My family was waiting outside, convinced I would end up in jail, if I were even allowed into the country. They were so relieved to see me. I was shaking with pent-up anxiety.

We got into a taxi and started towards Cherry's house. In the morning light, I looked upon a monochrome city that reminded me of Paris immediately after World War II. All the color in Tehran had been sucked out by the Revolution. Everything looked either black or gray, except for the huge portraits of Khomeini and other leaders that hung from public buildings. I thought back to the days before the Revolution, when the women were dressed in colorful clothing, bare-headed, free to go where they wanted. Those that wore *chadors* tended to wear pretty colors, pretty floral patterns, not these black, flapping, crow-like garments traditionally associated with death. The civilian men all looked as though they were in uniform, and I had never seen so many beards. The city was full of police with rifles on their shoulders. It looked like a place under siege.

As we approached my sister's home, I thought of my mother, who died in 1979, during the Revolution. Had she not died, I would be going to her house to stay. I remembered how she would be waiting for me on my other trips home. During her last twenty years, she was crippled and couldn't walk, so she would wait at her home for me, right by the door. The plane would always arrive in Tehran after midnight, but for my mother there was no time. She sat and sat until I arrived, no matter how long it took.

On the way to Cherry's home, we passed our old house. How I missed my mother. Tehran did not seem the same without her. I couldn't even come to say good-bye to her in 1979, as she lay dying. I had lost all that love that she gave unconditionally to me all my life. How we all take it for granted, as though our parents are going to live forever and there will always be time to thank them for their love. This chance to see my remaining brother and three sisters was heavenly, but of course none of them could take the place of my mother.

I stayed one month in Tehran. I left Cherry's home very rarely. Getting around was such a production that it hardly seemed worthwhile. I felt as though I couldn't see properly, all wrapped up in my black camouflage, making the uneven pavement, the crush of people, and the cars flying past just too hard to navigate. The legendary Tehran traffic seemed to have grown even more terrible with the rapid growth in population. It was not helped by the *Pasdaran* stopping taxis to check the passengers inside. Every now and then they would arrive in a great group in the street and apprehend young women for infractions. Theoretically, as a post-menopausal woman, many of the strictures no longer applied to me, but I was not going to test that theory. Police targeted women, especially the young ones. It seemed to give them great satisfaction to humiliate women and keep everyone in a state of anxiety.

Of course, Iranians are a defiant people and many took delight in finding ways around the system. New satellite dishes sprang up on roofs as quickly as their predecessors were confiscated. People held parties with music and dancing and home-brewed wine and spirits, despite the occasional raids. Chic women wore the latest fashion under their *chadors*. Despite this, theocracy lay like a dead hand on the city. It felt stifling.

After a month, I anticipated my return to the U.S. with enormous relief. But leaving Iran proved to be as complicated as arriving there. The day before departure, you were required to give your passport to the *Pasdaran*. Just as with the incoming flights, planes left at an ungodly hour and you had to be at the airport well before dawn—the only advantage being that the traffic was bearable at that hour. Once you arrived at the airport, you had to collect the passport from the police. If you had not been cleared to leave, your passport was not there. The manipulation was elegant in its simplicity.

I hardly slept for several nights for fear that I would not be allowed to leave. To my great relief, my passport was at the airport and after an hour, I finished with emigration and was ready to depart. My American passport still burned a hole in the false bottom of my bag, but its hiding place was undetected. After the unnecessary trauma of worrying about it, on future trips I left my U.S. passport with a friend in Paris.

As the plane took off, I found that I was weeping; though I thought I had forgotten my old memories of fear and oppression, my body had not. I might have been back in Shahrbani prison with Mehrdad, almost passing out with terror as the guard patted our little bodies before letting us visit our father in his tiny dark cell. I looked at the Alborz Montains surrounding Tehran. Everything had changed except those eternal mountains. The snow covering the peak of Damavand gleamed in the early morning sun and I thought of my father's fiery tribute to the mountain as a symbol of freedom. Though the Revolution had removed the monarchy against which he struggled, sadly the words from *Damavandieh* still rang true:

A warrior's silver helmet adorns your head,
But a slave's iron band encircles your waist.

An hour or so after departure, the pilot announced we were no longer over Iranian territory. The whole plane sighed with relief. I had heard that sometimes a plane is recalled when the authorities realize that by mistake they have allowed someone to leave whom they wished to detain. This time I was able to enjoy the transformation of the women as they tore off their *chadors* and coats and scarves and disappeared into the ladies' room, reappearing with makeup and coiffed hair, their crow personas left behind in the Islamic Republic.

After this first trip to Iran in 1982, I started to have more courage and went every year. I always stayed with my youngest sister, Cherry. Each time I looked for any changes that had transpired since my last visit. I could see that, little by little, the *Pasdaran* were a less visible presence in the streets. The young women still wore a version of *hejab*, Islamic clothing, but they seemed to be pushing the limits. Colored scarves replaced the depressing black, and some girls pushed their scarves back to show their lustrous hair. The *chador* or long robe was replaced by shorter robes or even fitted jackets. Makeup appeared. In the parks of Tehran I saw girls and boys walking and talking together; even a few daring couples holding hands. The ugliness I saw in my early visits almost disappeared. There were still many *chadors*, but the overwhelming feeling of restriction and oppression was dropping away for many young people. And young people are by far the largest demographic group, largely the result of Khomeini's successful call for women to have many children "for the Revolution."

According to the World Bank, the under-thirty group comprises two thirds of the population, and a quarter of the population is under fifteen.[7] When I was born, the population of Iran was about ten million; when I left for the United States in the early 1950s, it was just less than twenty million. Today the population is more than seventy-five million and still climbing, making Iran one of the twenty most populous countries in the world.

Schools that were co-ed before the Revolution are now completely segregated. The little girls going off to school have to wear a scarf, but they do *go* to school and the literacy rate for females has more than doubled since the Shah's reign. Many of the urban schools have two shifts a day to accommodate the huge number of children.

To matriculate, you must pass a test, and girls have outscored boys and won more places in universities. The revolutionary attitude that a woman's role is in the home raising children has changed by necessity: The government slowly realized that the country needs educated women. At the beginning of the Revolution, universities did not allow women to study science, engineering, technology, or medicine but have now opened these fields up to women. Now there is a shortage of educated men in the sciences, and quotas have been introduced to balance the numbers. Women now comprise about 65 percent of the students enrolled in Iran's universities. Like me, they have come to see education as their way out of oppression.

I saw women doing all kinds of work in Tehran, from driving buses and tractors to working for the government or entering politics. There was an atmosphere of hope in the air. The reformist President Khatemi seemed to embody a new progressive view and the dead hand seems to have lifted off the people's backs.

Heartened by what I saw around me in Iran, I started to write my memoir in English, so my children would know where they had come from and could learn about my father and my life. A publisher in Iran approached me to write the book in Persian. This was quite difficult for me as I had left the country with only an eighth-grade education, and my Persian was not sophisticated at all. To my surprise, I found writing in Persian liberated me. It took me back to the places I remembered with an immediacy I had not been able to achieve when writing in English. The voices came back to me and I heard again the conversations, smelled the garden, and wandered in my mind through the rooms of our family house. The writing was very simple and straightforward and honest, as though I had never learned to see the world with anything but a child's honest gaze.

To my great amazement, the memoir was published in 2004 in Iran and became a best seller, not only in Iran but also in countries with Persian-speaking communities like Tajikistan and Afghanistan. I even received a letter from the minister of education in Afghanistan, congratulating me on writing about my father and continuing his legacy.

For me, this success gave new meaning to my life and encouraged me to organize an apartment in Tehran, where I could continue to write for several months a year. After fifty-three years of living away from Tehran, I had "a room of my own." It was very exciting. My apartment had one bedroom, a living-dining room, a very nice kitchen, and a bathroom. All the windows opened to the Alborz Mountains. When I sat behind my desk, which was also my dining table, looking at the mountains and writing, I was filled with energy. At night I could see lights right up to the snow line; hotels and restaurants and apartments rose up before my eyes. When I was a child, we were in the last line of houses and the mountains were far away with no buildings visible between us and them. I furnished the apartment very fast, perhaps reflecting the mixed feelings I had about being anchored once more to my birthplace. Although I was born and grew up there and could speak the language, I felt like an outsider, not conversant with the changed society. I had to learn the culture like any foreigner would.

In 2006, I went to Tehran in winter, my first winter there for decades. I asked one of my friends to take me to the ski resort on Mount Damavand, about forty-three miles from Tehran. We drove up into the mountains for an hour, passing many villages. When I was young girl, these really were rural hamlets, but no longer. Now they are filled with apartment houses and new stores, serving as dormitory towns for Tehran.

When we arrived at the resort I felt a wonderful calm come over me. It was such a relief to escape the pollution of the city air and the thick fog of politics, and I felt free and clean. I discovered many young women and men dressed in ski clothing and skiing together. I asked my friend how this could be. She said the government tried to enforce separate ski slopes, but it was too impractical, not to mention difficult to police, so they let them ski together. It was a beautiful image: There on top of the highest mountain in Iran, the symbol of freedom and resistance throughout the long history of Persia, only there on the glorious, snow-covered volcano, Damavand, could men and women throw off the "slave's iron band" and be free to be themselves.

On this trip I abandoned scarf and robe and took to wearing a hat and coat instead. Sporting dark glasses, I walked freely in the streets and museums. Perhaps I was taken for a tourist, but I was never bothered. Little by little I realized how many women were working. Everywhere I went—museum, bank, subway, government office—I saw working women, some occupying senior positions. I was surprised, because when I was a teenager in Tehran, I never saw women working outside their homes. Only one or two of my classmates went on to university. A handful of women held top government positions under the Shah, but it was unusual.

But today's women have awakened to the liberating power of financial self-sufficiency. They see that, without an education, their rights will be denied them and they will be powerless. The women of Iran have staged a non-aggressive revolution of their own. Of course, there have been activist women dating back to the Constitutional Revolution in which my father was involved a hundred years before, and the list is long of magnificent and brave Iranian women who have worked against gender discrimination. Until finally crushed by Reza Shah as dangerous and subversive, there were women's organizations, women's interest newspapers and journals, and activists, poets and writers who called for equality and changes to the laws that shackled women to their fathers and husbands. But even under the repressive conditions the quiet push for equality never went away.

During the reign of the last Shah, slow but steady progress was made in revising laws prejudicial to women, led by public figures such as Farrokhroo Parsa, the brilliant physician who became a member of parliament and minister of education. But after the Revolution, all this changed and most of the hard-won gains were lost overnight. Removal of women from the workplace and a strict interpretation of Sharia—even to the point of bringing back polygamy, stoning for adultery, and the practice of short-term marriages or *sigheh*—seemed to spell the end for progress for women's rights. It was a bit like the U.S. after World War II—only more sinister—when women who had gained independence through the workplace were effectively thrown back into the kitchen and the bedroom.

One of the tragic casualties was Farrokhroo Parsa. For her work to get the vote for women and to enact the Family Protection Act of 1975 to improve the legal position of women and children, she was executed by firing squad on May 8, 1980 in Tehran, charged with the crime of "spreading vice on earth and warring against God."

In her last letter from prison, Dr. Parsa wrote to her children: "I am a doctor, so I have no fear of death. Death is only a moment and no more. I am prepared to receive death with open arms rather than live in shame by being forced to be veiled. I am not going to bow to those who expect me to express regret for fifty years of my efforts for equality between men and women. I am not prepared to wear the *chador* and step back in history."[8]

I met this courageous and passionate woman several times when I was president of the Iranian Women's Association of the United States. Her strong conviction that women should stand side by side with men as free and equal partners in democracy echoed my father's beliefs, and filled me with determination to follow in their footsteps.

For the growing number of women of Iran who have refused to accept their lot, the stakes are very high. As soon as Khomeini's intentions became known, there were demonstrations by Iranian women's rights activists and they have continued despite mass arrests and imprisonments, torture, and even death. The protests have been peaceful, but the response has not.

Every year on International Women's Day, for example, rights activists march to raise awareness of gender apartheid and commemorate those who were arrested or lost in the previous march; the cycle is self-perpetuating. After every march, a long period ensues when planners and participants are arrested, tried for "endangering national security," and sent to jail or even exile. One recent feature in the struggle for women's rights, which is growing exponentially under the banner of "Change for Equality," is the Campaign for One Million Signatures for the Repeal of Discriminatory Laws, a peaceful movement started in August 2006 that highlights the broad opposition to laws discriminating against women. Another is the wearing of purple bracelets to symbolize unity: In universities, homes, shops, and public places, women (and men) are distributing purple bracelets and pamphlets and spreading the word about gender discrimination, enlisting a growing percentage of the population.

In the very tech-savvy population, news travels fast on cell phones and the Internet, connecting not just the various communities, towns, and regions of Iran, but the vast Iranian diaspora as well. Millions of Iranians—some estimate as many as seven million—live outside Iran, with by far the largest number living in the U.S. While the One Million Signatures movement has won many international awards, in Iran there have been harsh consequences for the organizers, all of whom have ended up in jail. But the genie cannot be put back into the bottle.

While I was in Tehran finishing my collection of short stories (*Abe Porteghal*[9]) I received a call from the Department of Literature at the University of Tehran.

They wanted to know if I could meet students and talk to them about my first book, *Morghe Sahar*, a memoir on which this book, *The Poet's Daughter*, is based. I gladly accepted. This was the esteemed academic department my father established. I wondered what he would think if he could see me.

A young man with a very short beard picked me up at two thirty in the afternoon. He was polite but did not shake hands, as this was against Islam; but he did open the door to let me in and out of the car. He sat next to the driver and I sat in the back. As we walked to the conference room, I noticed many posters with my picture on the walls, announcing "Bahar talks about Bahar." I asked him why they had chosen my book to present. He said that it was chosen for the editing class to study.

"But why my book?" I insisted.

"Well," he said, "there were two reasons. Firstly, women rarely write autobiographies in Iran, because it makes public their private lives. Secondly it was because of your father; Iran has not had a poet like him since the fourteenth century and people are hungry to know more about him."

At three o'clock the students began to enter the room. The seats filled quickly. The young man introduced me and I rose from my chair and sat behind a teacher's desk. As I looked around, I realized that almost all of the people in the room were women. The three men in the room were sitting with their wives in *chador*. The others had on colorful scarves, makeup, fashionable pants and jackets.

The very first words from my mouth were, "Seeing so many young women at the university makes my soul happy, and I am proud that I am also an Iranian woman." It was mostly the women who asked questions; they were very outspoken. Only one man was inquisitive, and he asked interesting and quite profound questions. I found these students informed, knowledgeable, and forthcoming. The three hours raced by, and ended with a presentation of a big basket of fresh flowers. Everyone wanted to have their photo taken with me.

One of the women was appointed to take me back home. On the way she turned to me and said, "Mrs. Bahar, I have a question to ask of you. My parents are retired and live near the Caspian Sea. When I wanted to go to university they advised me to become an electrical engineer so I would always be able to find a job. Now I am an electrical engineer, and head of the factory where I work; but

I love literature and go to classes at night. I share an apartment with my brother, but my parents want me to get married. What do you advise me to do?" I was very surprised by the question and suggested this was a personal decision. She countered that it was more than a personal decision.

"Marriage in Iran takes all your rights away," she said. "You cannot divorce your husband. If you have children, the husband can take them. I couldn't leave the country without the written permission of my husband. Under Islamic law, when a man dies everything goes to the children, nothing to the wife but one eighth of the house—not the land, just one eighth of the building. So marriage is a trap for breaking down women's freedom and independence."

I told her I was aware of this, but after my experience with marriage, believed that one should not marry to satisfy parents or society. Only if you really love someone and feel the marriage will be good for you. By this time we were approaching the apartment. She carried up the big basket of flowers. I hugged her and said good-bye. I was so proud of Iranian women. How hard they fight against the tyranny of society, government, and religion. I greatly believe that if and when Iran changes, it will be because of the women, not the men.

Just before this visit, Ahmadinejad was elected president. I have not been back since. What is happening in Iran today looks very much like a slide into the military dictatorship that was so intolerable to my family when I was a child. There are, of course, different players now, and the government has a different face, with turbans replacing the crown; but all the signs are there. People are being slaughtered in the streets and tortured in the prisons for their views. Even peaceful protests are put down with a level of viciousness never before seen in Iran.

The beautiful and hopeful young students that I met at Tehran University—what has become of them? Have they been beaten and shot at for asking for more freedom? I cannot bear to think about it.

In the time of His Imperial Majesty, Mohammad Reza Shah Pahlavi, King of Kings, Light of the Aryans, and Head of the Warriors, the royal family and their friends, and to a lesser extent the military, controlled the country and benefitted from its resources through a police state. Now Iran has a Supreme Leader, Ali Khamenei, and a president, Ahmadinejad, who started off as a hot-headed populist and has grown to fill the jackboots the Western press designed for him. An ever more powerful Revolutionary Guard controls most of the economy and supports an increasingly fascist state. Different faces, same tactics.

Yes, there was a revolution, a real one, too. But it seems that Iran, like Prometheus, has been condemned to an endless cycle of pain and bloodletting. Every time the fire of freedom and democracy burns bright, it is snuffed out.

The street demonstrations that have gone on since the questionable presidential elections of 2009 show the determination of the opposition, many of whom are women. They will not go away. But the cost is terrible. My father captured this willingness to suffer rather than submit in his poem, *Dar Tahamol Narkardan Zur* (Stand up to Oppression):

Imagine your body crushed in the coils of a boa constrictor.
Imagine being tied, spread-eagled, over a nest of fire ants.
Imagine being smothered with fragrant oil and pushed into a beehive.
Imagine climbing Mount Bisetoon, with no guide, on a pitch black night.
Imagine walking, naked and lashed by whips, for mile after mile,
Shaking with chills and wracked by fever,
Your lacerated body plunged into salt water, in the middle of winter.
It is conceivable that these hardships could befall you in life.
But I would rather accept all of them than to submit to the
    will of a tyrant.

The demonstrators sing and chant two songs as they march. One is Iran's most beloved song, my father's *Morghe Sahar* (Bird of the Dawn). The other is a new anthem, compiled from several of my father's poems and sonnets and set to music. Those who created this rousing anthem are anonymous. The person or people who put together the selection of Bahar's words, the two singers—one man and one woman—who sing together on the recorded version, the composer and the musicians who perform it, all are unknown, no doubt for their own protection. It is stirring and powerful, and could have been written yesterday, for this current crisis.

Iranians, beware!

Wolves are plundering your country!

But Iran is *yours*!

Iran is *yours*!

It breaks my heart to see Iran divided.

Don't you feel the agony too?

Rivers of blood pour from my anguished eyes.

But with it flows my revenge.

The tsunami of blood shed by the people

Will soon wash you away, you tyrants!

Just one bird still sings in the ravaged garden that was Iran;

I am trapped in my cage and can see the full horror.

The other birds have flown from this terrible reality.

Tyranny and oppression cut short the lives of our children.

For God's sake, you officials, give the people justice!

If my home is consumed by fire, that is alright.

But watch out, you flesh-eaters, your turn will come!

For love of country, many people have lost their head.

But without you, my beloved Iran, I have neither life nor soul.

While it heartens me to hear my father's words once more ringing out on the streets in protest, it breaks my heart to see that the same sad cycle, people reaching for democracy only to be crushed by tyranny, continues to play out. The dream of my father, that Iran would one day join the free nations of the world as an equal and noble partner in democracy, seems further away than it has ever been. I know I will never return to my home. There is nothing there for me now.

In November of 1967, while I was a graduate student, students from five universities in the Washington area converged on Catholic University's basketball stadium for an anti-war meeting, and I was asked if I would cover the meeting for the student newspaper. I arrived a little late, with my camera and notepad, to find the place packed. Students filled the seats and spilled over onto the floor; others stood against the walls. As a reporter, I was allowed onto the stage, but even there the floor was so filled with people that I had to lean against the wall behind the speakers.

The first speaker was a PhD candidate in the history department who gave the background to the then-current situation in Vietnam. One of the other speakers was a young man who had lost his brother to the conflict. Between speeches, the students shouted slogans and the stadium practically rocked with the emotion and anti-war fervor of the hundreds present.

The final speaker was a young man who had lost a leg in Vietnam. He was a poet. He started reading a long poem he had written against the war, leaning into the podium and declaiming passionately the words he had written. Watching him and listening to his fervent voice took me back, back to the day that my father had addressed the peace movement in Iran and read *The Owl of War*. As I stared at the young veteran, I went into a trance-like state. His words began to be my father's words:

Beware the leader who takes his country to war!
Beware, the devil is war's true leader.
For soon you hear the angry roar of tanks,
See bombs raining merciless down,
Turning our lives upside down,
Opening wide the doors to hell
To let loose all its fiery dragons
To take their blood-drenched pleasure
On helpless villages and their inhabitants.
Come! It is time to behead the owl of war
And cast its head at its feet.

The poet's voice became my father's voice, growing stronger and stronger as he went on. It was no longer the young man leaning into the podium; it was my father, clinging in his weakened state to that other podium for support so that he could deliver his message to those who opposed violence and war. There was thunderous applause at the end of the poem, just as there had been after *The Owl of War*. I closed my eyes, giving myself up completely to the memory. When I opened them again, I found myself alone in that great stadium. Everyone else had gone, and I was still leaning against the wall on the stage, tears coursing down my cheeks.

Outside, a gentle rain was falling. As I walked through the campus on that soft evening, still half in the present and half in the past, I saw that my father had never really left me. His words still filled my mind, the images and memories of him were still within reach. His teaching still informed my life.

And it has continued thus, in the more than forty years since that day. I still participate, when I can, in anti-war rallies and marches for women's reproductive freedom. I support strong women candidates for public office. I drive elderly voters to the polls, even though I am getting dangerously close to qualifying for the same assistance!

I have been enormously gratified by the resurgence of interest in my father's work, particularly in Europe, at a time when the scourges of war, pain, and suffering beset so many of the world's people. I love almost every moment of the great gift of life and liberty that I have been granted. I have tried to "walk slowly and joyfully through the lush greenery and the roses," and I am predisposed to "see a hundred flowers but not one thorn." My father's legacy to me—a love of freedom, a respect for human dignity, and an irrepressible joy in existence—has been the solid core around which I have built my life.

Not a day passes when I do not thank him, not a day when I do not find inspiration in the passionate words that poured from his great soul. When I hear a bird singing the rapturous anthem of being, I hear my father's words. *Morghe Sahar* (Bird of the Dawn) is an existential cry from a poet whose voice has been stifled but whose heart flies free.

Come, bird of the dawn, start singing!
Your silvery song echoes the pain of my isolation.
May the piercing purity of your voice

Sweep all this away and let me start anew.
Shatter my cage with your crystal notes.

We birds of the night are imprisoned.
Our wings are clipped.
We yearn to escape this cage
And sing the universal song of human freedom.
Your scintillating voice can shatter this nightmare,
Reveal the work of the oppressors,
And the vicious cruelty of the hunters
Who destroyed my home and stole my life.
Oh God! Universe! Nature!
Whatever you are,
Please make my dark night dawn.
Please send light and herald a new day.

I know it must be springtime;
All the flowers must be blooming
But bitter tears fill my eyes and cloud my vision.
I fear my heart begins to resemble this cage:
Constricted and black and fetid.

Hurl the fiery spears of your song
To purify my caged heart and set me free!
Everything will be renewed by the cleansing fire.
Imagine the sweet lovers and the fresh new flowers—
I must focus on beauty and hope
And not on the shriveled flower of my life!

Bird, has your heart also shriveled?
Then why don't you start singing
And make separation from my beloved shorter, shorter, shorter?

* * *

What happened to liberté, égalité, *fraternité*?
Have they, too, withered and died?
Commitment and integrity have disappeared.
Is all that is left oppression and decay?
The lover's sweet endearments,
The coquettish sighs of the beloved…
Have even these turned to meaningless lies?

The rampant corruption and self-righteous hypocrisy
Encourages the people to become thieves and traitors,
Trumpeting their empty patriotism and piety.
It makes me weep to see this defilement.
The landowners oppress the peasants who work the land,
And clutch all the fruits of their honest labors.
Their complacent cups overflow with wine,
While my cup is filled with bitter bile.
Oh God, I am so tired of these people.
Equality? Equality is extinguished.
Oh feathered cup-bearer, pour me heartening wine!
My aching heart is already your slave.
Now sit down and play some sweet music.
Or perhaps you are singing a dirge, bird;
The searing pain I hear in your voice
Sets my heart on fire.

ENDNOTES

1. Referring to Russia and Britain.

2. Rai is the old name for Tehran.

3. Two famous leaders who were put in jail.

4. The shah during Ferdowsi's time.

5. "Shin" and "sin" are two letters in the Persian alphabet equivalent to "sh" and "s" in English.

6. Women and Development: Articles, Books and Research Papers Indexed in the Joint World Bank–International Monetary Fund Library, Washington, D.C. (Boston, MA: G.K. Hall, 1987)

7. World Bank, Development Economics, Development Data Group, *Iran: Country Brief*, Washington, D.C., June, 2009

8. Bahrami, Ardavan (May 9, 2005), *A woman for all seasons: In memory of Farrokhrou Parsa*, <http://www.iranian.com/ArdavanBahrami/2005/May/Parsa/index.html>

9. Parvaneh Bahar: *Abe Porteghal* (Rockville, MD: Sherkat Darko, 2010)

INDEX

ABOUT THE AUTHORS AND
The *Poet's* Daughter

PARVANEH BAHAR AND JOAN AGHEVLI have been close friends since 1976. Their collaboration on *The Poet's Daughter* began in 2005, in large part to assuage their grief after the untimely death of Bijan Aghevli, Joan's husband and Parvaneh's friend.

The project began as creating an English version of Parvaneh's Persian memoir, *Morghe Sahar: Khaterate Parvaneh Bahar*, published in Iran in 2004. It soon became a much more ambitious project—offering a wealth of information about the history, politics, and social context in Iran (and the U.S.), and personal information about Parvaneh and her father that was not in the original memoir. It also includes their own translations of more than two dozen of Bahar's poems, only two of which previously existed in English.

Each author brings a variety of skills to the project. After arriving in the United States as a young wife and mother in 1953, Ms. Bahar earned a bachelor's degree in English literature at American University in 1961 and an M.L.S. from Catholic University in 1965, and worked as a research librarian for the IMF's Joint Bank Fund Library from 1973–1992. Ms. Aghevli earned her B.A., and Diploma in Education, from Sydney University, and her M.S. (Urban Planning) from the London School of Economics. In 1996 she received her Master of Education (Counseling and Development) from George Mason University. In 1972, she joined the International Monetary Fund as a research assistant and published several economic research papers while there.